Contents

Citation Information	ix
Notes on Contributors	xi
Series Editors' Foreword	xiii

1. Sport and Revolutionaries: Reclaiming the Historical Role of Sport in Social and Political Activism — 1
   John Nauright and David K. Wiggins

2. Cricket and the Radical — 4
   Brian Stoddart

3. The Radicalisation of the Gaelic Athletic Association in Ulster, 1912–1923: The Role of Owen O'Duffy — 12
   Dónal McAnallen

4. Bolsheviks, Revolution and Physical Culture — 32
   Susan Grant

5. Game Changer: The Role of Sport in Revolution — 43
   Thomas F. Carter

6. Building Character and Socialising a Revolutionary: Sport and Leisure in the Life of Ernesto 'Che' Guevara — 55
   Charles Parrish

7. 'The Struggle That Must Be': Harry Edwards, Sport and the Fight for Racial Equality — 68
   David K. Wiggins

8. Kwementyaye (Charles) Perkins: Indigenous Soccer Player and Australian Political Activist — 86
   Daryl Adair and Megan Stronach

9. The Universe is Shaped like a Football: Football and Revolution — 103
   Alon K. Raab

Index — 123

Sport and Revolutionaries

This collection examines the role of sport in the lives of key revolutionary thinkers and leftist activists. In contrast to those who take a more romantic view of sport and believe in its apolitical nature, the chapters in this book help make clear how sport has served as a site for political activism and the revolutionary thought and practices of such individuals as Henry Mayers Hyndman, Vladimir Lenin, Fidel Castro, Ernesto 'Che' Guevara, Harry Edwards, Charles Perkins, and Darius Dhlomo. Written by noted scholars, each chapter in turn provides insights into the close connection between sport, politics, and revolutionary movements in countries varying widely in their history, governmental policies, and treatment of individuals and groups. This book, which adopts a very broad definition of revolutions, is written with the hope of encouraging more serious thought regarding the transformative potential of sports, which can be individually liberating, as well as responsible for co-opting the lower classes and helping maintain power among the political and economic elite in capitalist as well as socialist societies.

This book was published as a special issue of *The International Journal of the History of Sport*.

John Nauright is Professor of Sport and Leisure Management, Director of the Centre for Sport, Tourism and Leisure Studies, and Head of Research in the School of Sport and Leisure Management at the University of Brighton, UK. He is also a Visting Professor of Sport Management at the University of Ghana and an Advisory Board Member of the John Paul II Foundation of Sport. John is the author and editor of sixteen books and numerous refereed articles in Sports Studies.

David K. Wiggins is Professor and Co-Director of the Center for the Study of Sport and Leisure at George Mason University, Washington DC, USA. He is also a former Editor of Quest and the Journal of Sport History, and Fellow of the National Academy of Kinesiology. He is the author and editor of numerous books and essays on the history of sport.

Sport and Revolutionaries

Reclaiming the historical role of sport
in social and political activism

Edited by
John Nauright and David K. Wiggins

Routledge
Taylor & Francis Group

LONDON AND NEW YORK

Sport in the Global Society: Historical Perspectives
Series Editors: Mark Dyreson and Thierry Terret

As Robert Hands in *The Times* recently observed, the growth of sports studies in recent years has been considerable. This unique series with over one hundred volumes in the last decade has played its part. Politically, culturally, emotionally and aesthetically, sport is a major force in the modern world. Its impact will grow as the world embraces ever more tightly the contemporary secular trinity: the English language, technology and sport. *Sport in the Global Society* will continue to record sport's phenomenal progress across the world stage.

Titles in the Series

A Global History of Doping in Sport
Drugs, Policy, and Politics
Edited by John Gleaves and Thomas Hunt

American National Pastimes – A History
Edited by Mark Dyreson and Jaime Schultz

Delivering Olympic and Elite Sport in a Cross Cultural Context
From Beijing to London
Edited by Fan Hong and Lu Zhouxiang

East Asia, Geopolitics and the 2012 London Games
Edited by J. A. Mangan and Marcus Chu

Encoding the Olympics
The Beijing Olympic Games and the Communication Impact Worldwide
Edited by Luo Qing and Giuseppe Richeri

Gymnastics, a Transatlantic Movement
From Europe to America
Edited by Gertrud Pfister

London, Europe and the Olympic Games
Historical Perspectives
Edited by Thierry Terret

'Manufactured' Masculinity
Making Imperial Manliness, Morality and Militarism
J.A. Mangan

Mapping an Empire of American Sport
Expansion, Assimilation, Adaptation
Edited by Mark Dyreson, J.A. Mangan and Roberta J. Park

Militarism, Hunting, Imperialism
'Blooding' The Martial Male
J.A. Mangan and Callum McKenzie

Olympic Aspirations
Realised and Unrealised
Edited by J.A. Mangan and Mark Dyreson

Post-Beijing 2008: Geopolitics, Sport and the Pacific Rim
Edited by J.A. Mangan and Fan Hong

Representing the Nation
Sport and Spectacle in Post-Revolutionary Mexico
Claire and Keith Brewster

Rule Britannia: Nationalism, Identity and the Modern Olympic Games
Matthew Llewellyn

Soft Power Politics – Football and Baseball in the Western Pacific Rim
Edited by Rob Hess, Peter Horton and J. A. Mangan

Sport and Emancipation of European Women
The Struggle for Self-fulfilment
Edited by Gigliola Gori and J. A. Mangan

Sport and Nationalism in Asia
Power, Politics and Identity
Edited by Fan Hong and Lu Zhouxiang

Sport and Revolutionaries
Reclaiming the Historical Role of Sport in Social and Political Activism
Edited by John Nauright and David K. Wiggins

Sport, Bodily Culture and Classical Antiquity in Modern Greece
Edited by Eleni Fournaraki and Zinon Papakonstantinou

Sport in the Cultures of the Ancient World
New Perspectives
Edited by Zinon Papakonstantinou

Sport in the Middle East
Edited by Fan Hong

Sport in the Pacific
Colonial and Postcolonial Consequencies
Edited by C. Richard King

Sport, Literature, Society
Cultural Historical Studies
Edited by Alexis Tadié, J. A. Mangan and Supriya Chaudhuri

Sport, Militarism and the Great War
Martial Manliness and Armageddon
Edited by Thierry Terret and J. A. Mangan

Sport Past and Present in South Africa
(Trans)forming the Nation
Edited by Scarlet Cornelissen and Albert Grundlingh

The Asian Games: Modern Metaphor for 'The Middle Kingdom' Reborn
Political Statement, Cultural Assertion, Social Symbol
Edited by J. A. Mangan, Marcus P. Chu and Dong Jinxia

The Balkan Games and Balkan Politics in the Interwar Years 1929–1939
Politicians in Pursuit of Peace
Penelope Kissoudi

The Beijing Olympics: Promoting China
Soft and Hard Power in Global Politics
Edited by Kevin Caffrey

The History of Motor Sport
A Case Study Analysis
Edited by David Hassan

The New Geopolitics of Sport in East Asia
Edited by William Kelly and J.A. Mangan

The Politicisation of Sport in Modern China
Communists and Champions
Fan Hong and Lu Zhouxiang

The Politics of the Male Body in Sport
The Danish Involvement
Hans Bonde

The Rise of Stadiums in the Modern United States
Cathedrals of Sport
Edited by Mark Dyreson and Robert Trumpbour

The Triple Asian Olympics
Asia Rising - the Pursuit of National Identity, International Recognition and Global Esteem
Edited by J.A. Mangan, Sandra Collins and Gwang Ok

The Triple Asian Olympics - Asia Ascendant
Media, Politics and Geopolitics
Edited by J. A. Mangan, Luo Qing and Sandra Collins

The Visual in Sport
Edited by Mike Huggins and Mike O'Mahony

New Directions in Sport History
Edited by Duncan Stone, John Hughson and Rob Ellis

Women, Sport, Society
Further Reflections, Reaffirming Mary Wollstonecraft
Edited by Roberta Park and Patricia Vertinsky

First published 2015
by Routledge
2 Park Square, Milton Park, Abingdon, Oxfordshire OX14 4RN

and by Routledge
711 Third Avenue, New York, NY 10017, USA

First issued in paperback 2017

Routledge is an imprint of the Taylor & Francis Group, an informa business

British Library Cataloguing in Publication Data
A catalogue record for this book is available from the British Library

ISBN 13: 978-1-138-05810-1 (pbk)
ISBN 13: 978-1-138-85493-2 (hbk)

Typeset in Times New Roman
by RefineCatch Limited, Bungay, Suffolk

Publisher's Note
The publisher accepts responsibility for any inconsistencies that may have
arisen during the conversion of this book from journal articles to book chapters,
namely the possible inclusion of journal terminology.

Disclaimer
Every effort has been made to contact copyright holders for their permission to
reprint material in this book. The publishers would be grateful to hear from any
copyright holder who is not here acknowledged and will undertake to rectify
any errors or omissions in future editions of this book.

Citation Information

The chapters in this book were originally published in *The International Journal of the History of Sport*, volume 31, issue 7 (April 2014). When citing this material, please use the original page numbering for each article, as follows:

Chapter 1
Sport and Revolutionaries: Reclaiming the Historical Role of Sport in Social and Political Activism
John Nauright and David K. Wiggins
The International Journal of the History of Sport, volume 31, issue 7 (April 2014)
pp. 693–695

Chapter 2
Cricket and the Radical
Brian Stoddart
The International Journal of the History of Sport, volume 31, issue 7 (April 2014)
pp. 696–703

Chapter 3
The Radicalisation of the Gaelic Athletic Association in Ulster, 1912–1923: The Role of Owen O'Duffy
Dónal McAnallen
The International Journal of the History of Sport, volume 31, issue 7 (April 2014)
pp. 704–723

Chapter 4
Bolsheviks, Revolution and Physical Culture
Susan Grant
The International Journal of the History of Sport, volume 31, issue 7 (April 2014)
pp. 724–734

Chapter 5
Game Changer: The Role of Sport in Revolution
Thomas F. Carter
The International Journal of the History of Sport, volume 31, issue 7 (April 2014)
pp. 735–746

Chapter 6
Building Character and Socialising a Revolutionary: Sport and Leisure in the Life of Ernesto 'Che' Guevara
Charles Parrish
The International Journal of the History of Sport, volume 31, issue 7 (April 2014) pp. 747–759

Chapter 7
'The Struggle That Must Be': *Harry Edwards, Sport and the Fight for Racial Equality*
David K. Wiggins
The International Journal of the History of Sport, volume 31, issue 7 (April 2014) pp. 760–777

Chapter 8
Kwementyaye (Charles) Perkins: Indigenous Soccer Player and Australian Political Activist
Daryl Adair and Megan Stronach
The International Journal of the History of Sport, volume 31, issue 7 (April 2014) pp. 778–794

Chapter 9
The Universe is Shaped like a Football: Football and Revolution
Alon K. Raab
The International Journal of the History of Sport, volume 31, issue 7 (April 2014) pp. 795–814

Please direct any queries you may have about the citations to
clsuk.permissions@cengage.com

Notes on Contributors

Daryl Adair is Associate Professor of Sport Management at the University of Technology, Sydney, Australia. He has interests in sport, race, ethnicity and Indigeneity.

Thomas F. Carter is Principal Lecturer in Sport and Anthropology in the Centre of Sport, Tourism and Leisure Studies at the University of Brighton, UK. He has conducted research on Cuban sport for 20 years and written extensively on Cuban sport. His research on Cuban baseball led to an award-winning book–*The Quality of Home Runs: The Passion, Politics, and Language of Cuban Baseball* (2008).

Susan Grant is an Irish Research Council CARA/Marie Curie Co-fund Postdoctoral Fellow, University College Dublin, Ireland and University of Toronto, Canada (2011–2014). She recently published her book, *Sport and Physical Culture in Soviet Society: Propaganda, Acculturation, and Transformation in the 1920s and 1930s* (Routledge, 2012). Her current project, for which she was awarded the postdoctoral fellowship, examines nursing in Russia and the Soviet Union, 1914–1941.

Dónal McAnallen is an occasional lecturer in Sport at the Ulster Sports Academy, Co. Antrim, Northern Ireland. He is a co-editor of *The Evolution of the GAA: Ulaidh, Éire agus Eile* (2009) and the author of *The Cups that Cheered: A History of the Sigerson, Fitzgibbon and Higher Education Gaelic Games* (2012).

John Nauright is Professor of Sport and Leisure Management, Director of the Centre for Sport, Tourism and Leisure Studies, and Head of Research in the School of Sport and Leisure Management at the University of Brighton, UK. He is the author and editor of 16 books and numerous refereed articles in sports, leisure and tourism studies.

Charles Parrish is Assistant Professor of Sport Management at Western Carolina University, North Carolina, USA. He served as coeditor and contributing author for the award winning four volume *Sports Around the World: History, Culture, and Practice*. His most recent book is *Soccer Around the World: A Cultural Guide to the World's Favorite Sport* (2014). His published articles appear in a variety of peer-reviewed journals, including *Soccer and Society*, *Sport History Review*, and *Journal of Convention & Event Tourism*.

Alon K. Raab teaches in the department of Religious Studies at the University of California, Davis, USA, and his true religions are football and bicycles. He is co-editor of *The Global Game: Writers on Soccer* (2008) and *Soccer in the Middle East* (2014) and author of articles, essays, and encyclopaedia entries about sport and society.

Brian Stoddart is a former Vice-Chancellor at the University of Melbourne, Australia, and has written several works on the history and culture of cricket in several settings.

Megan Stronach is a Ph.D. graduate in Sport Management at the University of Technology, Sydney, Australia. She has interests in sport and Indigeneity in Australia.

David K. Wiggins is Professor in the School of Recreation, Health, and Tourism at George Mason University, Virginia, USA. His primary research interest is the history of sport in the USA, particularly as it relates to the interconnection among race, sport, and American culture. He has published many journals articles and written or edited nine books. He is also the former editor of *Quest* and the *Journal of Sport History*.

Series Editors' Foreword

On January 1, 2010 *Sport in the Global Society*, created by Professor J.A. Mangan in 1997, was divided into two parts: *Historical Perspectives* and *Contemporary Perspectives*. These new categories involve predominant rather than exclusive emphases. The past is part of the present and the present is part of the past. The Editors of *Historical Perspectives* are Mark Dyreson and Thierry Terret.

The reasons for the division are straightforward. *Sport in the Global Society* has expanded rapidly since its creation with over one hundred publications in some twelve years. Its editorial teams will now benefit from sectional specialist interests and expertise. *Historical Perspectives* draws on *International Journal of the History of Sport* monograph reviews, themed collections and conference/ workshop collections. It is, of course, international in content.

Historical Perspectives continues the tradition established by the original incarnation of *Sport in the Global Society* by promoting the academic study of one of the most significant and dynamic forces in shaping the historical landscapes of human cultures. Sport spans the contemporary globe. It captivates vast audiences. It defines, alters, and reinforces identities for individuals, communities, nations, empires, and the world. Sport organises memories and perceptions, arouses passions and tensions, and reveals harmonies and cleavages. It builds and blurs social boundaries, animating discourses about class, gender, race, and ethnicity. Sport opens new vistas on the history of human cultures, intersecting with politics and economics, ideologies and theologies. It reveals aesthetic tastes and energises consumer markets.

By the end of the twentieth century a critical mass of scholars recognised the importance of sport in their analyses of human experiences and *Sport in the Global Society* emerged to provide an international outlet for the world's leading investigators of the subject. As Professor Mangan contended in the original series foreword: 'The story of modern sport is the story of the modern world – in microcosm; a modern global tapestry permanently being woven. Furthermore, nationalist and imperialist, philosopher and politician, radical and conservative have all sought in sport a manifestation of national identity, status and superiority. Finally for countless millions sport is the personal pursuit of ambition, assertion, well-being and enjoyment.'

Sport in the Global Society: Historical Perspectives continues the project, building on previous work in the series and excavating new terrain. It remains a consistent and coherent response to the attention the academic community demands for the serious study of sport.

Mark Dyreson
Thierry Terret

Sport and Revolutionaries: Reclaiming the Historical Role of Sport in Social and Political Activism

John Nauright[a,b] and David K. Wiggins[c]

[a]Sport and Leisure Management, Centre of Sport, Tourism and Leisure Studies, University of Brighton, Eastbourne, UK; [b]School of Sport and Service Management, University of Brighton, Eastbourne, UK; [c]The Center for the Study of Sport and Leisure in Society, George Mason University, Manassas, VA, USA

While there was an active group of scholars in the 1970s and 1980s exploring sport and society from the left, particularly those influenced by the theoretical work of Karl Marx and Antonio Gramsci and the more recent work in cultural studies by Raymond Williams and in social history by E.P. Thompson,[1] leftist critiques of sport in society largely became subsumed by a postmodern mishmash by the 1990s and early 2000s. There was a brief period where historical sociology opened up space for the understanding of the role of sport in the construction and maintenance of class differences and in the resistance to forms of domination. Douglas Booth argues that this emerged out of political activism in sport that appeared in the 1960s, which influenced an 'emerging generation of sports historians'. He argues further that the work of Raymond Williams, particularly his approach to hegemony gave 'left-leaning sports historians ... the tool to escape the reductionism and determinism of structural Marxism and include expressions of agency *while* accounting for the ongoing dominance of capitalist structures'. He goes further to suggest that the appeal of hegemony 'owed just as much to the politics of disappointment in the face of growing conservatism in the 1980s'.[2] Most historians of sport largely focused on criticising leftist works drawing on social theories as not adhering closely enough to historical 'evidence' as they strove to reconstruct the sporting past. In particular, much attention was given over to 'mining the sources' and while class did appear in a number of excellent works of sport history since the mid-1990s, those works have largely been marginalised in favour of studies examining race, gender, space and place, representation, etc. Those on the left sought to explain the role of sport in the co-opting of working classes and in the maintenance of capitalist hegemony.

In this collection we seek to return to a critical examination of the place of sport in resistance without succumbing to an overly pessimistic view. Indeed, sporting and other bodily movement practices might be reclaimed as oppositional forces and certainly as sites where critical thought could be developed.

Given the overt focus on the functionalism of sport being taught around the world in sport management programmes, it is crucial that we stand against the tide of the neoliberal juggernaut and bring alternative ways of thinking in and through sport and physical activity to bear on our field. Indeed, sport played a key role in shaping the experiences of many leftist thinkers over the past 150 years. While there is still keen debate on the left about the role of sport as an opiate of the masses, we seek to demonstrate that sport cannot be left to reactionary forces on the right, whether past, present or future. Collectively, we explore the role of sport in the lives of key revolutionary thinkers and leftist activists including Vladimir Ilyich Lenin, Ernesto Che Guevara, Fidel Castro, the Irish Republican Army, Black Power movements, concluding with the role of sport in the Arab Spring.

In the opening essay, Brian Stoddart examines the connection between cricket and revolutionary thought and practices. Although acknowledging that cricket is a rather conservative game both socially and politically, a number of participants in the sport have been immersed in politics and revolutionary movements. Stoddart appropriately begins his essay by discussing Henry Mayers Hyndman, a wealthy cricketer from England who established the radical Social Democratic Federation, which was later transformed into the National Socialist Party. From there, Stoddart points out the involvement of such cricket players as Frank Hyett and Tom Cartwright in radical politics and movements directed at social change. No discussion of cricket and its connection to the radical left would be complete without mentioning C.L.R. James, and Stoddart gives relatively much space to the great Marxist-influenced intellectual and political activist who wrote the enormously important *Beyond A Boundary*. In the process, Stoddart also provides much information about Learie Constantine, an outstanding cricket player from Trinidad and a protégé of James who became a member of one of the first race relation's boards in England and eventually the first Black member of the House of Lords.

Vladimer Ilyich Lenin, who greatly influenced James' life and career, is a central figure in Susan Grant's essay on physical culture and revolution among the Bolsheviks. Using an impressive array of primary and secondary sources, Grant makes clear that the revolutionary struggle in the Soviet Union was closely bound with Lenin, physical culture, sport, and to a broader Bolshevik psychology. Grant, adroitly pointing out the influence of the 'new man' concept inspired by the character Rakhmetov from Nikolai Cherny-shevsky's novel *What is to be Done?*, writes convincingly that Lenin and the Bolsheviks firmly believed that sport and physical culture played key roles in revolutionary culture. Both were important in transforming individuals while at once benefiting society. In other words, physical culture and sport, whether participated in at schools, the workplace or in the military, were crucial to the Bolsheviks who believed they contributed to both individual and state success.

Thomas Carter, like Susan Grant in her essay on sport and the Bolsheviks, employs the concept of the New Man in his analysis of the role of sport in the Cuban Revolution. First pointing out more generally how sport has been used in twentieth-century political revolutions, Carter then turns to an examination of the various ways and under what circumstances sport has been adopted during the social and political transformation of Cuba. He notes that sport served as a way for the revolutionary leadership to express their cultural identity while at once distancing themselves from previous regimes. Sport was also considered and cast by Cuban nationalists as a means to prepare guerrillas and enrol revolutionaries in the larger struggle to reshape individuals and society more generally. Sport was used, moreover, by Cuban revolutionaries to secure legitimacy, providing a forum for them to publicly display athleticism and physical prowess. One of these was Fidel Castro himself who was a lover of sport and understood its power to transform individuals and by extension the state.

Charles Parrish examines an aspect of Ernesto 'Che' Guevara's life and career not previously studied by historians. While other academicians have analysed Guevara's involvement in Fidel Castro's new Cuban government and revolutionary efforts in the Congo and Bolivia, among other things, Parrish focuses on the role sport and leisure played in the early years of Guevara and how it contributed to his later life as a revolutionary and guerrilla fighter. Parrish contends that Guevara's participation in swimming, football (soccer) and rugby instilled in him the character traits necessary to become a successful revolutionary and seeker of social justice. Correctly noting the influence of the British Amateur Sporting Ideal on Argentina culture, particularly its schools and educational system, Parrish surmises that Guevara's involvement in sport and leisure may have developed in him such personal qualities as perseverance, self-discipline, leadership, courage, loyalty and the ability to deal with adversity and map strategy. In essence, participation in sport and leisure served as a socialising agent and contributed to Guevara's development as one of the world's most famous revolutionary.

The impact of sport was just as great in the life and career of Harry Edwards as it was in 'Che' Guevara's. Perhaps even more so. As David Wiggins points out, Edwards, a PhD from Cornell and long-time professor of sociology at the University of California, Berkeley, was a serious student of sport who used it in the fight for racial equality and freedom of opportunity. He wrote the first scholarly book on the sociological study of sport and was largely responsible for the founding of sport sociology as a legitimate academic discipline. More famously, Edwards, through an organisation he established called the Olympic Project for Human Rights (OPHR), led a proposed boycott of the 1968 Olympic Games in Mexico City. Recognising the worldwide attention that could be generated by disrupting what Edwards termed the 'sacred institution' of sport, the OPHR included mostly international calibre Black athletes who threatened a boycott of the Games unless Muhammad Ali had his heavyweight championship restored to him, South Africa was barred from the games because of its apartheid policies and several other demands were met. Importantly, OPHR athletes chose not to boycott, but instead lodged protests during the Games that resulted in the expulsion of Tommie Smith and John Carlos from Olympic competition and the demonisation of Edwards for his part in the whole affair. The changing nature of sport and society more generally and the mere passage of time has helped to heal old wounds, but Edwards is still remembered as the angry revolutionary who used sport in a larger cause. Similarly, in Australia Charles Perkins fought against discrimination against Aborigines and for social justice and transformation in Australian society as Adair and Stronach demonstrate.

In the final essay, Alon Raab provides a number of examples of football (soccer) players, coaches, teams and fans who have fought for social justice and betterment of mankind. Included here are such famous players as Darius Dhlomo and Matthias Sindelar and renowned teams such as Dynamo Kiev and the Ultras. Also included here is an assessment of how soccer has created a culture of fraternity and served as a means for seeking independence as well as dignity and first-class citizenship. Like the collection as a whole, Raab's essay adopts a very broad definition of revolutions, recognising they sometimes involve radical changes in the way things are done, sometimes involve both peaceful means and bloodshed and sometimes involve pronounced social, economic and political transformations. We hope this collection reopens debate about sport and revolutionary politics and will reinvigorate the notion of the transformative potential of sports.

Notes

1. For good examples, see earlier work by Richard Gruneau, John Hargreaves, Stephen Jones, Alan Ingham and Steven Hardy.
2. Booth, "Theory," 17.

Reference

Booth, Douglas. "Theory." In *The Routledge Companion to Sports History*, edited by S. W. Pope, and J. Nauright, 12–33. London: Routledge, 2010.

Cricket and the Radical

Brian Stoddart

Australia India Institute, University of Melbourne, Melbourne, Australia

Cricket is normally construed as a socially and politically conservative game based upon its origins in the English aristocracy and later the middle class. This article provides insight into areas where the more radical turn has been present in cricket, either through individuals or through collectives at different points in the game's history. The conclusion is that, for the most part, these exceptions prove the rule of cricket's essential conservatism.

In many respects and at first sight, cricket could be regarded as the sport that has been least affected by what might be termed broadly as the 'revolutionary' dimension. The game began in its pre-organised form in Britain (and more specifically England) as a bucolic activity then, as it took more organised and regulated form during and after the industrial revolution, became a replica of a classed and stratified society. That was best demonstrated in the Gentlemen versus Players matches (professional vs amateur, upper classes vs lower orders) that survived until 1962, after which the game transformed into a more professionalised and commercialised shape. It was that socially stratified form of the game that went around the British Empire to be taken up in a largely mirrored way, so that colonial outposts frequently saw contests with England as more than just cricket matches.

There were, however, important and significant exceptions to that dominant form, and in those may be seen the strands of a radicalism that both questioned and threw into relief the dominant organisational model. Those exceptions also demonstrate once again how sport has been used ingeniously to comment upon and even change the course of development.

A first important task here is to consider the word 'revolutionary'. In its specific sense, of course, it has a distinctly and overtly political implication, and invariably on the so-called 'left' of politics. That immediately places it with Marx and Engels, and traverses through, say, the Russian and Chinese 'revolutions' as well as through a myriad of other similar movements. Here may be mentioned, as examples, Cuba and other South and Latin American jurisdictions as forever symbolised by Che Guevara, Chile and the Shining Path, the Naxalites in India and, of course, the most recent outbreaks in the form of the 'Arab Spring' via Tunisia, Libya, Egypt and Syria. The aim with all these and all the other movements is, effectively, the dislodgement of the *status quo* in the political and social sense.

It is at that point, for this story at least, that a significant variation arises, but one that is still well within the range of cricket and the 'revolutionary'. In cricket, and throughout sport more widely, changing the *status quo* has taken many significant forms that all, it is here argued, have a social revolutionary impulse in that they change social practice, part of but beyond the immediately political. The point, then, is that the 'political' provides a good starting point, but also enables access to other key areas such as class and race where, in cricket, there have been several 'revolutionaries' of note.

H.M. Hyndman

Henry Mayers Hyndman is a useful starting point.[1] He played undistinguished first-class cricket for Cambridge and Sussex in 1864–1865: 13 matches, 20 innings, highest score 62 and an average of 16.2. He came from a rich, upper middle-class family, his grandfather having been a slave owner in the Caribbean where the family came to own several plantations, mainly in British Guiana. Hyndman grew up in that wealth, was educated privately by a tutor who later also schooled Ranjitsinhji. He then went to Cambridge where he played as well as turning out for Sussex. In one match against the Gentlemen of Gloucestershire he bowled to one W.G. Grace. The first ball was lobbed to a fielder, who dropped the catch, Grace going on to make 278. Hyndman later recalled that one of the biggest disappointments of his life was not being selected to play for Cambridge against Oxford.

Hyndman was part of an era where cricket was distinctly gentlemanly so that his social circle was an elite one. But despite his background and upbringing, Hyndman went off to Europe as a war correspondent, observed a lot more of life and began to read Karl Marx. He returned to England where he established what was first known as the Social Democratic Federation which later transformed into the National Socialist Party. In later nineteenth century England, this was radical to the point of revolutionary – a man from the privileged realms establishing a party that, among other things, called for the nationalisation of the means of production. He was clearly standing against everything his background and profile stood for, as well as against many if not most of the social circle of which he had been part.

Inevitably, he was something of the gentleman socialist, and at his death in 1921 many of the socialist memorials had the line that he should be remembered for what he had started rather than for what he had done.[2] As one example, during the 1885 elections it became known that he and a fellow 'socialist' had accepted funds from the Tories in order to try and split the vote going towards the Liberals. It was an incipient socialism, at best, that saw the Tories as perhaps a better ally than the Liberals. That was, of course, because Hyndman was still trying to run a political reform from within his original social context.[3] As part of that, he remained a member of the MCC for almost his whole life.

The point here was that the 'radical' inclination in politics was, in some ways, swayed or even stayed somewhat by the social connections through cricket. The social practice, then, had an effect on the political one.

Australian Radicalism

There were variations on that pattern in many locations around the world, as Frank Hyett demonstrated in Australia.[4] He grew up in a working-class environment in the Melbourne suburb of Brunswick where his great friend was John Curtin who later became an Australian Labor Prime Minister. They both played cricket and football locally, but Hyett later shifted affiliation to Carlton as a wicketkeeper batsman who was good enough to play for Victoria in 1914–1915, making 108 not out against Tasmania. By then, however, he had long been a member of the Victorian Socialist Party, involved in the intricate deliberations that saw the socialists align with the more electable Labor Party. Hyett's power base was as an organiser of the railway unions, and he was widely reckoned as the most effective unionist in the state. When he died young in the Spanish flu epidemic in 1919, 5000 people attended his funeral at which the coffin was draped in the red flag.

With both Hyndman and Hyett, in their different locations, the jarring of the radical political movement with the socially contexted cricket milieu never really arose as an apparent contradiction, and there have been interesting reverberations of this down to the present time. In the late 1970s, for example, Malcolm Caldwell, a specialist on Southeast Asian politics and more widely remembered as an apparent apologist for the Pol Pot regime in Cambodia, did a lecture tour of Australia. At the end of that, in Perth, the one time he lifted in a tired interview was at a discussion about cricket. He was a paid member of one of the most socially elite county cricket clubs in England, and saw no incongruity between that and his politics.[5] Then, the ability to blend those two seemingly contradictory traditions was captured in the last episode of season three of *Downton Abbey*. Lord Grantham places great store in the house versus village cricket match, and recruits his radical Irish son-in-law to play against the latter's wishes. However, the radical takes a great catch and the pair are joined in a mutual endeavour to save the estate alongside the more socially acceptable other brother-in-law. While this is a fictionalised depiction, of course, it sits well in the framework of what has gone before here.

Some groups, like the Royal Park Reds Cricket Club, also in Melbourne, took this one step further and theorised the coalition of these seeming opposites.[6] Originating in annual cricket matches between the Communist party of Australia and the International Socialists, the Reds recognised the 'imperialist' nature of cricket but argued that it was compatible with the socialist agenda. What other game offered so much time for debate? Captains were elected by team members and for a couple of seasons rotated game by game, in line with a syndicalist approach. The team turned out in support of trades union activities and strikes, and set itself up as a different culture from the 'beery sexist' ones said to pervade mainstream cricket clubs.

English Alternatives

Just as clubs like the Reds have been rare, so, too, have cricketers with a strong left view. One of the few in English county cricket was Tom Cartwright who played just five tests for England but was a legend in Warwickshire where he played from 1952 to 1969, then Somerset between 1970 and 1976. He was the quintessential professional player who scored over 13,000 runs and took more than 1500 wickets during his career, but was also widely renowned as a 'socialist'. He grew up in a strong working-class environment that he never abandoned, and in the days when professional cricketers still needed winter employment he worked on car assembly lines in Coventry. That outlook turned him into a great player advocate and activist. When he was asked to tour South Africa with England in 1969, he claimed injury prevented him from doing so but, in reality, an earlier tour had transformed him into an opponent of apartheid. His withdrawal led to the selection of Basil D'Oliverira, a coloured player of South African descent. South Africa objected and the tour was cancelled.[7]

John Arlott, the legendary English cricket commentator, was in much the same vein, except that he stood as a candidate for the Liberal Party on two occasions, when the Liberals were the mid-point choice between Tory and Labour. Arlott was a strong proponent of social change and especially in and through cricket. He supported the boycott of South Africa over apartheid, and refused to commentate South African matches in England in 1970. Arlott was also a great player advocate and was voted by the players union as its lifetime patron.[8]

All these figures, and others who were similar, had an essentially 'political' dimension about them that saw either their politics taken into cricket, or effectively being run separate from their cricket affiliations in an attempt to maintain the Victorian fiction that the game was apolitical. Others, however, proved radical in a different way, in that they tested the social boundaries of the game in such a way that it could never revert. Much of this had to do with race, and with change driven from within the British Empire, that entity that many thought was the doing of cricket, rather than the other way round.[9]

Alfred Holsinger

At that time, Ceylon had another interesting sports export in Alfred Holsinger. Born in 1880, Holsinger was from the prestigious St Thomas College and said to be the fastest bowler on the island.[10] He was a prolific wicket taker in schoolboy and senior cricket, then in 1899 became Ceylon's first exported professional cricketer, travelling to England in search of fame and fortune. He never really found either, struggling away in the county leagues.[11] He probably played first on the Isle of Wight because he married there in 1901, sadly lost his newly born son there in 1905, but was soon trooping his wife and daughters through the Yorkshire and other leagues. Holsinger was said to have taken a wicket with his very first delivery in England, then gone on to take six wickets in six deliveries.

In 1907–1908, he played several matches for Lincolnshire in the Minor Counties championship. His best bowling came in a 1908 match against Staffordshire for whom former England player S.F. Barnes appeared – Holsinger took 6/37 off 27 overs. In some of his earlier appearances he did not bowl, inexplicably, raising questions about how he was treated as a 'coloured' player long before they became common in the leagues. He also played against William Tyldesley who would later die in Belgium towards the end of World War I and who was the brother of England player Dick Tyldesley.

At the 1911 census, though, Mrs Holsinger was recorded as residing in Mirfield in the Yorkshire West Riding, with at least three daughters and a male (presumably Alfred) also in residence. Alfred Holsinger was certainly playing for Mirfield in 1915 because he took six wickets against local rivals Hopton Mills for whom he also played at some point. By then, Holsinger had played for many teams including Burnley St Andrews in the Lancashire League, Batley in the Central Yorkshire League, Liverpool Nomads, Lincoln Lindrum, Llanelly in Wales and would also play for Eppleton in the Durham League by the time his playing career ended somewhere around 1920..

Holsinger spent 20 years pursuing this tough life, taking his family into what must have been frequently an uncomfortable, unwelcoming environment. Upon retirement, however, he stayed in the area and died in the Spen Valley in 1942, the first case of a Sri Lankan turning what was thought to be a social training tool into a working life, even if a precarious one.

In 1902, Holsinger saw another black player arrive in England to play permanently, in the form of C.A. Ollivierre.[12] He had toured with the first West Indies side to visit England in 1900, and did enough to attract attention so he stayed on, qualified to play for Derbyshire and represented that county from 1902 to 1909, while Holsinger was toughing it out in the leagues. He played as an amateur, and was funded by an office job with a local lawyer-politician. Ollivierre was the first West Indian to play county cricket and was moderately successful before fading eyesight forced him out of the first-class game though he later played in the leagues, then spent some time coaching in Holland. There is some evidence he endured some racist pressure at Derbyshire, in the same way that Holsinger would have in his pioneering journey. Ollivierre died in England in 1949.

He would have played against C.B. Llewellyn who turned out successfully for Hampshire in 10 seasons up until 1910 after which he went to the leagues from which he did not retire until 1938 when aged 62.[13] LLewellyn was a controversial figure, still reckoned the first non-white player to represent South Africa where he was born the illegitimate son of a union between a white father and a black mother. He encountered a lot of hostility in South Africa though he rose to test level, so decamped to England where he could pass off as white and had an outstanding career with Hampshire.

Learie Constantine

Those two, in many ways, were the radical harbingers of what was to come, beginning in 1929 with the arrival in England of Learie Constantine who reshaped the English leagues.

Constantine was the son of Trinidadian and West Indies player Lebrun Constantine who was also on the 1900 tour to England.[14] The family was lower middle-class black, so for a while Lebrun focused his son's attention on a professional law rather than cricket career. However, Learies's talent was too obvious to ignore and he was selected for tours of England in 1923 and 1928. On the last of those, he was approached by the Nelson club in the Lancashire League, and he played for that side from 1929 until 1938 and lived there until 1949. He was one of if not the highest paid sportsman in the country through that period as Nelson gained a stranglehold on the title through his efforts as an all-rounder. Constantine continued to play for West Indies and toured England as well as Australia, but it was in the leagues that he made a mark.

Constantine had two major influences besides his actual play.

The first was that he began an influx of black West Indian players, in particular, to the leagues. Among them were such brilliant and fast bowlers like Manny Martindale and George Francis, and the man still referred to as the 'Black Bradman' (others called Bradman the 'white Headley') George Headley. Francis toured England in 1923 although he had never played first-class cricket in the Caribbean, mainly because he was a 'professional' in Barbados. He routed several county sides, and continued to do so on his return in 1928 even though he was then past his best. When he went to the leagues, he was still good to have an impact. The rise of those players continued after World War II when the galaxy of starts like Frank Worrell, Everton Weekes and all the rest arrived to light up the leagues, beginning the social changes in the composition of English cricket that would later be reflected in the national test sides.

C.L.R. James

The second impact was associated but more powerful, and associated mainly with C.L.R. James. There was still considerable racial exclusion in Caribbean cricket as late as the 1960s, and most of these league stars arrived to make a living they could not earn at home. The further dimension was that it was clear county cricket would not admit them, and while the ostensible reason was qualification necessity, the perception was that a colour bar existed that even these brilliant players could not break.[15] That was where C.L.R. James came in.

There has been much said and written about James, especially in recent years, and his work has been applied, often unsuccessfully, into many other cultures and sports apart from the Caribbean and cricket which was the subject of his massively influential *Beyond a Boundary* which appeared first in 1963 after a lifetime of activity as a leftist in West Indies, the UK and the USA.[16] Put simply, James depicted the social trajectory of Caribbean cricket from the post-emancipation period through to the dawn of regional independence, but with an argument that the overshadow of the plantation and its cultural formations was ever-present. He depicted a world in which club cricket in Trinidad was marked by the intersection of race and class, and from which those entrapped found it difficult to escape. That transferred to the national level where those vectors were added to by a parochial one, and all still watched over until the 1950s by a white elite. That led in activist terms to James' campaign to have Frank Worrell selected as the first non-white captain of West Indies, which in itself was the foundation for the emergence of West Indies as the eminent world cricket power from the late 1970s until the mid-1990s.[17]

The origins of the book and of James' work lay in his time as a non-paying lodger in Nelson with his fellow Trinidadian, Constantine. James was in London, ran out of money and work, Constantine took him in. James got a post with the *Manchester Guardian* through Constantine's connections, and Constantine himself drew from James a far broader conception of what his journey as a black cricketer meant in social terms in an England unused to such a presence. Constantine, too, with James' assistance, began to write a series of cricket books that were a lot more than sports ones.

Constantine went on to a political career, and was appointed to one of the first race relations boards in England as part of his campaign against racism more broadly, and which he located in some of his less pleasant experiences as a black cricketer in a white environment. He later returned to Trinidad to be part of Eric Williams' independent government there, became Trinidad's High Commissioner back to the UK, then remained in England to take up his race relations work. Knighted in 1969, he was later made a life peer, becoming the first black member of the House of Lords. It was a very long way from his humble beginnings back in Trinidad, and was a testament to the radical opportunities offered by cricket but so often not taken up. If James was the theoretician, Constantine was the implementer.

Modern Trends

The issue of race itself has continued in several forms, with a poetic one involving Brendan Nash. Nash was born in Australia and played state cricket for Queensland before a poor run of form saw him dropped and given the message it would be hard for him to fight a way back in. His father was Jamaican, so Nash travelled there to play in 2008 and was selected for Jamaica, in the face of what was said to be some severe racist criticism in the mistaken view he was a 'white boy'. Players like Constantine and Weekes had to struggle because they were black, now Nash had to because he was white. The much criticised and maligned Chris Gayle is said to have supported Nash during that initial phase, and Nash went on to be selected for West Indies and played for four seasons.

All that, in turn, created the platform for the well-known and well-worn story of the cricket struggle with apartheid which eventually saw South Africa re-enter the game after a period of suspension following episodes like the Basil D'Oliveira episode, and with a new system of selection that has led to the emergence of such wonderful players as Hashim Amla, the Muslim of Indian descent with flowing beard and an exemption from having to feature alcohol advertising on his gear. His rise has not been unmarked, though: the mercurial if talented Kevin Pietersen left South Africa for England because of what he thought of as the bias towards players like Amla in the selection policies.

From there, of course, it is just a quick few steps to the ongoing intersection between cricket and politics, with activists keen to see a repeat of the South African story to bring about change in Zimbabwe, Sri Lanka and, to lesser extent, Pakistan where former star Imran Khan is now a leading political opposition figure. The Zimbabwe case has been predicated on the overthrow of the Robert Mugabe regime which, among other things, has been alleged to have far too much control over institutions like Zimbabwe cricket where former captain Andy Flower resigned in protest at government policies. This has been aggravated at International Cricket Council level where Zimbabwean representative Peter Chingoka, a Mugabe ally, has been banned from entry to several countries including the UK and Australia which means that ICC meetings cannot be held there.[18]

The Sri Lankan case has been the most recent and is gaining strength. Opponents of the Mahinda Rajapaksa regime argue that Sri Lankan cricket is a stronghold for ethnic Singhalese domination so that only a handful of outstanding Tamil players, like Muthiah Muralidaran, have been able to come through.[19] Moreover, leading players like Sanath Jayasuriya have become politicians in the Rajapaksa party that is alleged to have carried out human right abuses on the Tamil population towards the end of the civil war, and to be now engaged in the ethnic cleansing of Tamils. This is a clear sequel to the South African story and has some way to run, but it is also a descendant of the movement through which social practice was challenged by prominent cricketing figures.

That broader dimension of the place of cricket in a national culture, and in a Jamesian tradition, was further illuminated by Mike Marquesee who traced the malaise of English cricket of the 1980s into the 1980s to a broader demise in what he considered the fabric of British society.[20] Seeing it as a post-Thatcher consequence, the American-born Marquesee directly located cricket and its modern English evolution inside a wider set of social shifts that were transforming British society.

Conclusion

The story throughout, then, is of an essentially conservative game, in the social and political senses, having been reoriented over a long period by a series of individuals whose lives and actions have shifted the practice of cricket. While there have been few true radicals in the most specific sense of that word, there have been several more who have turned the social course taken by the game. In turn, that has had substantial social impact on the take-up of cricket in several settings and in the way the game interacts with the social construct wherever it is found.

Notes

1. Hyndman, *The Record*.
2. Hyndman, *The Evolution of Revolution*.
3. Hyndman, *England for All*.
4. Scarlett, "Hyett."
5. Anthony, "Lost in Cambodia."
6. Roberts, "Royal Park Reds."
7. Foot, "Tom Cartwright."

8. Allen, *Arlott*.
9. Warner, *Imperial Cricket*.
10. Stoddart, "Sport."
11. Pallister, "The Centenary."
12. Derbyshire Life, "Charles Ollivierre."
13. Merret, "Sport and Race."
14. Mason, *Learie Constantine*.
15. Constantine, *Colour Bar*.
16. James, *Beyond a Boundary*.
17. Constantine, *The Changing Face*; Constantine, *Cricket Crackers*; Constantine, *Cricket in the Sun*; Constantine, *Cricketer' Carnival* and Constantine, *Cricketers' Cricket*.
18. Briggs, "Zimbabwe."
19. Grant, "The Case for Boycotting."
20. Marquesee, *Anyone but England*.

References

Allen, David Ravern. *Arlott: The Authorised Biography*. London: Aurum, 2004.

Anthony, Andrew. 2010. "Lost in Cambodia." *The Guardian*, 10 January. http://adb.anu.edu.au/biography/hyett-francis-william-frank-6783

Briggs, Peter. 2010. "Zimbabwe Cricket Is Still Suspect Despite a Number of Welcome Improvements in the Coaching Structure." *The Telegraph*, February 25. http://www.telegraph.co.uk/sport/cricket/international/zimbabwe/8348657/Zimbabwe-Cricket-is-still-suspect-despite-a-number-of-welcome-inprovements-in-the-coaching-structure.html

Constantine, Learie. *The Changing Face of Cricket* [with Denzil Batchelor]. London: Eyre & Spottiswoode, 1966.

Constantine, Learie. *Colour Bar*. London: Stanley Paul, 1954.

Constantine, Learie. *Cricket Crackers*. London: Stanley Paul, 1950.

Constantine, Learie. *Cricket in the Sun*. London: Stanley Paul, 1941.

Constantine, Learie. *Cricketer' Carnival*. London: Stanley Paul, 1949.

Constantine, Learie. *Cricketers' Cricket*. London: Eyre & Spottiswoode, 1949.

Derbyshire Life. "Charles Ollivierre - West Indian Cricketer." http://derbyshire.greatbritishlife.co.uk/article/charles-ollivierre—west-indian-cricketer-derbyshire-county-cricket-club-21300/

Foot, David. 2007. "Tom Cartwright." *The Guardian* May 1. http://www.guardian.co.uk/news/2007/may/01/guardianobituaries.cricket

Grant, Trevor. 2012. "The Case for Boycotting Sri Lankan Cricket." *GreenLeft*, December 10. http://www.greenleft.org.au/node/53028

Hyndman, H. M. *England for All: The Textbook of Democracy*. New York: Barnes & Noble, 1974.

Hyndman, H. M. *The Evolution of Revolution*. London: Richard, 1920.

Hyndman, H. M. *The Record of an Adventurous Life*. London: Richard, 1911.

James, C. L. R. *Beyond a Boundary*. London: Hutchison, 1963.

Marquesee, Mike. *Anyone but England: Cricket and the National Malaise*. London: Verso, 1994.

Mason, Peter. *Learie Constantine*. London: Signal, 2008.

Merret, C. "Sport and Race in Colonial Natal: C.B. Llewellyn, South Africa's First Black Test Cricketer." *The Cricket Statistician*, 128 (Winter 2004).

Pallister, Ray. "The Centenary of the Durham Senior League, 2002." http://www.durhamseniorleague.org.uk/centenary.htm

Roberts, Tony. "The Royal Park Reds: Bringing the Class Struggle to the Cricket Field." *Baggy Green* 1, no. 1 (November 1998). http://www.anu.edu.au/polsci/marx/interventions/cricket.htm

Scarlett, A. "Hyett, Francis William (Frank) (1882–1919)." *Australian Dictionary of Biography*. http://adb.anu.edu.au/biography/hyett-francis-william-frank-6783

Stoddart, Brian. "Sport." In *An Encyclopedia of the Sri Lankan Diaspora*, edited by P. D. Reeves. Singapore: Didier Millet, pp. 44–48. 2014.

Warner, P. F. *Imperial Cricket*. London: Press Association, 2012.

The Radicalisation of the Gaelic Athletic Association in Ulster, 1912–1923: The Role of Owen O'Duffy

Dónal McAnallen

Ulster Sports Academy, University of Ulster, Jordanstown, UK

The early history of the Gaelic Athletic Association (GAA) has been described by Richard Holt as 'certainly the outstanding example of the appropriation of sport by nationalism' in a British imperial context.[1] This statement is most apt to define the association's part in the radicalisation of Ireland in the decade leading up to the independence of most of the island in 1922. In Ulster, the GAA became increasingly embroiled in the political issues of the day, as the spectre of the partition of the northern province came into view and became a reality from 1920. The rapid transformation of the sporting and political landscape was embodied by the career of Owen O'Duffy, whose star rose through the ranks of the GAA in Ulster from 1912 and the revolutionary movement from 1917. This article will explore the nature and extent of change through which the northern province of the GAA passed in the years 1912–1923, and will demonstrate that the personal role of O'Duffy in this process was profound but very opportunistic. Whereas the interlocking of GAA leadership and republican activity propelled O'Duffy to high office in the new Irish Free State regime for the next decade, it produced a much less favourable legacy for GAA members to the north of the Irish border living under an arch-Unionist regime.

Introduction

This article aims to enhance understanding of the complex position of the Gaelic Athletic Association (GAA) in the northern province of Ulster during the Irish revolutionary period from 1912 to the early 1920s. It proposes to examine whether the reputation of the association as a protagonist in this transformative decade is fully merited in respect of Ulster. The radicalisation of the GAA in this period has been discussed in several scholarly articles, but no published study has focused at length on the subject at a provincial level. As Ulster was the province most profoundly affected by the national reconfiguration, due to the division of its territory into two new adversarial states, it warrants a special academic appraisal. The process is analysed through the prism of the early career of Owen O'Duffy,[2] one of the foremost sporting revolutionaries in Irish history, whose term as Ulster GAA secretary corresponds exactly with the revolutionary era, 1912-1923. Although Fearghal McGarry's acclaimed biography of O'Duffy (2005) details some of his ascent through the Monaghan and Ulster ranks of the GAA and republicanism, some aspects such as the ramifications of his ongoing role as an Ulster GAA official after 1920 (until 1934) are underexplored.

This article will draw from newly available sources, principally the archives of the Ulster Council of the GAA from 1917 onwards – written by O'Duffy himself – as well as a wide range of newspapers from all over Ulster, and several recent academic articles about radical activity in the GAA. It will be shown that the association in the north moved from a stance of relative moderatism before 1917 to central involvement in the republican (para)military movement over the next five years, largely as a result of the manoeuvres and machinations of O'Duffy. Furthermore, it will be revealed that his involvement continued to have a significant legacy for the GAA in Ulster for years after the revolutionary period.

When the Ulster Council of the GAA appointed Owen O'Duffy as its secretary in November 1912, it was four months shy of its 10th anniversary. The previous decade had seen a great degree of growth and achievement: the inception and popularisation of the Ulster championships in the games of hurling and Gaelic football; the establishment and consolidation of clubs and county boards throughout the north where none had been affiliated at the outset of the 1900s; and Ulster at last taking its place in the national administration and competitions. The feat of the Antrim football team in reaching consecutive All-Ireland finals in 1911 and 1912, albeit ending in ultimate defeat, was widely considered to represent a general improvement in playing standards within the province.

For all of these positive developments, Ulster remained the weakest province of the GAA in several respects. None of its counties, other than Antrim of late, had appeared in an All-Ireland final, and in hurling they were hopelessly adrift from their southern compatriots. At all levels there was poor organisation, with clubs and county boards drifting in and out of existence, having few assets and barely any playing facilities to call their own. Despite being the overarching body for the nine counties and having a regular source of income from its inter-county competitions, the Ulster Council floundered in debt and failed on some basic duties. The council neglected even to run its flagship provincial championships in 1911.

O'Duffy's Appointment as Ulster GAA Secretary, 1912

The context of the appointment of Owen O'Duffy, a 22-year-old assistant surveyor with Clones Urban District Council in County Monaghan, demonstrated how disordered the provincial body had become. Since joining the GAA in 1910, O'Duffy had done little of consequence until his selection in September 1912 – seemingly without prior knowledge of his nomination – as the honorary secretary of the Monaghan County Board. Two months later, the Ulster Council had to fill its own secretarial vacancy. Patrick Whelan, the Ulster president and a Monaghan man, had already taken notice of O'Duffy's energy and interest in Gaelic culture, and proposed his name for the post. Fluency in the Irish language was his foremost credential, for the council had determined to conduct all of its business through Irish by 1915. Once again he was chosen for the chief clerical role of a GAA body with which he had no prior involvement. Accepting the office, O'Duffy promised 'to do his best to keep the flag of the Gael flying in the province of Ulaid'.[3] By further happy convenience for him, Clones, close to his new residence and having the central railway junction of the province, was the Ulster Council's principal meeting place. Hence, he could combine the burden of the provincial workload with his existing duties. (The previous Ulster secretary, P.J. Magill, had taken seriously ill after a short period in office and would die prematurely in 1913.)

The problems facing the GAA in Ulster extended far beyond internal mismanagement. External opposition underlay much of its infrastructural weakness. Hostility to the playing of Gaelic games on Sundays, which did not exist in the predominantly Catholic southern provinces, surfaced in a range of ways in the mainly Protestant north-east. Sabbatarian loyalists staged several protests and attacks on Gaelic sports teams, supporters and grounds. The forceful resistance to GAA teams playing on Sundays near Lisburn, Banbridge, Cookstown and Armagh became the subject of parliamentary questions at Westminster in the 1903–1906 period. Sabbatarian sentiment continued to underlie a boycott by the largely unionist local press on Gaelic games, the refusal of Protestant landowners and local councils to facilitate such games on Sundays, and the scarcity of trains to matches on Sundays.

The tensions raised by the third Home Rule Bill of April 1912 and subsequent events embroiled the GAA in Ulster in political contention once again. During a Westminster debate in July, James Craig, the Unionist MP for East Down (and later premier of Northern Ireland), condemned a Sunday sports meeting under GAA rules at Shaun's Park, Whiterock Road, as a 'provocative action' in 'the heart of Protestant Belfast', which could reignite sectarian riots that had recently led to 3000 Catholics being expelled from their workplaces.[4] The establishment of unionist militia corps, which coalesced under the banner of the Ulster Volunteer Force (UVF) in January 1913, stoked the flames further. By November of that year, the nationalist Irish Volunteers were formed in response, with the purpose of safeguarding the implementation of Home Rule. Both Volunteer movements quickly drew in hundreds of thousands of young men from opposing sides of the political divide, and began to engage in military drill and gather arms. The GAA president, James Nowlan of Kilkenny, publicly encouraged members to join the Irish Volunteers to 'learn to shoot straight'.[5]

The GAA became increasingly entangled in Volunteer activity as the year developed. By the summer, approximately 150,000 men had joined up, many of them being members of the GAA. The Volunteers became very much a mainstream nationalist concern, to the extent that Irish Parliamentary Party leader John Redmond gained control of them in June 1914. In a like fashion, Patrick Whelan, the Ulster GAA president who came from a constitutional nationalist viewpoint, became the 'prime mover' of the Volunteers in County Monaghan.[6] At an Ulster championship match in April, he led hundreds of Volunteers parading with bayonets.[7] Volunteer parades of local battalions became regular sights at headline Gaelic games. Such marches took place at a game in Derry City in June[8] and at a tournament at Roslea, County Fermanagh, in July.[9] Urban grounds under the GAA's control also became central rallying points. Shaun's Park, the main Gaelic park in the north, featured a drill competition for 16 Volunteer companies as part of a GAA sports day in July. This was 'no mere show', explained the *Irish News* Gaelic columnist, 'but a test of proficiency both for officers and men in … the elementary stages of the work before us'.[10] City regimental inspections also took place at Shaun's Park when no sport was scheduled.[11] Some other sports were similarly affected by the militarisation of nationalist Ireland. Indeed, whether Volunteer parades should be held on Saturdays or Sundays caused discord between soccer and GAA officials in Belfast, as each sought to prevent clashes with their own games.[12]

It is interesting, in the light of his later republican career, to review Owen O'Duffy's actions during 1914. After attending the initial meeting of the Volunteers in Monaghan in January, he remained detached from them and focused on sporting governance. Due in part to his efforts to inculcate a united county identity where internal divisions were rife, Monaghan won its first Ulster football championship title in seven years and then its maiden Ulster hurling championship. The Ulster Council, meanwhile, began to make administrative and financial progress, as more clubs affiliated and crowds grew in size. O'Duffy's 'relentless energies and self-sacrifice' for the GAA did not go unnoticed. 'He certainly made matters hum … not alone in Monaghan but throughout Ulster', wrote a local observer.[13] In November, he resigned as Monaghan secretary but accepted the less arduous post of county vice-chairman. Some of O'Duffy's glowing reputation owed to a courtship of the local press, and his written columns on Gaelic games often reflected a penchant for self-publicity.

The Outbreak of the First World War

The outbreak of the First World War in August 1914 had massive repercussions for Irish sport. From the mainstream political parties, newspapers and other institutions arose a broad consensus that supporting the war effort was the right thing to do for Ireland and for Empire. Crucially, in September John Redmond appealed to Volunteers to enlist in the British army on the basis that their efforts would be rewarded with the implementation of the Home Rule Act of 1914. Towards this end, some 142,000 men joined the new National Volunteers, leaving just 10,000 men in the Irish Volunteers. For most sporting organisations, the decisions to be made were quite straightforward. Because Ireland's national teams in sports such as rugby, hockey, cricket, golf and soccer were confined to the grid of the 'Home Nations' – England, Ireland, Scotland and Wales – and the other national associations opted for an immediate cessation of activity, withdrawal from international games was a *fait accompli*. As in Great Britain also, the bulk of domestic games were suspended: Irish rugby, hockey and cricket officials, among others, called a prompt halt out of a sense of imperial loyalty first and foremost, for the majority of their adherents held pro-Union sympathies and many enlisted. Moreover, their organisations promoted recruitment and made donations to war charities.[14] In slight contrast, Irish League professional soccer stopped in autumn 1915, once the financial realities of reduced participation and gate-receipts during wartime became evident. Although there was a greater diversity of political opinion within Irish soccer, most of those from a nationalist perspective shared the Redmondite view.

A very different dynamic was at work within the GAA. While IPP supporters constituted a large section of its membership, there was also a substantial body of advanced nationalists who were apathetic if not hostile to the British war effort. For this reason, senior GAA officials avoided publicly taking sides in the Volunteer split,[15] and the association sought to continue its games schedule regardless of war. Even this decision was viewed by the GAA's opponents as tantamount to tacit or surreptitious siding with the minority Volunteers. At an Ulster Council meeting in late September 1914, a Fermanagh delegate refuted press depictions that 'we are anti-Party men and that we are against the men joining the army. Times have changed', he said, and 'it should be known that we are not that way'. P.L. McElgunn, who chaired the meeting, replied simply that, 'Men of all ideas are in the GAA'.[16]

Yet the war impacted more profoundly on the GAA and its membership, especially in Ulster, than has been acknowledged heretofore. In several respects, much of their conduct over the next few months tended to lend succour to the recruitment and training of the Irish Brigade of the British army. Celtic Park in Derry City continued to be used for rallying and drilling by the National Volunteers: on an October Sunday, marching and counter-marching with bayonets and an address by Joseph Devlin MP attracted hundreds to the ground;[17] and another large crowd turned out in November to watch inter-battalion competitions on the park.[18] The collapse of GAA competitions in the city that autumn was no coincidence. A parallel period of GAA inactivity occurred in Tyrone. '[T]he Volunteer movement had knocked it out' in both counties, Owen O'Duffy explained in his Ulster secretary's report in spring 1915. By then, and for similar reasons, just one club was operating in Down also.[19]

It may be surmised that more erstwhile GAA members fought in British uniforms than in Irish republican corps over the next couple of years. Exactly how many recruits 'responded to the call of the Empire' from the GAA gene pool is unclear, but within nine months they numbered probably well into three figures in Ulster alone. By May 1915, 20 players of St Peter's GAA Club, Belfast, had enlisted – 14 in the Irish Brigade and 6 in the regular army – 'a fairly good record for a Gaelic football club', the committee agreed, though its senior team had to fold.[20] Seven members of Armoy GAA club were then stationed with the Irish Brigade at Fermoy.[21] This tally of 27 men from two lower-rank clubs in Antrim suggests that scores of other soldiers from that county had worn GAA colours. An early casualty of war was Private Patrick Corey of Cookstown, an ex-County Tyrone Gaelic footballer and member of the Royal Inniskilling Fusiliers, who was killed by shellfire at Bethune, France, in July.

In spite of these facts, the impression grew that while other sporting bodies and their members were rendering noble service, the GAA was reneging on and undermining the war effort. Some Unionists took aim at the GAA. In April, Sir Frederick Banbury, a Conservative MP for London, enquired what the War Office would do about the exclusion of British troops from GAA membership.[22] There are no known instances of this rule being enforced against recruits at this time, but as the war dragged on, GAA officials expressed more openly their desire that members remain in Ireland. In his report on 1915 in Ulster, Owen O'Duffy referred to 'games as usual and all things as before'.[23] A GAA official in Belfast elaborated further: 'By having business as usual, ... we help to counteract the depressing effects of the constant strain', and give members 'something to keep them at home'.[24] The enlistment of moderate members gave greater sway in the GAA to more radical elements who stayed at home, including the Irish Volunteers in certain Belfast clubs who began to use games for cover.[25] Their influence should not be overstated, however. Most members had no sedition in mind, and remained keen to maintain the association's law-abiding profile. Patrick Whelan, the Ulster president, decried the deployment of police reinforcements at an inter-county game at Clones in July as tending 'to cast suspicion on the Gaels of Ulster'.[26] The Royal Irish Constabulary (RIC) abounded at GAA games in the north, but seldom got free admission. 'In Clones they always pay of course', said O'Duffy.[27] For all their presence, the observing policemen seemed to accept that the GAA posed no direct threat to the state, as intelligence files of the pre-1916 decade say little to incriminate the association. The ringing endorsement that the Catholic Bishop of Down and Connor, Joseph MacRory, gave to Gaelic games in a lecture at Belfast in March 1916,[28] also indicated the increased status of the GAA in Ulster.

The 1916 Easter Rising and the GAA in Ulster

The participation of scores of GAA members in the Easter Rising of 1916 is so well documented[29] that the association's direct role in this defining week of Irish history may be slightly overstated. When the GAA's annual congress took place in Dublin on Easter Sunday, delegates such as Owen O'Duffy were unaware that insurrection was about to break out. Most of the GAA members who took part in the Rising were from Dublin and a handful of others were from the southern provinces, but very few northern residents fought, and just one from GAA ranks – young Newry clubman Patrick Rankin, who cycled to Dublin to join in.[30] The Ulster GAA's only real links to the action were small clusters of sometime members from Belfast and Derry whose wishes to fight were thwarted – by countermanding orders from Volunteer leader Eoin MacNeill causing confusion, in the case of the former group who assembled at Coalisland, County Tyrone;[31]

and by disagreement regarding tactics in the case of the latter group in Derry City.[32] In fact, in April 1916 more former GAA members fought on the battlefields of Europe than in the Irish republican struggle. Of 13 soldiers from St Peter's GAC, Belfast, 7 were then wounded and 6 still on duty in France;[33] one of them, John Drain, died in action five months later.[34] In the week before the Rising, a soldier identifying himself as a former player of Ben Madigan GAC in the city wrote an open letter to his ex-colleagues asking them to send some mouth organs to the trenches.[35]

Yet the GAA was singled out for special treatment on the back of the Rising. A week later, the military authorities banned all public meetings, including sports, which had no police permit. GAA members in Ulster, showing remarkable deference, sought and waited for permits to be granted before restarting games, first in Monaghan in late May and other counties thereafter. Clubs disliked the sacrifice of principle, but, as Ulster Council officials agreed, it was 'better to play under permit here to try to keep the game alive'.[36] Fears of impending partition of the province – a political proposal which was beginning to gain currency – fed into northern pragmatism: an *Anglo-Celt* writer made the jocular but telling comment that Derry officials wanted a game with Cavan 'before they are "excluded" from the rest of Ireland'.[37] Unionist and British MPs, meanwhile, tabled several pointed questions about the GAA in parliament. Unionist leader Sir Edward Carson urged the Chancellor of the Exchequer, Reginald McKenna, to refuse exemption from entertainment tax to the 'Gaelic Athletic League' [sic], as it was closed to the Crown forces but open to 'men who are in open rebellion against this country'.[38] At the official inquiry into the Rising at Westminster, on 18 May, the resigning Under-Secretary for Ireland, Sir Matthew Nathan, blamed the GAA in part, as it had always been 'anti-British' and denied soldiers entry to its events.[39] Patrick Whelan, the Ulster president, distanced the GAA in Ulster from the Rising – as Central Council officials had done – but he condemned the 'mad and reckless insanity' of the authorities' reaction.[40] Owen O'Duffy also denounced Nathan's 'falsehood'; 'I have been at hundreds of meetings … and I never yet heard a word of politics'. But the mud seemed to stick. In July, the Chancellor declared that the 'Gaelic League' [sic] had 'no title to exemption' from tax on games.[41] The repeated use of misnomers for the GAA by pro-Union politicians tended almost to lump all cultural nationalist groups together in sedition.

The emergence of the GAA in Ulster into a position of open defiance during 1916 came not in direct response to the Rising or consequent emergency security measures, but rather the imposition of entertainment tax as a means to fund the war effort. This taxation question became the springboard for the meteoric rise of Owen O'Duffy as a rebel figure. With Gaelic games back in full swing in most counties by the autumn, excise commissioners in London began to demand tax returns, but the Ulster Council and other northern GAA branches and officials refused to pay,[42] claiming exemption as bodies 'reviving national pastimes' were entitled to.[43] If the GAA became 'tax-gatherers for England', whose garrison had just executed Irish martyrs, Irish nationalists would desert it, argued O'Duffy. Further, he boasted that, contrary to some members' advice, he 'never condescended to acknowledge' any tax invoices.[44] Simultaneously, amid various fuel restrictions of that time, rail firms restricted excursion trains to GAA and other Irish sporting events, apparently at Dublin Castle's behest, but O'Duffy, ever the propagandist, remarked that, 'evidently the idea is to destroy our Association' by 'underhand methods'.[45] Similarly, O'Duffy and others voiced outrage that some northern GAA officials were interned after the Rising simply *because of* their GAA roles,[46] though this claim was highly questionable. A perception of punitive government policies was bringing the GAA to a position of grand defiance of the state.

Moderation still prevailed around the north in early 1917, nonetheless. County GAA officials remained mostly of the nationalist establishment, from teachers to justices of the peace, with Catholic clerics as patrons.[47] From his Ulster GAA presidential platform, Patrick Whelan entreated the government to drop plans for compulsory tillage with national service, and instead to free Irish internees and send agricultural officials to consult with the GAA – whose large membership comprised 'the chief factors in the food production of this country' – to plan how to stave off famine, quell 'Irish disloyalty', and lay 'the foundations of a peace and prosperity ... to Ireland and England'.[48] Efforts 'to crush the spirit of the Gael' would backfire, he warned, but fair legislation would inspire 'good order and absolute toleration' in the GAA in the north. All the while, a trickle of rank and file members continued to join the British army. Well-known players from several Belfast clubs enlisted that spring,[49] despite the steady stream of news about the war dead. Seven members of O'Neill Crowley's GAC, Belfast, had died in action in Europe by July 1917.[50] Lance-Sergeant William Manning of the Royal Dublin Fusiliers, who had played for Antrim in the 1912 All-Ireland football final, was shot dead in France in May 1918.[51]

For most members, it seemed, local rivalries continued to be greater concerns than political issues. There were a plethora of incidents of rough play, foul-mouthed crowds, rows about medals, post-match protests in committee and triumphalist poems to the press.[52] Such was the degree of controversy engulfing games in Belfast that in May 1917 the *Irish News* – the only daily nationalist newspaper in Ulster – took the extraordinary decision to drop its Gaelic games column.[53] Until the turn of the decade, the only regular reporting of Belfast Gaelic matches came in *Ireland's Saturday Night*, from the unionist *Belfast Telegraph* stable.

But the events since the Easter Rising had undeniably aroused a heightened national identity among younger generations of Ulster Catholics. From early in 1917, moreover, elements of the GAA began to contribute to the growth of a communal resistance in Ireland. 'GAA influence is causing disaffection to spread amongst the young men', stated a police report from Co. Monaghan in February.[54] Clubs were being named after new martyrs, like Pearse's and O'Rahilly's in Tyrone,[55] and raising funds for dependants of Rising participants. A change of mood was palpable even in Catholic seminaries. After years of playing soccer, leading colleges suddenly switched allegiance to Gaelic games. A football diary kept by pupils of St Patrick's College, Armagh, records that in spring 1917, 'influenced by the Irish spirit of the age we abandoned "socer" [sic], which seemed to savour of anglicisation, and we started to play Gaelic ... from a national point of view'.[56] With other schools following suit, an initial Ulster colleges' championship was planned.[57]

Ulster Unionists renewed and increased their accusations of the GAA evading tax, wasting petrol on Sunday games for 'thousands of young men of military age' and being 'largely organised for the purpose of spreading seditious teachings'.[58] These hostile views overstated the GAA's part and underestimated the state's role in causing radicalisation at that point. The perception of victimisation created by the frequent stopping of teams on their way to games,[59] the jailing of GAA members – such as Antrim secretary Séamus Dobbyn in March, for statements made in a private letter – and the pursuit of some GAA officials for tax evasion (leading to a prosecution in Co. Cavan in March),[60] all played a part too. Similarly, the public ban on marching with *camáin*, introduced in August 1917 after an RIC inspector was struck and killed by one, popularised the hurling stick as never before.[61] Drilling and marching with *camáin* increased in Ulster; many Cavan men were prosecuted for doing so months later. This was one of several manifestations of the reviving Irish Volunteers encroaching onto GAA activity. In Belfast, some skeleton Volunteer companies were re-formed around GAA clubs, for camouflage.[62]

O'Duffy Joins the Irish Volunteers, 1917

Step forward Owen O'Duffy, who would take such tactics to another level. In May 1917, the Ulster GAA secretary joined the Volunteers and became a commander in the Clones company, then the only branch in County Monaghan. He set about trying to recruit 'virtually every able-bodied member or supporter of the GAA into Volunteer activities'.[63] Within a month, the local police reported that the 'GAA is the most active political organisation' and its matches were being used to extend the Sinn Féin movement.[64] By September O'Duffy was elected captain of the expanding company and moved to form companies in two nearby villages. At a Sinn Féin rally at Monaghan in October, *camáin* were used to guard the meeting, as they would increasingly be used by the party in the coming months;[65] O'Duffy, presumably present, seemed unperturbed that the flaunting of a hurling stick as a weapon might politicise the GAA's image in the eyes of outsiders.

From around the time of his first meeting with Michael Collins in Dublin in November and his initiation into the Irish Republican Brotherhood (IRB), O'Duffy became more powerful in both republican and GAA circles. By spring 1918, O'Duffy had effective control of the Ulster Council, while the president Patrick Whelan faded into the background, for reasons unknown. In his annual report, O'Duffy portrayed how the GAA surmounting 'all sorts of threats, pains and penalties' from the authorities, and yet 'Croke Park is still in the possession of the Gaels'. He tendered his resignation, stating that it was impossible to carry on this increasingly onerous role, as 'my time is not my own'. The Ulster convention would not accept his resignation, however, and pledged to provide assistance if he would continue.[66] Such histrionics would become an annual feature of O'Duffy in high sporting and public office.

As the state took ever stiffer actions to try to contain potential unrest, the more the nationalist population and bodies such as the GAA resorted to open disobedience of official orders. Following the government's threat to impose conscription in April 1918, the GAA's Central Council, echoing a pledge by the Irish Anti-Conscription Committee, vowed 'to resist by any and every means in our power the attempted conscription of Irish manhood'.[67] The apex of the GAA's passive resistance came that summer. Public meetings in most areas were proscribed under emergency measures,[68] so a police permit was needed for Gaelic games. O'Duffy et al. relished the chance to defy the ruling, believing that efforts to suppress their sports since 1916 had 'hopelessly failed' and inspired a host of new clubs in Ulster.[69] But many Ulster GAA players proved poor rebels. Before an unpermitted Ulster championship game at Cootehill on 7 July, the Cavan and Armagh teams refused to field, despite O'Duffy's entreaties, in the face of dozens of armed policemen and soldiers occupying the ground.[70] A week later, numerous club ties were likewise obstructed by force,[71] though a few others were held under permit, after some RIC constables offered compromises on the regulations.[72] In order to overturn the permit requirement, the GAA's Central Council (apparently at the behest of O'Duffy and Ulster) designated a national day of unpermitted games concurrently to overburden the Crown forces. With a few days to go, the government suddenly declared that only sports featuring political speeches required permits. On 'Gaelic Sunday', 4 August, hundreds of matches took place uninterrupted, including dozens in Ulster; teams nicknamed the 'Kaffirs' and 'Hottentots' played at Clones, under O'Duffy's direction, with many police watching.[73] GAA members had asserted their right to play as they wished, and the permit demand vanished. O'Duffy gloated that the association could 'entirely ignore the proclamations of the British Government' on permits as on taxation.[74] A few weeks later, he and his protégé Dan Hogan were arrested and charged with the 'illegal assembly' of 30 men on their way back from a football match in Cootehill. On his way to trial he received a hero's welcome in the villages of Monaghan. The two men refused to put up sureties for good behaviour and were thus imprisoned in Belfast Gaol. Subsequently, O'Duffy misrepresented the episode to boast of his price that 'it was for GAA activity he was taken away'.[75]

No one had done more than he to blur the lines of demarcation between the GAA and republicanism. Redmondite GAA members resented the growth of Sinn Féin attempts to capitalise on the popularity of Gaelic sports to attract new members and funds.[76] Tensions between republican- and Hibernian-aligned GAA clubs led to violence in games in south Armagh. The *Dundalk Democrat* complained that Gaelic sports 'descended more and more into the troubled sea of politics until they were simply recognised as so many Sinn Féin demonstrations'.[77]

The general election of December 1918 occasioned a landslide victory for Sinn Féin. In the same month, the GAA's Central Council took its most politically minded decision yet by deciding to expel members who took the (newly introduced) oath of allegiance for civil servants. As a consequence, Patrick Whelan, a justice of the peace (JP), had to resign after 15 years as Ulster president. At the Ulster GAA convention of March 1919, a new president was elected: Séamus Dobbyn of Belfast, who was also the head IRB man in Ulster and a recent internee. The *de facto* revolutionary takeover of the Ulster Council was reinforced by the appointment of O'Duffy's brigade deputy and IRB colleague,[78] Dan Hogan, as the council's assistant-secretary.[79] The top level aside, however, Ulster was far from universally radical. The ban on oath-takers from membership – which would exclude many such as teachers – caused much commotion in the north, with some branches ignoring the edict altogether, and Cavan leading a revolt against it.[80] Even the Ulster Council stayed neutral on the issue until congress in April 1919 cemented the ban.

O'Duffy and the Irish War of Independence

Political developments and opinion were in a constant state of flux, however. On the same day in January that the first Dáil parliament of Sinn Féin *Teachtaí Dála* (TDs, or members) convened in Dublin, the Irish Republican Army (IRA) assassinated two policemen in County Tipperary and thus began the Irish War of Independence. This war remained confined to the south for several months. O'Duffy kept on spreading the Gaelic gospel with a radical agenda. In April, he organised a meeting to form the first GAA county board in Donegal in over a decade; the election of two former internees and two Sinn Féin TDs to its offices signposted the inclinations of the new board.[81] Three months later, he attended a meeting to reorganise the GAA in Tyrone. He also intensified his public criticisms of other sports and their promoters. In letters to the press, he alleged that the government was using 'bribery and corruption' to popularise soccer so as to expedite its 'attempt to divide Ireland into two colonies'.[82] The rapid entanglement of the GAA with Sinn Féin continued apace at local level. Some Gaelic clubs in republican areas, like Camlough in south Armagh, were openly pro-Sinn Féin,[83] or the party and the Volunteers used sports to garner popular support in areas where their natural base was relatively small. Party *cumainn* advertised 'GAA Athletic Sports', when the track-and-field rules were the only link to the GAA.[84] Several sports-*aeridheachta* (outdoor festival days) with political speakers were proclaimed by the authorities: one such event at Fintona (Tyrone) was duly cancelled,[85] but two in Down went ahead in some form anyhow.[86] After a game at an *aeridheacht* at Wattlebridge, County Fermanagh, Fr. Terence Caulfield advised the crowd to join the Volunteers, declaring that 'the more they were persecuted the stronger they grew, and the more England jailed them the more vigorous they became'.[87] A possible case in point occurred when a group of Crossmaglen players assaulted two RIC men who had shadowed them after a game.[88]

In 1920, the GAA suffered the serious consequences of its intertwining with the revolutionary movement in Ulster and elsewhere. The War of Independence spread to the north early in the year. In February, O'Duffy acted as the ringleader of a successful arms raid by the IRA at Ballytrain, Co. Monaghan, and went on the run. The GAA in Ulster had fallen hostage to the plots, ploys and personal fortunes of O'Duffy and other republicans in its ranks. He attended the Ulster GAA convention at Clones in March anyhow. 'It is at very considerable risk to my freedom that I am present today', he wrote. 'I have been advised from 100 sources not to come but my desire to meet in conference my fellow workers in the movement I cherish surmounted everything else'. For the third year in a row, he offered his resignation but was prevailed upon to continue as secretary.[89] Within weeks, Ulster GAA president Séamus Dobbyn was 'taken by the enemy' to prison again; and at the next council meeting, at Armagh in April, O'Duffy was dramatically arrested by what the minutes termed 'armed aliens' (soldiers).[90] O'Duffy was detained in Belfast Gaol, where he promptly organised a successful hunger strike, and was released the next month. Dobbyn, also freed, declared at a meeting in July that he was 'proud to know that the GAA was powerful enough to merit attention on the part of the foreign rulers of Ireland'.[91] From July onwards, the Ulster Council underwent a lengthy lull in meetings, partly due to certain officers' non-sporting distractions.

The strains of the 'Tan War' took their toll on the GAA. Games ground to a halt in most parts of the other provinces from late spring, and in much of Ulster from the late summer onwards. Due in the main to harassment by Crown forces, sectarian violence and paramilitary activity, play stopped in all but Cavan, south Down, east Donegal, Belfast and Derry City – where a revival owed to the urban corporation recently coming into Nationalist-Sinn Féin control and making the municipal Brandywell ground available for Gaelic matches. Gaelic teams were regularly stopped and searched.[92] In north Armagh, a man returning from a GAA sports day was killed by a sniper.[93] A Tyrone county footballer, Patrick Loughran, became the first northern IRA martyr, dying during an attack on an RIC barracks.[94] Another Tyrone player, a non-combatant, survived being shot; and a recent county secretary, Patrick Crawford, was jailed for possession of arms.[95] A former Ulster GAA secretary (1909–1911), William Gilmore, was driven from his family home in Lisburn in a wave of reprisal for the assassination of RIC inspector Oswald Swanzy in August;[96] the Gilmores, like many other local Catholics, fled to Dublin. In September, John McFadden, whose brother Patrick was deputising for O'Duffy as Ulster GAA secretary, was killed in a reprisal in Belfast; neither brother was a combatant.[97] The action of Black and Tans and Auxiliaries on 'Bloody Sunday', 21 November 1920 – invading Croke Park and opening fire on a large crowd, causing the deaths of a footballer and 13 spectators[98] – probably also deterred players from returning to northern GAA fields. When Joseph Devlin, Nationalist MP for Belfast (Falls), raised the atrocity in parliament, he was supported by just one Nationalist MP (Jeremiah MacVeagh, South Down), and opposed by a mass of Unionist and English MPs, who believed that the crowd fired first. Devlin even got involved in a brawl, while other MPs chanted 'kill him'.[99]

The Partition of Ireland, 1920–1921

The passing of the Government of Ireland Act in December 1920 divided the country into the Unionist majority 6 counties of Northern Ireland and the Nationalist-majority 26 of Southern Ireland, with each state to have devolved parliaments, subject to imperial rule from Westminster. Ulster would be split in two, with only three of its nine counties – Donegal, Monaghan and Cavan – going to the southern state. The Belfast parliament opened in June, with James Craig as the new Prime Minister. Disillusioned Nationalist and Sinn Féin MPs boycotted the Belfast polity, and to many ordinary nationalists, GAA members included, the new alignment was anathema. The sectarian nature of the new arrangement would place them in a hostile environment, isolating and threatening the future of their culture and identity. Moreover, the Unionist-run regime, in the face of vigorous republican opposition, developed a 'siege mentality', fixating on the security of the state.[100] A paranoia emerged about all nationalist bodies as potential bases of popular dissent. The GAA, as the largest nationalist organisation, with salient republican elements, automatically fell under suspicion.

South of the border, the dominant Sinn Féin party carried on with its own Dáil, ignoring the proposed political apparatus of the Government of Ireland Act, while the War of Independence reached its violent crescendo in the first half of 1921. Due to the widespread declaration of martial law from late 1920 (to summer 1921), with curfews and restrictions on public meetings making it illegal or unsafe to play,[101] official GAA activities ceased for the corresponding period in most of Munster and Connacht and a swathe of Leinster – Dublin playing on was a notable exception. Members who were in the IRA were also unavailable, as they moved in 'flying columns' or went 'on the run'. O'Duffy was now a major player in the conflict on either side of the border. Under his command, the IRA in Monaghan became more ruthless in pursuit of members of the Crown forces. His brigade deputy, Dan Hogan, was also reportedly trigger-happy after Bloody Sunday, when his brother Michael was shot dead (hence the name of the Hogan Stand today). In March, O'Duffy was promoted to commandant of the Second Northern Division, operating in counties Tyrone and Derry, while Hogan took charge of Monaghan. Dozens of Ulster GAA members were now fighting for the IRA, and some used the clubs covertly to further paramilitary objectives. Members of the IRA's Belfast Brigade predominated in O'Donovan Rossa's GAA Club and used it as a base for some attacks – notably the killing of inspector Swanzy.[102] Patrick Shiels, the (largely nominal) Derry GAA County Board chairman (1918–1923), was the IRA commandant in Derry City, who spent several weeks on hunger strike in Mountjoy Jail that summer.[103] In many rural areas too there was strong overlap. Some GAA and political meetings were co-located, so that delegates could attend both; at Castlewellan in April, P.M. Moore was chosen as a county vice-president at the adjourned Down GAA convention and as an electoral candidate by a Sinn Féin conference on the same afternoon.[104]

The troubled state of the country underlay the GAA's inactivity in much of the north-east in 1921. The vast majority of northern GAA members remained outside the IRA ranks, but the range of sporting-military links gave the Crown forces ample reason to shadow GAA affairs. For most of the year, county board structures lay dormant in the rural mid Ulster cockpit of Monaghan, Tyrone, Armagh and Fermanagh, with only sporadic local club games to show on the field of play. Even where board structures remained active, such as Derry City, general measures such as the imposition of curfew hours hindered meetings.[105] (One could obtain police permits to be out during curfew hours, but GAA officials would not apply for them.) Yet greater aggravation was caused by the partisan and often excessive conduct of the security forces. The Ulster Special Constabulary was entirely unsuitable for the central law enforcement role entrusted to it by the imperial government in December 1920. The 'Specials' were untrained, largely unsupervised, and nearly all Protestant recruits from the UVF and the Orange Order.[106] They subjected Catholics to frequent personal and property searches, interrogations and even physical assaults.[107] Immediately, the GAA felt the brunt of their wrath. Anyone attending a Gaelic game was liable to face security-force hostility or actual violence. In January 1921, a party of 'Specials' interrupted a game at Killowen, Co. Down, and searched players and spectators.[108] In April, the Duffin brothers, of O'Donovan Rossa's GAA Club, were shot dead at home in west Belfast, in revenge for the killing of two Auxiliaries that day. Daniel was an IRA lieutenant; Patrick was not in the IRA at all.[109] On the other side of the border in south-west Ulster, similar problems arose. 'Tans' and Auxiliaries reportedly harassed GAA personnel in various incidents, such as forcing players at a game in Cavan to fill trenches in May, searching and interrogating spectators at a game in Belturbet, and seizing and destroying hurling *camáin*, GAA books and documents in Cavan and Monaghan.[110] In Cavan, unlike Monaghan, games continued nonetheless.

Owen O'Duffy had many other things on his mind, though. Meteorically, he rose to national prominence through his election (unopposed) as a TD for Monaghan in May, and his appointment as IRA GHQ director of organisation in June.[111] He was in Dublin for only a few weeks when a truce on 11 July ended the War of Independence and caused his reassignment as IRA chief liaison officer in Ulster. He was posted to Belfast, where he found that the truce had no effect. In fact, sporadic attacks, reprisals and sectarian killings escalated in the north, with the GAA being caught in the crossfire. After the IRA shot dead a policeman in west Belfast on the weekend of the truce in July, there came a furious response. The RIC reported finding a rifle and 1000 rounds of ammunition in St Gall's GAA club, before a fire ravaged the building. The weapons find was denied by the club, and nationalists ascribed the fire to arson in reprisal for the ambush.[112] In the same weekend, loyalist mobs and Specials colluded to kill 16 Catholics and burn 161 Catholic homes in west Belfast. Also that week, Crown forces shot dead, among others, civilian GAA members from Carey, County Antrim, and Killeavy, near Newry; the former, Patrick McCarry, was also a JP.[113] In August, the IRA in Belfast was directed by O'Duffy to strike back. But while on an IRA operation shadowing a policeman who was allegedly in a loyalist 'murder gang', Fred Fox, an O'Donovan Rossa's GAA player was shot dead.[114] Clearly embittered by the sectarianism of Belfast, O'Duffy, while speaking alongside republican leader Michael Collins at Armagh in early September, warned that if loyalists flaunted arms the IRA could 'use the lead against them'. His comments inflamed unionist feeling once again in Ulster.[115]

Later that month, O'Duffy was appointed Deputy Chief of Staff of the IRA and became active again as the provincial GAA secretary. Flanked by the reliable Dan Hogan, now Commandant of the IRA's Fifth Northern Division, O'Duffy set about reorganising both the IRA and Gaelic games in Ulster. In October, the Ulster Council convened a reorganisation meeting at Clones, after a 15-month hiatus. O'Duffy was absent, being 'very busily engaged in important work', explained the chairman (and IRB colleague), Séamus Dobbyn.[116] Republicans became ever more conspicuously at work at GAA events. IRA men stood on duty at a GAA sports meeting in Derry in September, attended by the (abstentionist) Sinn Féin MP for Derry, Eoin MacNeill.[117] Meanwhile, the Donegal county football final was deferred until interned players returned from jail.

The signing of the Anglo-Irish Treaty on 6 December 1921 was a seminal political event. The Treaty provided for the creation of the Irish Free State as a self-governing dominion in the 26 counties and the continuation of the Northern Ireland government within the UK. The border would remain, subject to minor modifications at most. The treaty created deep divisions within Sinn Féin. O'Duffy became a crucial figure in the ensuing debate. Despite abhorring partition, he lobbied heavily for support for the treaty. In the tense Dáil debates, he used striking Gaelic games metaphors. The treaty would bring 'the ball inside the fourteen yards' line' and 'by keeping our eye on the goal the major score is assured'.[118] On 7 January, he was one of the slim Dáil majority who voted to accept the agreement, 64-57. O'Duffy was reassured by the personal determination of his leader and treaty signatory, Michael Collins, to undo partition through a combination of political ploys, economic boycott and surreptitious IRA assaults on the border.[119]

O'Duffy, the IRA's Border Campaign of 1922, and the GAA

As soon as prisoners were freed under the terms of the treaty, an IRA border campaign was plotted, and the overlap between republicans and players ensured that the GAA was wrapped up in it. Gaelic matches proved apt settings for comrades to regroup. A club game in Belfast occasioned the reappearance of Joe McKelvey, an officer of the IRA's Third Northern Division, and three men who were reprieved from execution, one of whom, Tom Fox, scored the first point.[120] The Monaghan and Cavan teams that contested the Ulster football semi-final at Clones on 1 January contained players 'who had been in different internment camps for a considerable time past, [and] had a warm hand-shake from each other'.[121] Nine days later, O'Duffy was promoted to Chief of Staff of the IRA.[122] Far from keeping his IRA and Ulster GAA business separate, he blurred the lines between them quite deliberately.

The entangling of the two organisations culminated in an infamous incident on 14 January. Ten members of the Monaghan Gaelic football team were arrested by 'B Specials' at Dromore, County Tyrone, en route to the Ulster final in Derry. Four revolvers and ammunition were found in their cars.[123] Around then about half the team were in the IRA – which was the *de facto* southern state army since the treaty took effect – and they included Commandant Dan Hogan (the team captain) and four divisional officers.[124] They claimed that they had the right to carry the guns under the truce and did so for self-defence through hostile Protestant areas.[125] It seems though that they tried to use the game as cover for a reconnaissance mission aimed at an eventual jailbreak for three condemned prisoners in Derry.[126] O'Duffy, as Ulster GAA secretary and the IRA Chief of Staff, was ideally placed to coordinate events with his sidekick Hogan, who had overseen the rescue of an IRA prisoner 10 months earlier. The fixture was highly unusual also: never before or since was an Ulster football final appointed to Derry; and, oddly, the Ulster Council picked the venue before the finalists were known, at a meeting in November 1921. It may even have been initially intended to co-ordinate the Derry–Antrim semi-final with a prior jailbreak attempt: the November meeting had fixed this game for Derry, on 11 December, and decided to arrange for O'Duffy or Seán Mac Eoin, the renowned IRA commandant from Longford (who would become deputy director of the IRA's 'Ulster Council' in January), to attend this game or the final.[127] However, this first failed jailbreak went ahead earlier, on 2 December. Even without proof of the Monaghan players' plans, a northern military court remanded them in custody.[128]

Their detention had grave repercussions over the next three weeks. In early February a shadowy IRA 'Ulster Council', under the command of O'Duffy and Collins along with Frank Aiken, was set up at Clones. Parallels with the GAA Ulster Council that was already based at Clones under O'Duffy could not be more obvious. The IRA proceeded to kidnap 42 loyalists in border areas of Fermanagh and Tyrone as hostages for the Monaghan players. The Belfast government reacted by sealing the border with Specials. But when a detachment of Specials on a train crossing the border at Clones was confronted by the IRA, a gun battle broke out in which five constables and Matt Fitzpatrick, a local IRA commandant and leading Fermanagh footballer, were killed.[129] Then in the three days after the Clones shootout, 30 people were killed in Belfast. They included Frank McCoy, an IRA member and recent Antrim county footballer, who was shot dead by persons unknown.[130] Collins, now the leader of the Provisional Government in Dublin, demanded the Monaghan footballers' release to defuse the tension. London echoed this call: Winston Churchill MP, the Secretary of State for the Colonies, criticised their ongoing detention while no serious crime was alleged, and read a letter from O'Duffy blaming Specials for the Clones fatalities.[131] Once legal advice to free the footballers was received, James Craig in Belfast vowed to resign if the royal prerogative were used over his head. Reluctantly, however, he consented to their release in March.[132]

This episode was disastrous for the GAA in Ulster. Unionists seized on it to vindicate their scepticism about the GAA. Robert Lynn MP, for one, referred to 'the so-called footballers ... with arms and ammunition ... and bombs and all the other paraphernalia generally associated with Gaelic football'.[133] O'Duffy's machinations had helped to ensure the GAA would receive harsh treatment north of the border for the near future. Nevertheless, the County Monaghan GAA convention in March welcomed Dan Hogan's team as heroes, and passed a resolution hailing their 'noble part ... in the late war for the freedom of our country'. Hogan declared that they would go to Derry to play the final within the month.[134] A fortnight later, O'Duffy missed the Ulster convention at Clones, being 'detained in Dublin on other work'. Delegates realised that he could no longer commit to his GAA role, but wanted to keep him on board. Hence, they decided to retain him as secretary, even 'if only in an honorary way', and to appoint an assistant-secretary/treasurer to tackle the workload proper.[135]

But now that the security forces were on red alert towards the GAA, such a match was unlikely. Heavy-handed treatment of GAA members on their way to and from games and meetings increased. Special constables reportedly beat up delegates returning from a GAA board meeting at Claudy, Derry, in February,[136] arrested a 'well-known Gael' from Kilcoo, Co. Down, in March,[137] searched spectators at an Ulster championship match at Warrenpoint in May and stopped supporters' cars everywhere.[138] Matters worsened in May when the Minister for Home Affairs, Dawson Bates, a staunch loyalist who was notoriously distrustful of Catholics, directed the internment of over 900 nationalists without trial, including numerous GAA members. Less than 10% of internees were active in the IRA.[139] A few of the prominent GAA-member internees were in the IRA, such as Hugh Corvin and David Matthews of Belfast. Most, however, were selected as influential community leaders, whose removal could further demoralise nationalism.[140] John H. King and J.J. McKenny, the Down GAA chairman and secretary, were not IRA men, but were rounded up because of their political allegiance and their abilities as cultural organisers.[141] Dan Dempsey, an ex-Antrim GAA chairman, was interned on the basis that he 'kept the company of prominent Sinn Feiners' and supported the party.[142] Peter Tohall, a recent Tyrone GAA Board treasurer and well-respected chemist, escaped internment only because he was away from home.[143] Hence, many GAA officials and other local nationalist figures laid low or went 'on the run'.

From May, organised games lapsed in south Armagh and south Down as teams feared to turn out. In June, the Newry and District League was asked by a referee to make no fixtures 'until the times change. ... as we are surrounded by A, B and C Specials'.[144] For the rest of 1922 very few Gaelic games were played in rural areas of the six counties, with Belfast and Derry City alone playing on. The advent of the Royal Ulster Constabulary (RUC) in June compounded nationalists' worries. From the off, the RUC was an overwhelmingly Protestant-unionist force, known for partisanship.[145] The repeated stopping and overnight detention of the Derry football team on the way to Cavan in

August[146] typified the obstacles before the GAA north of the border then. In stark contrast, the new southern security forces stood proudly in support of Gaelic games. Members of the Civic Guard and the National Army patrolled the sidelines of the Monaghan–Antrim Ulster championship match at Clones in May.[147]

The outbreak of the Irish Civil War on 28 June – a week after the pro-treaty side won the southern general election – brought a swift end to the IRA's campaign against the northern state, and the GAA's entanglement therein. In July, O'Duffy moved to Limerick to take charge of the south-western command of the National Army, and he proved to be hawkish in policy. Following the assassination of Michael Collins in August, the Dublin government became preoccupied with domestic problems, abandoned plans to bring down the northern state and began to neuter the northern campaign instead: some 900 northern IRA men were enticed in August to train with the Free State Army, and then split up.[148] Collins' death represented a personal tragedy for O'Duffy and an end to his hopes of smashing partition. September brought to him a new position and fresh opportunity, however, as the Commissioner of the Civic Guard. In this police force, soon renamed *An Garda Síochána*, he instilled a greater discipline and sense of national duty. He promoted Gaelic games relentlessly too. 'A candidate's best recommendation, in my eyes', he wrote, 'was athletic fitness and keenness such as a GAA record shows'.[149] At his insistence, Gaelic games were established as the official Garda sports. Garda teams soon achieved a nationwide reputation for excellence, and, as encouraged by O'Duffy, officers built numerous handball alleys for local communities. His championing of Gaelic games over the next decade as a Garda officer did much to elevate the GAA to its position of sporting primacy in the Free State. By championing the retention of the association's ban on players engaging in soccer and rugby, counter to a strong lobby of mainly pro-treaty members seeking its deletion, O'Duffy also retained a certain respect among his republican political opponents.

O'Duffy's Involvement with the GAA in Ulster after 1923

At last O'Duffy was relieved of the duty of the Ulster GAA secretaryship in March 1923, and his replacement, Patrick McFadden, would receive a new stipend based on commission. O'Duffy's ties with his home province were certainly not cut, however. In July, he attended the opening of Breifne Park, Cavan, a landmark event in the development of the GAA in Ulster. This was not merely a first stadium for Gaelic games in the province. Its launch, just two months after the end of the Civil War, symbolised new hope for the association and society south of the border. This was the first time since the conflict that pro- and anti-Treaty TDs (O'Duffy and Frank Fahy) shared a platform. O'Duffy called on the GAA to 'bring together all sections of the Irish people' and suggested that security north of the border was bring relaxed, and he joked that 'the RUC have presented a set of medals to the Crossmaglen hurlers'.[150] Not for the first or last time, however, O'Duffy somewhat misread the political map north of the border. There the GAA faced a much more difficult future. While a calm in tensions fostered a revival during 1923 and by the late 1920s it was stronger than ever all over the six counties, the dynamics and trajectory differed greatly from those in the Free State. The denial of playing fields for Sunday games in many areas, tensions with the security forces, chronic unemployment and emigration among Catholics, and various other factors stunted the progress of the GAA within the Northern Ireland state.

In the post-revolutionary decade, O'Duffy, though based in Dublin throughout, was a totemic figure for the GAA in Ulster for several years. Ulster conventions re-elected him annually, repeatedly *in absentia*, as one of the province's three representatives on the Central Council. Even officials from the six counties who despised the border that O'Duffy's forces protected, and increasingly the Free State regime of which he was a lynchpin, insisted that he was the best man to represent them at Croke Park.[151] His reputation as a brilliant Ulster GAA official since 1912, his ongoing support of the GAA in a key public office, and his frequent anti-partition and anti-'foreign' games rhetoric, all secured their respect. His entry at the 1925 Ulster convention triggered a standing ovation from delegates.[152] Two months later, the Ulster Council suddenly appointed O'Duffy as its honorary treasurer[153] – its first standalone treasurer in two decades. This was a ruse to convince the tax authorities in Belfast that Ulster's financial affairs were conducted entirely from Croke Park, but it failed.

For the next seven years, O'Duffy remained as Ulster's nominal treasurer, but in an increasingly detached manner and amid growing controversy. He did not attend regular meetings, and on the few occasions that he attended GAA events north of the border, the RUC kept watch. Meanwhile, the posting of star Garda players from the southern provinces led to unprecedented success for Monaghan and festering resentment in the other northern counties who saw O'Duffy's hand at work. When Monaghan reached the All-Ireland football final for the first time in 1930, the match was popularly billed as 'the last battle of the Civil War', due to the apparent Garda/O'Duffy connection of the Ulster side and the presence of several leading republicans in the Kerry team; Kerry won easily in a bad-tempered clash. Dublin-based Garda and Irish Army teams made numerous visits to north during this period, to rapturous local acclaim. Yet by 1932, some republican voices north of the border began to call for the exclusion of Garda and Irish Army members from the GAA, citing political reasons, and the Antrim county convention passed a motion to that extent. In response, the Ulster Council released a statement to extol the part of the southern servicemen in promoting the GAA in Ulster and especially the 'patriotic labours' of their colleague, Garda chief O'Duffy, and the motion was withdrawn. A year later, under the new Fianna Fáil regime in Dublin, O'Duffy was dismissed as Garda Commissioner. He reacted by forming the Army Comrades Association (the 'Blueshirts') in July 1933, and in September he took office as the inaugural president of the Fine Gael party. His contentious re-entry into the political sphere led to his being voted off the Ulster Council in February 1934. After making an inglorious foray into the Spanish Civil War, his public career waned, and he died in 1944. For all that his reputation has since been tainted, there endures a certain respect for his immense part in developing the GAA in Ulster, as memorialised by the O'Duffy Terrace at the principal provincial ground, St Tiernach's Park in Clones.

Conclusion

There can be few examples in the world of someone interweaving sport and revolutionary activity so successfully as Owen O'Duffy and the GAA in Ulster. What was probably the most moderate province of the association in 1912, mirroring contemporary moods within nationalism, became radicalised through the course of political events until it acted as a central player in the War of Independence. Halfway through this period, O'Duffy re-imagined and modelled himself as a rebel leader, pushing himself and the GAA in Ulster to the van of the republican movement – but still, expediently, presenting both as martyrs of unjust rule. Many other republican leaders catalysed the politicisation of the GAA in the north and elsewhere, but none drove the transformation of their branches to such a profound or prolonged extent as O'Duffy. Nor did any Irishman benefit more than he from the role of sporting revolutionary, for his past administrative record with the GAA and military celebrity with the IRA propelling him to senior public office in the independent part of Ireland. The ironic flipside to his success in accelerating independence for the Irish Free State, this new dispensation, replete with partition, was anathema to his personal beliefs and came at the expense of his loyal GAA supporters in the six north-eastern counties.

Notes

1. Holt, *Sport and the British*, 240.
2. This article uses Owen as the spelling of O'Duffy's first name, as the contemporary documents researched indicate that he signed his name this way, rather than Eoin (as it appears in most historical texts to date).
3. *Irish News*, November 11, 1912.
4. UKHC, 5th series vol. 44, cols 2118–2119, July 31, 1912; *Irish News*, July 30, 1912.
5. Mandle, *The Gaelic Athletic Association*, 166–7.
6. McGarry, *Eoin O'Duffy*, 20.
7. Short, *The Ulster GAA Story*, 61.
8. *Derry People*, June 27, 1914.
9. *Anglo-Celt*, July 18, 1914.
10. *Irish News*, July 28, 1914.
11. Ibid., August 17, 1914.
12. Ibid., August 18, 1914.
13. *Dundalk Democrat*, November 19, 1914; McGarry, *Eoin O'Duffy*, 12–3.
14. Garnham, *Association Football*, 167–9; O'Callaghan, *Munster Rugby*, 45–9.
15. Mandle, *The Gaelic Athletic Association*, 171–5.
16. *Anglo-Celt*, October 3, 1914.
17. *Derry People*, October 26, 1914.
18. Ibid., November 28, 1914.
19. *Irish News*, April 19, 1915. See also *Anglo-Celt*, March 27, 1915.
20. *Irish News*, May 26. 1915.
21. Ibid., May 19, 1915.
22. UKHC, 5th series vol. 71, cols 704–705, April 28, 1915.
23. *Dundalk Democrat*, February 19, 1916.
24. *Irish News*, November 25, 1915.
25. McDermott, *Northern Divisions*, 8–9.
26. *Anglo-Celt*, July 24, 1915.
27. *Dundalk Democrat*, February 17, 1917.
28. *Irish News*, March 14, 1916.
29. Murphy, "The GAA," 67–8.
30. *Newry Democrat*, September 7, 2005.
31. Hepburn, *Catholic Belfast*, 172–4.
32. *Derry Journal*, May 4, 1953; May 6, 1953.
33. *Irish News*, April 12, 1916.
34. Ibid., October 4, 1916.
35. *Ireland's Saturday Night*, April 29, 1916.
36. *Anglo-Celt*, June 10, 1916.
37. Ibid., July 1, 1916.
38. UKHC, 5th series vol. 81, cols 2597–2598, May 2, 1916. See also an editorial in *The Times*, April 18, 1916.
39. De Búrca, *The GAA*, 102–3.
40. *Anglo-Celt*, June 3, 1916; June 10, 1916.
41. UKHC, 5th series vol. 83, col. 1519, July 5, 1916.
42. *Dundalk Democrat*, August 19, 1916; August 26, 1916. See also *Dungannon Democrat*, August 1, 1917.
43. Mandle, *The Gaelic Athletic Association*, 178–9.
44. Ulster GAA secretary's report for 1917, Ulster Council GAA minutes, Cardinal Ó Fiaich Library and Archive, Armagh (hereafter CÓFLA).
45. *Dundalk Democrat*, December 2, 1916.

46. *Anglo-Celt*, June 3, 1916.
47. *Irish News*, November 30, 1916; January 29, 1917.
48. *Dundalk Democrat*, February 17, 1917.
49. *Irish News*, April 11, 1917; April 16, 1917.
50. Ibid., May 16, 1917; *Ireland's Saturday Night*, July 21, 1917.
51. *Ireland's Saturday Night*, April 20, 1918.
52. *Irish News*, January 10, 1917; January 31, 1917; February 17, 1917; May 2, 1917; *Dungannon Democrat*, February 28, 1917; April 25, 1917.
53. *Irish News*, May 29, 1917.
54. McGarry, *Eoin O'Duffy*, 28.
55. *Dungannon Democrat*, January 17, 1917.
56. Entry for 1916/1917, football-diary of pupils of St Patrick's College, Armagh, 1903–1919, CÓFLA.
57. *Irish News*, December 17, 1917.
58. UKHC, 5th series vol. 93, cols 2464–2465, 2480, May 24, 1917.
59. *Anglo-Celt*, May 19, 1917.
60. *Ireland's Saturday Night*, March 10, 1917; *Anglo-Celt*, March 31, 1917.
61. *Frontier Sentinel*, August 4, 1917.
62. McDermott, *Northern Divisions*, 14.
63. O'Duffy, "Days That Are Gone," 177.
64. McGarry, *Eoin O'Duffy*, 28.
65. *Dundalk Democrat*, October 13, 1917. See *Irish News*, April 2, 1918, for similar use of *camán* at Dungannon.
66. Ulster secretary's report for 1917, Ulster Council GAA minutes of convention of March 16, 1918, CÓFLA.
67. McElligott, *Forging a Kingdom*, 269.
68. De Búrca, *The GAA*, 109; Mandle, *The Gaelic Athletic Association*, 183.
69. *Gaelic Athlete*, June 30, 1918.
70. Ulster secretary's report for 1918, Ulster Council GAA minutes, CÓFLA.
71. *Dungannon Democrat*, July 17, 1918; *Frontier Sentinel*, July 20, 1918.
72. O'Duffy, "Days That Are Gone," 173, 175; Ulster Council GAA minutes, meeting of 24 August 1918, CÓFLA. See also *Derry People*, July 20, 1918.
73. *Anglo-Celt*, August 10, 1918. See also *Frontier Sentinel*, August 10, 1918; *Freeman's Journal*, August 6, 1918; and McGuire and Hassan, "Cultural Nationalism," 8.
74. Ulster Council GAA minutes, meeting of August 24, 918, CÓFLA.
75. McGarry, *Eoin O'Duffy*, 36–7; *Anglo-Celt*, September 21, 1918. See also O'Duffy, "Days That Are Gone," 175–6.
76. *Anglo-Celt*, March 2, 1918.
77. *Dundalk Democrat*, August 10, 1918.
78. McGarry, *Eoin O'Duffy*, 32.
79. Ulster Council GAA minutes, meeting of November 15, 1919, CÓFLA.
80. *Freeman's Journal*, March 13, 1919; *Anglo-Celt*, August 16, 1919.
81. *Derry People*, April 12, 1919.
82. O'Duffy, "Days That Are Gone," 169, 171.
83. See *Frontier Sentinel*, June 21, 1919.
84. *Ulster Herald*, July 24, 1920; August 21, 1920.
85. Ibid., August 16, 1919.
86. *Frontier Sentinel*, August 2, 1919; August 16, 1919.
87. *Anglo-Celt*, July 26, 1919.
88. *Frontier Sentinel*, July 12, 1919; October 18, 1919; November 1, 1919.
89. Ulster Council GAA minutes, Ulster secretary's report for 1919, and convention of March 17, 1920, CÓFLA.
90. Ulster Council GAA minutes, meeting of April 17, 1920, CÓFLA. See also Louis Walsh, "General Eoin O'Duffy: His Life and Battle," 40, National Library of Ireland, P6539.
91. *Ulster Herald*, July 17, 1920.
92. See, for example, *Derry Journal*, August 13, 1920.
93. *Frontier Sentinel*, August 21, 1920.
94. *Ulster Herald*, June 26, 1920.

95. Ibid., October 30, 1920.
96. Lawlor, *The Burnings 1920*, 116.
97. McDermott, *Northern Divisions*, 60–1, 285. See also *Irish News*, September 27 and 29, 1920.
98. De Búrca, *The GAA*, 118; Mandle, *The Gaelic Athletic Association*, 193–4.
99. UKHC, 5th series vol. 135, 39–42, November 22, 1920; *Freeman's Journal*, November 23, 1920.
100. Follis, *A State under Siege*, 54, 68, 81, 91; Buckland, *Factory of Grievances*, 71.
101. De Búrca, *The GAA*, 119.
102. Lynch, *The Northern IRA*, 71, 75; McDermott, *Northern Divisions*, 51.
103. *Derry Journal*, March 10, 1922; Lynch, *The Northern IRA*, 54; *Irish News*, January 19, 1922.
104. *Derry Journal*, April 16, 1921.
105. *Derry Journal*, April 15, 1921.
106. Hopkinson, *The Irish War*, 158.
107. Farrell, *Arming the Protestants*, 154–66, 299–304 *passim*.
108. *Frontier Sentinel*, January 29, 1921. See also *Dungannon Democrat*, May 18, 1921.
109. *Irish News*, April 25, 1921.
110. *Anglo-Celt*, March 11, 1922.
111. McGarry, *Eoin O'Duffy*, 74–5.
112. McDermott, *Northern Divisions*, 101. See also *Irish News*, July 11 and 12, 1921.
113. *Irish News*, July 19, 1921.
114. McDermott, *Northern Divisions*, 108.
115. McGarry, *Eoin O'Duffy*, 78–81.
116. Ulster Council GAA minutes, meeting of October 22, 1921, CÓFLA.
117. *Derry Journal*, September 19, 1921.
118. McGarry, *Eoin O'Duffy*, 93.
119. Phoenix, *Northern Nationalism*, 189–91, 209–12.
120. *Irish News*, January 23, 1922.
121. *Anglo-Celt*, January 7, 1922.
122. McGarry, *Eoin O'Duffy*, 95.
123. *Irish News*, January 17, 1922; February 16, 1922.
124. Lynch, *The Northern IRA*, 100; Clogher Diocesan Historical Society, *Cuimhneachán Mhuineacháin*, 92–4.
125. *Freeman's Journal*, January 17, 1922.
126. Lynch, *The Northern IRA*, 100.
127. Ulster Council GAA minutes, meeting of November 11, 1921, CÓFLA.
128. *Irish News*, January 17, 1922.
129. Livingstone, *The Fermanagh Story*, 303–4.
130. *Frontier Sentinel*, February 18, 1922; February 25, 1922.
131. UKHC, 5th series vol. 150, col. 1009, on February 15, 1922; McGarry, *Eoin O'Duffy*, 100.
132. Buckland, *Factory of Grievances*, 209.
133. Northern Ireland House of Commons debates (*Hansard*; hereafter referred to as NIHC), vol. 2, col. 26, March 14, 1922.
134. *Anglo-Celt*, March 11, 1922.
135. Ulster Council GAA minutes, Ulster convention of March 17, 1922, CÓFLA.
136. *Derry Journal*, February 15, 1922.
137. *Frontier Sentinel*, March 11, 1922.
138. *Anglo-Celt*, May 13, 1922.
139. Kleinrichert, *Republican Internment*, 335–68 *passim*.
140. Ibid., 52, 62.
141. Ibid., 337, 341, 350, 352, 353, 354, 359, 360–2. See also W. F. Curry, District Inspector's Office, RUC Newcastle, to CI, Co. Down, March 24, 1923, PRONI HA/5/2325.
142. Intelligence file on recommended internment of Daniel Dempsey, *circa* June 1922, PRONI HA/32/1/155.
143. Intelligence file on Peter Tohall, Moy, Co. Tyrone, PRONI HA/5/1237.
144. Joe Connellan, "Down's Early Days," in *Ulster Games Annual*, 1966, 121.
145. Ryder, *The RUC*, 59, 60–1.
146. *Derry Journal*, August 18, 1922.
147. *Frontier Sentinel*, May 13, 1922.

148. Lynch, *The Northern IRA*, 190–7.
149. McGarry, *Eoin O'Duffy*, 118.
150. *Anglo-Celt*, July 28, 1923.
151. See *Anglo-Celt*, March 21, 1925; and *Frontier Sentinel*, March 20, 1926.
152. *Gaelic Athlete*, March 21, 1925; Ulster Council GAA minutes, Ulster convention of March 15, 1925, CÓFLA.
153. Ulster Council GAA minutes, meeting of May 16, 1925, CÓFLA.

References

Buckland, Patrick. *Factory of Grievances: Devolved Government in Northern Ireland, 1921–1939*. Dublin: Gill and Macmillan, 1979.
Clogher Diocesan Historical Society. *Cuimhneachán Mhuineacháin 1916–66 Souvenir Programme*, edited by Fr. Laurence Marron. Clogher: Cumann Seanchais Chlochair, 1966.
de Búrca, Marcus. *The GAA: A History*. 2nd ed. Dublin: Gill and Macmillan, 1999.
Farrell, Michael. *Arming the Protestants: The Formation of the Ulster Special Constabulary and the Royal Ulster Constabulary, 1920–27*. Dingle: Brandon, 1983.
Follis, Bryan A. *A State under Siege: The Establishment of Northern Ireland, 1920–25*. Oxford: Clarendon Press, 1995.
Garnham, Neal. *Association Football and Society in Pre-partition Ireland*. Belfast: Ulster Historical Foundation, 2004.
Hepburn, A. C. *Catholic Belfast and Nationalist Ireland in the Era of Joe Devlin 1871–1934*. Oxford: Oxford University Press, 2008.
Holt, Richard. *Sport and the British: A Modern History*. Oxford: Clarendon Press, 1989.
Hopkinson, Michael. *The Irish War of Independence*. Montreal: Gill and Macmillan, 2004.
Kleinrichert, Denise. *Republican Internment and the Prison Ship Argenta, 1922*. Dublin: Irish Academic Press, 2001.
Lawlor, Pearse. *The Burnings 1920*. Cork: Mercier Press, 2009.
Livingstone, Peadar. *The Fermanagh Story: A Documented History of the County Fermanagh from the Earliest Times to the Present Day*. Enniskillen: Cumann Seanchais Chlochair, 1969.
Lynch, Robert. *The Northern IRA and the Early Years of Partition 1920–1922*. Dublin: Irish Academic Press, 2006.
Mandle, W. F. *The Gaelic Athletic Association and Irish Nationalist Politics, 1884–1924*. Dublin: Gill and Macmillan, 1987.
McDermott, Jim. *Northern Divisions: The Old IRA and the Belfast Pogroms, 1920–1922*. Belfast: Beyond the Pale Publications, 2001.
McElligott, Richard. *Forging a Kingdom: The GAA in Kerry 1884–1934*. Cork: Collins Press, 2013.
McGarry, Fearghal. *Eoin O'Duffy: A Self-Made Hero*. Oxford: Oxford University Press, 2005.
McGuire, Andrew, and David Hassan. "Cultural Nationalism, Gaelic Sunday and the Gaelic Athletic Association in Early Twentieth Century Ireland." *International Journal of the History of Sport* 29, no. 6 (2012): 1–12.
Murphy, William. "The GAA during the Irish Revolution, 1913–23." In *The Gaelic Athletic Association 1884–2009*, edited by Mike Cronin, William Murphy, and Paul Rouse, 95–111. Dublin: Irish Academic Press, 2009.
O'Callaghan, Liam. *Munster Rugby: A Social and Cultural History*. Cork: Cork University Press, 2011.
O'Duffy, Eoin. "Days That Are Gone." In *Gaelic Athletic Memories*, edited by Seamus Ó Ceallaigh, 161–191. Limerick: Gaelic Athletic Publications, 1945.
Phoenix, Eamon. *Northern Nationalism: Nationalist Politics, Partition and the Catholic Minority in Northern Ireland 1890–1940*. Belfast: Ulster Historical Foundation, 1994.
Ryder, Chris. *The RUC: A Force under Fire*. London: Methuen, 1989.
Short, Con. *The Ulster GAA Story 1884–1984*. Monaghan: Comhairle Uladh, 1984.

Bolsheviks, Revolution and Physical Culture

Susan Grant

School of History and Archives, University College Dublin, Dublin, Ireland; and Munk School of Global affairs, University of Toronto, Toronto, Canada

This article assesses the impact of the October Revolution of 1917 and the role of its leading revolutionaries on physical culture and sport. Foremost among these was Bolshevik leader Vladimir I. Lenin, and his contribution to the shaping of sport in the Soviet Union receives particular attention. Key to fully understanding Lenin's role in the development of physical culture and sport is the Lenin 'myth' and its interpretation in later Soviet sports discourse. The combination of the Lenin myth and Marxist–Leninist ideology was part of an ongoing Soviet effort to shape the ideal socialist citizen. The Bolshevik project was concerned with forging a new self and physical culture was an important part of this process. Thus, this article highlights intersections between the physical and emotional self, arguing that physical culture and sport were instrumental in contributing to revolutionary vision.

Introduction

In his excellent article on Vladimir Ilyich Lenin and sport, Carter Elwood concludes that the leader of the world communist revolution did not pursue his passion for active leisure in order to make himself a 'better revolutionary', but rather because he more than likely enjoyed the physical challenge of climbing, skiing, skating or cycling.[1] In the Soviet Union, quite a different view prevailed. Lenin's actual motivation became irrelevant. His love of sport and exercise was portrayed as being not 'an end in itself' but rather a means of increasing his labour capacity, his physical strength and will, and, importantly, 'helping him in the revolutionary struggle'.[2] Yet, this view was part of an important discourse construct, one that indelibly bound Lenin, the revolutionary struggle, and physical culture and sport together. As I argue here, this discourse did not just emerge as some form of late Soviet nostalgia, but was also an important facet of Bolshevik revolutionary discourse from the outset. Moreover, the nexus between sport and revolutionary struggle was often tied to a larger Bolshevik psychology. Sport and physical culture, inextricably connected to emotion and feelings, became a key component of this new Soviet psychology. Perhaps even more significantly, in Bolshevik terms, sport could provide a site for both individual and collective emotional expression. With the Bolsheviks in power, sport and physical culture became part of the revolutionary discourse, a vital political, social and cultural tool with which to introduce and promote the new communist lifestyle.

The Bolshevik obsession with knowing the 'mood' of its people has been well documented in recent works that explore issues of surveillance and information gathering, as well as the Bolshevik desire to ensure that those admitted to the party and holding party cards were those with a Bolshevik 'soul' and 'conscience'.[3] The inner realm of the individual, their self and their soul, was subject to constant investigation and review. But the physical self was just as important – appearance, behaviour and manner were also part of being a Bolshevik. To this end, involvement in sport and physical culture displayed an individual's faith in and commitment to the Bolshevik credo. To be a true Bolshevik meant total physical, emotional and intellectual submission to the socialist way of life. This immersion had to be demonstrable. Participation in sports, attendance at parades as well as observance of personal hygiene, diet and exercise were all central facets of being a good, 'practicing' Bolshevik.[4] In an era when the language of signs and symbols carried considerable meaning, the significance of one's comportment revealed a great deal. An outwardly healthy physical body mirrored an inwardly healthy soul. The moral character of an individual could be shaped through physical culture. Therefore, as this article will show, Lenin and the Bolsheviks considered physical culture and sport to be a key part of overall revolutionary culture.

Lenin, Ideology and Myth

Cohorts armed with knowledge of Marxism–Leninism and an understanding of what the Bolshevik project was about was not enough in the battle to establish a communist state; one had to embrace the entire revolutionary philosophy and master the new psychology. Lenin and the Bolsheviks required the new socialist world to be populated by new socialist people who were ready at any moment to meet the exacting needs of the party-state. In an endeavour to achieve this lofty goal of creating a new type of people, the concept of the 'New Man' was reborn in Bolshevik guise. The original inspiration behind the New Man was in large part derived from the character of Rakhmetov from Nikolai Chernyshevsky's nineteenth century novel *What is to Be Done?* Rakhmetov was the figure which every Soviet citizen was encouraged to emulate, his ascetic and abstemious lifestyle suited to the ideal revolutionary new person of the 1920s.[5] In order to transform his body, Rakhmetov devoted himself to building up his physical strength. The utopian ideas associated with the novel permeated Russian revolutionary thinking of the late nineteenth and early twentieth centuries, inspiring in particular Lenin, who had been so impressed by its revolutionary message. Elwood argues that while Lenin 'may have admired Chernyshevsky's aesthetic hero', he casts doubt over the view that Lenin would have considered 'good health to be the revolutionary's main asset'.[6] This may be true, but over the 70 years of Soviet power, what Lenin said or did was suffused in ideology. Lenin, the man, might not have emulated Chernyshevsky's hero, but Lenin, the myth, could be viewed as a direct descendent and a practitioner of his ideas. This is in large part because of the high stature in which *What is to be Done?* was held among Russian revolutionaries, with the concept of the New Man a powerful force in Soviet politics, art and literature.[7] It formed part of the healthy ideal, encouraging the masses to participate in sports to not only better themselves physically but also to show themselves as 'new people', born of the socialist revolution. Lenin, the 'myth', expanded exponentially after his death in 1924, when the cult of Lenin initiated some months beforehand assumed immense prominence.

As head of state, Lenin had sought to lead by example in the hope that his appreciation of a good work ethic and discipline would somehow transfer to his subordinates and indeed the Russian population at large.[8] After his death, the cult of Lenin lived on and was exploited to extol the virtues of the deceased leader of the socialist revolution, propelling him to saint-like status and often conflating the man and the myth. This is evident in the case of sport. Lenin's personal interest in sport and physical culture represented a direct link with state policy. In motivating Soviet citizens to participate in sport, the shadow of Lenin and his celebrated genius was often present, promoting physical activity and thus validating the Soviet sports system. It was a strange fusion of Marxism–Leninism. In the absence of any serious writings on sport by either Marx or Lenin, the latter's hobbies, personal musings and interests often came to substantiate articles and books on the significance of physical culture and sport. Of course, what had been hobbies for Lenin were in the Soviet context transformed into serious political activities for ordinary citizens. Physical culture, even during the very early years of Bolshevik power, was on its way to becoming a vast ideological machine that would produce physically ideal and robust Soviet citizens.

In his book on Lenin and the protection of the health of workers and physical culture, G. S. Demetr stated that Lenin considered the physical conditioning of the Bolshevik revolutionary to be of utmost importance. Lenin, physical culture and the revolution were tightly interlocked. This was the standard Soviet line. In his speeches and letters, Demetr notes, Lenin emphasised that the revolutionary Bolshevik – with their high moral qualities and complete devotion to the business of revolution – had to be in the best of health and be physically strong and tough to be able to withstand the deprivations associated with the revolutionary struggle, arrest and exile.[9] However, among the leading Bolshevik revolutionaries, physical fitness and a commitment to exercise were not widespread. Lenin was not widely emulated in his adherence to a strict regimen. The cafe culture enjoyed by revolutionaries in exile prior to October followed by the lean years of civil war was not conducive to a healthy lifestyle for Bolshevik leaders.[10] But the point here is that Lenin was *ex post facto* accredited with making individual commitment to the cultivation and maintenance of good health essential to the Bolshevik revolutionary.

Lenin, as argued by Demetr, frequently indicated that the revolutionary had to use physical culture for the strengthening of his or her health.[11] Walking, running, cycling, skating and gymnastics were to be a part of the revolutionary's personal armoury. Good health, if not the revolutionary's main asset, was, nonetheless, construed to have been an important one. Demetr's writings certainly suggest this. When discussing vital party questions, he noted, Lenin never failed to remind colleagues to take care of their health, advising them to exercise in order to preserve their health and strength for the revolutionary cause.[12] After his death, Lenin's views on exercise and health, expressed largely through personal correspondences, became co-opted to represent some sort of broader revolutionary outlook. As James Riordan put it in his work on sport, politics and communism, 'Lenin's sporting activity may seem to have little relevance for an understanding of sport in communist states', but what cannot be overlooked is 'the influence Lenin has had … as well as the Soviet establishment's cult of Lenin and penchant for looking to Lenin's personal example when seeking to justify current policies'.[13] Lenin was the means to an end.

Naturally, Marx and Engels were drawn upon to explain and legitimise Soviet physical culture and sport. So what had Marx to say about physical culture and sport? Not a great deal, in fact. When discussing the struggle for a normal working day, Marx had written that in its 'wolf-hunger for surplus labour, capital oversteps not only the moral, but even the merely physical maximum bounds of the working-day' and 'usurps the time for growth, development, and healthy maintenance of the body. It steals the time required for the consumption of fresh air and sunlight'.[14] Thus, it could be interpreted (as indeed it was in the Soviet context) that physical culture was important for workers because devoting time to physical activities such as games or exercises would help improve workers' health, making them more efficient in the workplace. Engels had also advanced physical culture as a means of improving health and physical fitness, advocating the curtailment of military service as the equivalent to 'the best physical education of youth'.[15] Engels (unlike Marx) had a personal interest in physical health, related to his interest in military theory and strategy. Indeed, he 'combined this intellectual preparation with a constant concern to maintain his physical fitness, to resume action on the ground when the time came'.[16] Neither Marx nor Engels came close to Lenin in their personal or philosophical views on physical culture. It was Lenin who tied Marxist doctrine and physical culture together.

As both Riordan and Demetr have argued, ideas associated with the development of the individual through physical culture were produced by Lenin after the revolution. Lenin's ideas formed the basis of the Soviet school that 'defined the tasks and goals of communist *vospitanie*[17] of the growing generation, the principles of methods of study, as well as all the problems related to education, and moral, aesthetic, and physical *vospitanie*'.[18] The post-Stalinist interpretation – as iterated by Demetr in typical Soviet parlance – argued that the classics of Marxism–Leninism laid the basis for the classical, party understanding of the 'social essence' of physical culture and only Marxist–Leninist methodology allowed for the 'fullest means' of defining the most effective route for the further development of physical culture and sport and for their use in the construction of communist society. Moreover, Lenin's works dedicated to the question of communist *vospitanie* offered the opportunity to 'fully value' the role of physical culture and sport as a means of constructing communism.[19] The impression produced is that the development and success of Soviet physical culture and sport owed entirely to the efforts of the 'great Lenin'. Symptomatic of the Lenin cult and its imputations, Soviet sport and physical culture had come to be considered an inseparable element of Marxist–Leninist doctrine.

The Physical and Emotional Self

When the Bolsheviks came to power in October 1917, they inherited a country devastated by war and in the throes of revolution. Violence did not end with the Bolshevik revolution and withdrawal from the First World War; civil war was soon to follow. The extreme political, social and economic turmoil that accompanied the widespread violence exacerbated the already fragile health of the population. Typhus, tuberculosis, cholera and other diseases and illnesses afflicted tens of thousands. Mass migration, famine and general upheaval caused even more chaos across Russia and its borderlands. It was against this backdrop that the Bolshevik party attempted to wield its power. Establishing a foothold was a priority. So too, however, was improving health. Participation in physical culture and sport, by allowing young men and women to raise their fitness levels and train in paramilitary activities, was in many ways a means to create a strong, active force ready to defend Bolshevik power.

As early as 1917, physical culture was placed under the control of Vsevobuch (*Vseobshchee Voennoe Obuchenie* or the Central Agency for Universal Military Training, 1917–1921) which set as its goal the military and reserve training of youth between the ages of 14–18.[20] This enabled the Red Army to train civilian youth and prepare them for military action.[21] According to its head, Nikolai Podvoisky, the creation of Vsevobuch, with its emphasis on physical training as an important step in the development of a more fully rounded individual, reflected Lenin's reading of Marx on physical culture.[22] Two important points should be noted here. First, pre-revolutionary Russia had a splay of developing sport and physical culture societies and groups (albeit not state organised). The Scouts, Maccabees, as well as a slew of sports clubs and associations already existed and then expanded after the 1905 revolution. Moreover, Vsevobuch could be regarded as the

Bolshevik successor to the Tsarist military sports organisation set up during the war to train young men for the battlefield. Second, the Leninist or Bolshevik 'take' on physical culture fitted into a broader European trend that looked to replace militarism and paramilitarism with health and hygiene as a means to revitalise society. Soon after the Civil War ended, Vsevobuch was dissolved and a body more suitable to civilian conditions was established. The need for the mass military training of young people was overtaken by the need to improve basic health and hygiene. Debilitated, diseased and disillusioned youth became a growing concern in the 1920s. The Supreme Council for Physical Culture and Sport, established in 1923, sought to channel mass energy and emotion into organised proletarian sport and exercise. By doing this, Lenin and his fellow revolutionaries attempted to exert a direct influence on the leisure time of young people, the party's vanguard.

The importance of involving people in sport and physical culture was perhaps also noted because Bolsheviks and other revolutionaries had used sport and sports clubs for their own revolutionary purposes in the past. In 1904, Bolsheviks in the famous Petersburg Putilov factory had lured young workers away from the 'bourgeois-democratic' sports club and instead organised their own circle or *kruzhok* for revolutionary worker sportsmen.[23] In Rostov in 1905, a worker's *kruzhok* for boxers had been established where, besides boxing, they also practised shooting and read Marxist literature. The worker sports clubs that emerged around this time often engaged in military activities, including bomb throwing.[24] It was no wonder then that the Bolsheviks were keen to establish their own organisation for physical culture and sport, which would include as much of the population as possible, but especially workers and youth. Drawing large segments of the population into physical culture and sport could, in theory at least, eliminate a whole host of potential social, cultural and political problems.

At the Third Komsomol (the Communist Youth League) Congress in 1920, Lenin called on youth to acquire valuable knowledge and nurture moral qualities necessary in the fight to construct the new, socialist society. He emphasised that the education and upbringing of young people had to present a model of communist morality – this had 'particular meaning for the development of physical culture as part of communist upbringing'.[25] By proselytising good hygiene habits, encouraging exercise and affirming discipline, physical culture was a vital aspect of communist education and upbringing. Lenin, a life-long enthusiast of outdoor pursuits and healthy living, appreciated the benefits of physical culture and its influence on the development of an individual. Of all the Russian revolutionaries associated with physical culture and sport, however, neither Lenin nor Lev Trotsky could claim to have had much direct involvement in its organisation or implementation. The two figures most closely connected to physical culture were Podvoisky and Nikolai Semashko.[26] It was the latter, in particular, who exerted immense influence over physical culture in the 1920s. Semashko, a physician and close friend of Lenin's since their time in European exile, was Commissar for Health and head of the body overseeing physical culture. His interest in health lent a strong prophylactic element to the direction which early Soviet physical culture was to follow. It was nonetheless Lenin who was more often than not lauded as the 'father of Soviet physical culture', who had outlined and defined the goals, tasks and path to its development.[27]

The educational and moral value of physical culture and sport was not lost on the revolutionaries. Lenin, as Podvoisky recalled, considered Vsevobuch to hold a very important social function – to foster among young boys and girls involved in physical culture a cultured and 'comradely' mutual relationship.[28] This notion of physical culture and sport as a healthy lifestyle choice for young people – and healthy forum for social interaction among the sexes – was developed further throughout the 1920s.[29] Young people in particular, according to Lenin, 'needed the joy and force of life'. This could be attained through '[h]ealthy sport, swimming, racing, walking, bodily exercises of every kind and many-sided intellectual interests' which would 'give young people more than eternal theories and discussions about sexual problems and the so-called "living to the full"'.[30] Sport could provide a healthy environment for social interaction between boys and girls, veering them away from alcohol and sexual encounters. At this stage, though, it was physical culture as opposed to sport *per se* which the Bolsheviks sought to promulgate. Sport had assumed negative connotations, associated with bourgeois competition and record-breaking. Soviet sport (and indeed worker sport more generally) was concerned with the health and well-being of the individual as well as the collective experience and enjoyment of physical exercise. Competitive sport was looked upon unfavourably and did not receive official sanction until the late 1920s and 1930s.

In the Soviet context, active participation in or observance of physical culture were not sufficient in and of themselves. Physical culture had to be conducted in the communist spirit with complete socialist consciousness and mental commitment to the cause of the revolution and the party-state. For the Bolsheviks, the body was not just an empty vessel, but also a physical entity to be preened and perfected. It was viewed as a rich symbolic bearer of political policy and ideological destiny. Sport was thus an ideal means of 'working on' the physical self. Soviet citizens were encouraged to become participants in the construction of communism through their physical and emotional involvement in *inter alia* agitation campaigns, shock work, Pioneer activities, sports, festivals and parades. According to official rhetoric, social and individual betterment were possible only through total immersion in socialist life. This was well described by Lenin's wife, Nadezhda Krupskaya, who wrote that 'a communist is, first and foremost, *a person involved in society*, with strongly developed social instincts ...'.[31] In the new socialist world, each person was assigned some sort of an ethical and moral responsibility. In this world, individual involvement in political, cultural and social life were instrumental to the collective well-being of society. Aside from moral and ideological commitments, as well as the channelling of emotional energy into sports, there were also, of course, practical reasons for the revolutionaries' interest in sport and physical culture.[32]

By the time he was writing 'On Cooperation' in January 1923, Lenin acknowledged the significance of culture. With the revolution won and political power attained, he wrote that the 'emphasis is changing and shifting to peaceful, organizational, "cultural" work' and, most significantly, to education.[33] Exercise and hygiene were directed to informing and educating young people, with the ideology of physical culture to provide them with a clearly defined programme for assuming the role of new socialist person. The objective of physical culture education and propaganda was to mould young people into healthy, physically strong citizens, and this was frequently accompanied by a moralising element that sought to influence the sexual and behavioural desires and actions of young people. In discussing the ideology of physical culture and the creation of the New Man, Trotsky referenced the 'evolution of a "new will-power", "courage", "speed" and "precision"'.[34] Bodily discipline and a desire to shape and assert control over one's physical self was attractive at a time when strong workers were needed to rebuild civil society. Responsibility for achieving much of this was placed on the physical culture organisations. When speaking at the congress of physical culture councils in 1924, Trotsky spoke of the 'future person' who would look back on the past and 'with gratitude recall the work done by the organizations of physical culture', which had prepared for and precipitated the arrival of this future person.[35] The desire for improvement formed part of the ideology of physical culture which, although stretching across a range of different disciplines, had the common objective of stabilising society by encouraging people to work on themselves to become healthier and thus better citizens.[36]

The Bolsheviks used physical culture and sport to target certain groups within society, tailoring physical culture to their needs and marketing sport as an attractive pastime. As discussed above, active sport for young people was deemed particularly important. Swimming, running, football and other sports were encouraged, with collective sport especially desirable. For young women, active sports – contrary to prevailing opinion in much of Europe at the time – were acceptable and widely promoted, but for older women or women in the countryside physical culture that spoke to maintaining standards of hygiene and healthy living were more commonplace, especially in the 1920s. National minorities and peasants were also encouraged to participate in physical culture. While there was already a rich physical culture heritage among both peasants and national minorities, this was not organised and so did not strictly fall within the rubric of Soviet sport and physical culture. One of the primary tasks of the All-Russian Supreme Council for Physical Culture and Sport was to coordinate and organise sport. Since the first days of the revolution, establishing political control had been the key objective. Within the cultural sphere, control was no less important and physical culture and sport were subject to constant organisation and re-organisation throughout the interwar period. Bolshevik revolutionary zeal manifested itself in many fields in the 1920s, and physical culture was one of these.

The Bolshevik interest in physical culture and sport draws attention to physical culture's power to transform the individual self, thereby benefiting both the individual and, most importantly, society. Physical culture in its Bolshevik incarnation was above all an ideology that promoted the right kind of 'physical' image with which the individual and collective could identify. As art historian Christina Kiaer has argued, 'the ideological images of sport succeeded ... because of the active participation of Soviet subjects'.[37] Participation was intrinsic to both individual, personal success and collective, state success. Through schools, workplaces, social outlets, military service and elsewhere, Soviet citizens came into contact with sports clubs and societies. Whether through the Komsomol (the Communist Youth League) or the trade unions, ordinary people living in the Soviet Union were encouraged to participate in sports classes, competitions and parades. Whether they wanted to or not, Soviet citizens found themselves drawn into sport as part of the wider socialist project. The emotional investment of participants in this project varied considerably. Some factory workers, for example, had little interest in attending the physical culture parades. As one worker commented, they did not know whether their weary legs could carry them home, let alone to the demonstration.[38] Another worker who had previously attended a parade remained unimpressed: 'I went once ... what did I get out of it? I just wanted to eat'.[39] At the other end of the spectrum were the genuinely enthusiastic who enjoyed participating in sports, whether or not they believed the Soviet propaganda that more or less always accompanied it. For example, N. Slivina, a Soviet diving champion, noted that participation in sports improved her physical and mental well-being.[40] Another woman, a factory worker, claimed that sport allowed her to exert more influence and control over her life, and that she felt better when involved in sport.[41] Irrespective of how those participating in sports or attending the parades actually felt, what was important now was image.

By the 1930s, it seemed as though the revolutionary dream was coming true with the New Soviet Man and Woman winning cult-like status of almost superhuman proportions. Images of strong and healthy sportspersons captured the dynamic forward movement of communism and the success of the revolutionary commitment to physical culture. Successful workers, heroically fulfilling the Five Year Plans and contributing to society, provided an image of vitality and discipline, characteristics resonant of participation in sport and physical culture. Reflecting this linear progression, the 1930s Soviet New Man was a more cultured and developed version of his 1920s predecessor, and was also to be a more exact embodiment of the ideals of physical culture – he was to be clean and smart, healthy and politically astute.[42] Even more significant was the development of such facets as endurance, persistence, self-sacrifice and control over one's emotions. This latter characteristic was deemed particularly essential. Mental strength was to be accompanied by the physical, with New Soviet Citizens to not only participate in, but also in fact excel at sport. Still incorporating the precepts of Marxism–Leninism, the 1930s held aloft the revolutionary spirit of physical development and discipline. The epitome of sporting achievement and demonstration of self-control and discipline in the Soviet case were the GTO[43] awards, the spartakiads[44] and the physical culture parades.

Conclusion

Physical culture and sport were an intrinsic part of the Bolshevik and Soviet project. Although physical culture had shallow roots in Marxist doctrine, it was not entirely absent and the writings of both Marx and Engels suggested that physical activities such as exercise and games contributed to worker satisfaction and consequently created better conditions for workers and society. Lenin, and Lenin's writings, put Marxism into practice and the Bolshevik revolutionaries implemented policies and decisions that saw to the establishment of a socialist or proletarian physical culture and sport. Marxist doctrine left no blueprint for how socialist sport should develop. In the absence of such a blueprint, Lenin's writings and his personal interest in sport and physical culture often served as substitute. Whatever the exact provenance of socialist physical culture and sport or its later Soviet interpretation, there is no doubting that it was born in the cauldron of revolution and initially forged by those revolutionary figures who assumed control after 1917, who adapted it to suit the immediate conditions with which they were confronted. Physical culture and sport during these early post-revolutionary years assumed a prophylactic nature as the newly empowered revolutionaries initially attempted to steady the Soviet ship before setting it upon its course for a glorious communist destination. The 1920s saw the growth and organisation of physical culture and sport as it underwent its metamorphosis from a form of fledgling proletarian physical culture to a mighty Soviet sports system. Within this system were countless individuals tasked with achieving their own personal kind of transformation, both mental and physical. The Bolshevik project, with its contorted fusion of ideology and dogma, as well as its preoccupation with transformation and expedience, was in theory a grand, if not utopian, vision. Through their participation and involvement in physical culture and sport, millions of Soviet citizens contributed to realising this revolutionary vision. They had, it seemed, answered Lenin's call to pursue sport and physical culture to make themselves better revolutionaries and then later, better communists.

Acknowledgements

I thank James Ryan and Sylvain Dufraisse, who read and commented on this paper. Any errors or omissions are the responsibility of the author.

Notes

1. Elwood, "The Sporting Life of V. I. Lenin," 94.
2. Prokofiev, "Fizicheskaya Kul'tura v zhizni V. I. Lenina." Quite bizarrely, and more than a little out of place, this article on Lenin and sport featured in a nursing journal.
3. Holquist, "Information is the Alpha and Omega of Our Work"; Halfin, *Red Autobiographies*.
4. For more discussion of some of these ideas, see Starks, *The Body Soviet*; Hoffmann, "Bodies of Knowledge: Physical Culture and the New Soviet Man," in Halfin, *Language and Revolution*.
5. That many did idolise those who had adopted the lifestyle of the 'New Soviet Person' is undisputed. Admiration and awe for these new Soviet warriors and bureaucrats have been recounted, predominantly among the young and impressionable. See, for example, Novak-Deker, *Soviet Youth*, especially 53–4.
6. Elwood, "The Sporting Life of V. I. Lenin," 93.
7. See Bowlt, "Body Beautiful." For further discussion of the New Man, see Fritzsche and Hellbeck, "The New Man in Stalinist Russia."
8. For more on the cult of Lenin, see Tumarkin, *Lenin Lives!*
9. Demetr, *Lenin ob okhrane*, 26. It is worth noting here that works produced in the Soviet period faced ideological restrictions. Some of those who wrote on physical culture and sport were members of the History and Organization Faculty of Physical Culture in the Moscow Institute of Physical Culture, and so were unlikely candidates for a neutral treatment of physical culture, no doubt being obliged to toe the party line and provide the 'accepted', ideologically correct history of the movement. See, for example, Samoukov, *Istoriya fizicheskoi kul'tury*; Chudinov, *Osnovnye postanovleniya, prikazy i instruktsii po voprosam sovetskoi fizicheskoi kul'tury i sporta 1917–1957*. See *Bibliograficheskii ukazatel' nauchno-issledovatel'skikh i nauchno-metodicheskikh trudov professorov i prepodavetelei instituta (1920–1961)* (Moscow, 1964).
10. There were some notable exceptions, for example Mikhail V. Frunze, Feliks E. Dzerzhinsky, Sergei M. Kirov and Anatoly V. Lunacharsky. See Demetr, *Lenin ob okhrane*, 28.
11. Ibid., 27.
12. Ibid., 29. In 279 published letters to relatives ('k rodnym'), more than 80 of these mentioned physical culture.
13. Riordan, *Sport, Politics, and Communism*, 23–4.
14. Karl Marx, *Capital*, Vol. 1 Chapter 10, Section Five. Accessed July 19, 2013. http://www.marxists.org/archive/marx/works/1867-c1/ch10.htm
15. Burban and Solodkii, "Dal'neishee razvitie KPSS i voploshchenie v zhizn' Leninskikh idei o fizicheskom vospitanii," 111.
16. Achcar, "Engels."
17. *Vospitanie* is not a term that translates directly into English. It means more than just education (which is 'obrazovanie') and refers to upbringing, habits, mores, etc.
18. Demetr, *Lenin ob okhrane*, 10. See Riordan, *Sport, Politics, and Communism*, 245.
19. Demetr, *Lenin ob okhrane*, 11.
20. Rossisskii Gosudarstvennyi Arkhiv Sotsial'no Politicheskoi Istorii (RGASPI), f.17, op.10, d.25, l.24. During the civil war, women were also participate in Vsevobuch training and activities. For more on this, see Wood, *The Baba and the Comrade*, 52–7. See also Sanborn, *Drafting the Russian Nation*, chapter 4. It should be noted here that other groups such as the Scouts remained in existence during this period and were gradually taken over by the Bolsheviks.
21. For more on Vsevobuch and the organisation of physical culture and sport in the Soviet Union, see Grant, "The Politics of Physical Culture in the 1920s" and *Physical Culture and Sport*.

22. Riordan, *Sport, Politics, and Communism*, 24.
23. Demetr, *Lenin ob okhrane*, 23.
24. For more on worker sport activities in Russia, see Riordan, "Worker Sport within a Worker State".
25. Demetr and Gorbunov, *70 let sovetskogo sorta/Liudi, sobytiya, fakty*, 12. The 'moral' dimension remained an important element of physical culture and sport throughout the Soviet period.
26. For more on the relationship between these two Podvoisky and Semashko, as well as other leading figures in physical culture and sport, see Grant, "The Politics of Physical Culture in the 1920s."
27. N. I. Podvoisky, "Lenin o fizicheskom vospitanii," *Krasnyi sport*, 1940 in *Uchenye zapiski*. Vypusk 1 (Trudy kafedry marksizma-leninizma, Volgograd, 1969), 126.
28. Demetr, *Lenin ob okhrane*, 57.
29. For more discussion on this, see my chapter on young people in *Physical Culture and Sport in Soviet Society*.
30. Zetkin, "Women, Marriage, and Sex."
31. From the journal *Iunii kommunist*, No. 8–9, 1922 in Rosenberg, *Bolshevik Visions*, 26.
32. It must be noted that physical culture and sport were not the only targets of 'Leninization'; the cult of Lenin was all-pervasive. Lenin and Leninism were so entangled that it was hard to separate the man from the ideology.
33. Lenin, *Collected Works*, Vol. 33, 467–75. Accessed July 19, 2013. http://www.marxists.org/archive/lenin/works/1923/jan/06.htm
34. Simpson, "Imag(in)ing Post-Revolutionary Evolution," 236.
35. "Rech' na s"ezde sovetov fizkul'tury 19 Aprelya 1924g," in *Trotsky L. Sochineniya kul'tura perekhodnogo perioda* (Moscow-Leningrad: Gosizdat, 1927), 103.
36. Bernstein, Burton, and Healey, *Soviet Medicine*.
37. Kiaer, "The Swimming Vtorova Sisters: The Representation and Experience of Soviet Sport in the 1930s," in Katzer et al., *Euphoria and Exhaustion*, 90.
38. TsASPIM, f.3, op.49, d.23, l.58ob. My thanks to Judith Devlin for this reference.
39. TsASPIM, f.3, op.49, d.67. l.71.
40. Slivina, "Mastera – organizatory massovoi ucheby."
41. "V XX godovshchinu mezhdunarodnogo kommunisticheskogo zhenskogo dnya shlem plamennyi privet trudyashchimsya zhenshchinam! (Chto govoryat rabotnitsy o fizkul'ture)," *Fizkul'tura i sport*, no. 13 (1930): 4–5.
42. For more detailed discussion of *kul'turnost'* and its associated advice literature in Soviet society, see Kelly, *Refining Russia, Advice Literature*, 230–311.
43. Get Ready for Labour and Defence (*Gotov k trudy i oborone*) was a programme introduced in 1931 that sought involve as many people as possible in sport and physical culture by setting out different sports norms for them to pass. Eventually, different levels for different age groups and different levels of difficulty widened the breadth and focus of the programme.
44. Spartakiads were the equivalent to the Olympics. There were grand national Spartakiads held every four years in Moscow but also smaller ones held on republic, regional and provincial levels.

References

Achcar, Gilbert. "Engels: Theorist of War, Theorist of Revolution." *International Socialism Journal* 97 (2002). Accessed July 11, 2013. http://pubs.socialistreviewindex.org.uk/isj97/achcar.htm#6

Bernstein, Frances, Christopher Burton, and Dan Healey. *Soviet Medicine: Culture, Practice, and Science*. DeKalb: Northern Illinois University Press, 2010.

Bowlt, John E. "Body Beautiful: The Artistic Search for the Perfect Physique." In *Laboratory of Dreams. The Russian Avant-Garde and Cultural Experiment*, edited by John E. Bowlt and Olga Matich, 37–58. Stanford, CA: Stanford University Press, 1996.

Burban, F. M., and V. A. Solodkii. "Dal'neishee razvitie KPSS i voploshchenie v zhizn' Leninskikh idei o fizicheskom vospitanii." *Leninskie idei v razvitii teorii poznaniya i praktike kommunisticheskogo stroitel'stva, Leninskie idei v razvitii teorii poznaniya i praktike kommunisticheskogo stroitel'stva*, Lvov, Izd-vo pri L'vovskom gos-om Universitete Izd-vogo ob'edineniya "Visha Shkola" 1981.

Chudinov, I. G. *Osnovnye postanovleniya, prikazy i instruktsii po voprosam sovetskoi fizicheskoi kul'tury i sporta 1917–1957.* Moscow: Fizkul'tura i sport, 1917.

Demetr, G. S. *Lenin ob okhrane zdorov'ya trudyashikhsya i fizicheskoi kul'ture.* Moscow: Fizkul'tura i sport, 1965.

Demetr, G. S., and V. V. Gorbunov. *70 let sovetskogo sorta/Liudi, sobytiya, fakty.* Moscow: Fizkul'tura i sport, 1987.

Elwood, Carter. "The Sporting Life of V.I. Lenin." *Canadian Slavonic Papers* LII, no. 1–2 (2010): 79–94.

Fritzsche, Peter, and Jochen Hellbeck. "The New Man in Stalinist Russia and Nazi Germany." *Beyond Totalitarianism: Stalinism and Nazism Compared*, edited by Michael Geyer and Sheila Fitzpatrick, 302–341. Cambridge: Cambridge University Press, 2009.

Grant, Susan. "The Politics of Physical Culture in the 1920s." *Slavonic and East European Review* 89, no. 3 (July 2011): 494–515.

Grant, Susan. *Physical Culture and Sport in Soviet Society: Propaganda, Acculturation, and Transformation.* New York: Routledge, 2013.

Halfin, Igal. *Language and Revolution: Modern Political Identities.* London: Routledge, 2002.

Halfin, Igal. *Red Autobiographies: Initiating the Bolshevik Self.* Seattle, WA: The Herbert J. Ellison Center for Russian, East European and Central Asian Studies, University of Washington, 2011.

Holquist, Peter. "'Information is the Alpha and Omega of Our Work': Bolshevik Surveillance in Its Pan-European Context." *The Journal of Modern History* 69, no. 3 (1997): 415–450.

Katzer, Nikolaus, Sandra Budy, Alexandra Kohring, and Manfred Zeller. *Euphoria and Exhaustion: Modern Sport in Soviet Culture and Society.* Frankfurt-am-Main: Campus Verlag, 2010.

Kelly, Catriona. *Refining Russia, Advice Literature, Polite Culture, and Gender from Catherine to Yeltsin.* Oxford: Oxford University Press, 2001.

Lenin, Vladimir. *Collected Works.* 2nd ed. Moscow: Progress, 1965.

Novak-Deker, N. K. *Soviet Youth: Twelve Komsomol Histories.* Munich: Institute for the Study of the USSR, 1959.

Prokofiev, N. Y. "Fizicheskaya Kul'tura v zhizni V. I. Lenina." *Medistinskaya sestra* 8 (1979): 4–6.

Riordan, James. *Sport, Politics, and Communism.* Manchester: Manchester University Press, 1991.

Riordan, James. "Worker Sport within a Worker State: The Soviet Union." In *The Story of Worker Sport*, edited by Arnd Kruger and James Riordan. Champaign, IL: Human Kinetics, 1996.

Rosenberg, William G. . *Bolshevik Visions: First Phase of the Cultural Revolution in Soviet Russia.* Ann Arbor, MI: University of Michigan, 1990.

Samoukov, F. I., ed. *Istoriya fizicheskoi kul'tury.* Moscow: Fizkul'tura i sport, 1956.

Sanborn, Joshua. *Drafting the Russian Nation: Military Conscription, Total War, and Mass Politics, 1905–1925.* Dekalb: Northern Illinois University Press, 2003.

Slivina, N. "Mastera – organizatory massovoi ucheby." *Fizkul'tura i sport* 16–17 (1931): 15.

Simpson, Pat. "Imag(in)ing Post-Revolutionary Evolution. The Taylorized Proletarian, 'Conditioning', and Soviet Darwinism in the 1920s." In *The Art of Evolution. Darwin, Darwinisms, and Visual Culture*, edited by Barbara Larson and Fae Brauer, 226–261. Hanover, NH: University Press of New England, 2009.

Starks, Tricia. *The Body Soviet: Propaganda, Hygiene and the Soviet State.* Madison, WI: The University of Wisconsin Press, 2009.

Tumarkin, Nina. *Lenin Lives! The Lenin Cult in Soviet Russia.* Cambridge, MA: Harvard University Press, 1983 [1997].

Wood, Elizabeth. *The Baba and the Comrade: Gender and Politics in Revolutionary Russia.* Bloomington: Indiana University Press, 1997.

Zetkin, Clara. "Women, Marriage, and Sex." In *Reminiscences of Lenin.* Accessed July 11, 2013. http://www.marxists.org/archive/zetkin/1924/reminiscences-of-lenin.htm#h03

Game Changer: The Role of Sport in Revolution

Thomas F. Carter

School of Sport and Service Management, University of Brighton, Brighton, UK

Sport is generally understood as a conservative social institution that reaffirms the established values and norms of a society. It is not seen as a mechanism for radical political or social change but a means for individual transformation within a society. This article explores that notion by examining how sport has been used by twentieth-century political revolutions. While considering twentieth-century revolutions, it takes the Cuban Revolution as a particular case study to illuminate the use of sport in remaking of society and persons. The article begins with a general discussion of revolution and sport's relationships to it before briefly considering the two most prominent twentieth-century revolutions, the Russian and Chinese. The thrust then focuses on how the idea of revolution was understood in Cuba prior to the success of 1959 as well as immediately after. The article then examines the Cuban revolutionary state's explicit emphasis on sport as a means for producing the New Man. In all, the article argues that contrary to the common assumption that sport and revolution do not mix, sport can play an important role in the major social and political transformations.

The so-called Arab Spring of 2012, in which a number of governments across North Africa were threatened by their populist challenges, if not actually brought down, is the latest example of unfinished political revolutions. Sport played little role in these upheavals, although Zamalek FC, a prominent football club in Egypt, was noted for its forthright and immediate support of the anti-Mubarak protesters in Tahrir Square and club members' connections underpinned part of that head of state's eventual removal. The role of this club, as a social institution, is unusual. Most sport-related institutions are known more for their support of established political regimes and embedded in state institutions such as the military and police, some infamously so. Two well-known examples are the East German Stasi's infiltration of all social institutions and the use of sport clubs by various state ministries in Ceacescu's Romania. In 1989, athletes (international medallists in target shooting) from the Steaua sport club famously shot at the Romanian secret police while members of the Dinamo sport club manned barricades protecting the Securitate.[1] These are unusual instances, though. In general, sport is not usually at the cutting edge of revolutionary violence or movements.

Nevertheless, sport has played significant roles in revolutionary movements and revolutions. Therefore, my intent is to outline the relationship between sport and revolution. This article argues that sport is not, in the main, a revolutionary activity because it simply is not suited for radical, transformative social change. Rather, sport is often a conservative set of institutional practices used to reinforce existing power relations.

Yet, sport could be party to more radical purposes as long as the values embedded in sporting activity also push for broader social change instead of solely immediate political change. I start by discussing the relationship between revolution and sport before moving to a specific case in which sport was explicitly made a prominent part of a revolutionary project. Sport and revolution were consciously linked by Revolutionary authorities and the purposes to which sport were used to facilitate revolutionary changes are revealing. Consequently, this article examines what is meant by revolution and how sport is usually incorporated into those political projects. In so doing, both the idea of revolution and the social meanings of sport in Cuba must be thoughtfully considered. The article then moves to a discussion of how revolution has been understood in Cuba, as this has been a historical discourse that preceded the eventual successful revolution led by Fidel Castro. Finally, an examination of how sport was deployed as a tool of revolutionary change in Cuba and how pre-existing values about sport were incorporated, modified and otherwise implemented to promote the construction of a new Revolutionary social body is undertaken.

Revolution and Sport

The concept of revolution has been overly popularised diminishing its salience. We hear about social revolutions, technological revolutions and other changes, innovations or other alterations in the circumstances of social life that allegedly are revolutionary. Revolution, though, is not merely a social change; it is the complete upheaval and transformation of society; its social relations, political hierarchies and institutions, economic forms and, quite simply, society's ways of being. A revolution also is frightening and dynamic because it is a complete break off from not just what is known, but what is taken for granted about everyday life.[2] A revolution is so novel that it transforms the basic assumptions people have about the ways their lives are ordered. With this caveat in mind, there are only a few revolutions that truly had an impact on the world in the twentieth century. Two that certainly did, perhaps the only two to truly be world-affecting political revolutions were the Russian and Chinese Revolutions. They profoundly affected Eastern Europe, the Caribbean and much of East and Central Asia, while shaping the way global politics was played throughout the twentieth century. Each had its own political aspirations to which sport became attached. While liberal democratic capitalist states maintained primarily a *laissez-faire* attitude towards sport, both revolutions provided challenges to capitalism's predominant principles of competition. Assessing these revolutions' impacts remains highly charged and, from a scholarly perspective, still premature. Their effects on the global political and global economic structures throughout the twentieth century and into the twenty-first century are sufficiently profound that these must be taken into consideration as to how sport is currently understood and structured in most of the world.

In a very real sense, sport is essentially meaningless. The acts of striking a ball, throwing an object or other competitive action in a game or contest are all acts that depend on the cultural context in which those actions occur. Those actions are imbued with specific meanings: social, religious, political or ideological. While sport can be harnessed to any particular political agenda or ideology, the idea that sport can be revolutionary rarely reflects the circumstances on the ground, even when a society is undergoing some form of revolution. As institutionalised practices, sport more easily embodies the more conservative aspects of a society. Sport is rarely transgressive. Instead, it is used to maintain the *status quo*, to inculcate specific values, mores and habituses in a populace, and linked to educational institutions to reinforce a dominant, if not hegemonic, world view. When sport has been used otherwise, it has come at times of social change and revolution. This is most apparent in the aforementioned revolutions.

The Russian Revolution and the subsequent organisation of sport in the emergent Soviet Union (USSR) is particularly striking. Drawing especially on the enormous contributions of Jim Riordan, the Soviets did not engage with capitalist sport or the nascent formations of global sport.[3] Instead, they rejected the capitalist values and principles supposedly inherent in sport in liberal democracies choosing instead to emphasise physical culture rather than sport. The emphasis on the betterment of the individual within physical culture instead of the winner-takes-all competitive values of sport would help shape the new socialist person working for the good of all. This did not mean that achievements were not to be made or records be broken; indeed, the goal was to improve performance. But physical cultural activities to be pursed were to be directly related to industrialised production. The reach of this Soviet influence was not limited to the country's borders. The internationalist workers movement organised different forms of sport designed to promote solidarity and related 'working class' or 'proletariat' groups with significant sport-related events throughout Europe in the 1920s and 1930s.[4] After World War II, however, the Soviets more fully engaged with the burgeoning Olympic prominence, seeing the Olympics and other elite international competitions as an ideological battleground in which to counter the undue spread of American hegemony. This Cold War competition permeated the nascent production of global sport. The Soviets and the USSR satellite states embraced this neo-Olympism and elite competitive sport as a soft power means of asserting greater legitimacy in the broader sphere of global politics.[5]

The collapse of the Soviet Union led to triumphal proclamations of an American hegemony that constituted 'the end of history'.[6] There simply was no other alternative to the rapidly expanding ideologies of neoliberal capitalist democracies on the global scale. President Bush proclaimed a New World Order with the USA firmly at the centre of this new order. International sport, run by a number of non-state international organisations, tapped into and adopted some of these neoliberal principles transforming the governance and organisation of sport around the world into a form of New Economic Order sport or NEOsport in which the idea of the global became the fetish by which rule was to be established.[7] Appearing in the last decades of the twentieth century and solidifying their hold over the production of global sport, international non-governmental organisations, in alliances with transnational corporations and certain governments, are in the process of getting the world to agree to play by their rules and to accept their dominance and control over how sport is organised and run, and how people could participate would become the domain of their sovereignty.[8]

The post-Mao Chinese authorities gradually embraced NEOsport ideals, driving its original notions of how sport should be implemented, what values its practices should inculcate and its guiding principles to the margins while emphasising the precepts of global sport envisioned through the International Olympic Committee and other global governing bodies.[9] Susan Brownell chronicles how the body was understood in Revolutionary China – a distinctly different conceptualisation than liberal democratic or Soviet socialist ideas about the body.[10] Those distinctions drew on Chinese notions of the body that were used to resist European colonisation and continue to engage with the now pervasive values of global sport promoted through the ideology of Olympism. The Chinese Revolution and its post-Mao transformations make it abundantly clear, the practices of various physical activities and the values inhered within them become essential to the very formation of social persons.

The use of sport is vital for the making of persons throughout the world. It was especially so in those countries that underwent socialist revolutions. Considered anathema to Western democratic ideals of both amateurism and professionalism, the central principles of sport that emerged in the Soviet bloc and China were predicated upon a notion of planned progress that extended beyond the horizon of capitalist-based democracies, a rational organisation of all spheres of life on a mass scale and a scientific, secular world view that conceived of the world as a coherent whole. Whatever the provenance of these revolutionary states, sport was assigned four essential roles: (1) a means for channelling self-development (states need healthy and obedient citizens); (2) ideally, this self-development was part of mass exercise programmes that fostered the inculcation of the collective over the individual; (3) such exercises mobilised the populace in an effort to foster unity and promote collective actions; and (4) these unified collective actions would foster allegiance to specific visions of the party-state reinforcing everyone's place in the political-economic system.[11] Sport in revolutionary Cuba, in this regard, was no different than sport in other socialist states. However, the inculcation of socialist values through sport did differ from other revolutionary states. The mass gymnastics displays performed in other socialist states to demonstrate the embodiment of said values[12] were not part of the Cuban Revolution's repertoire, although mass spectacle certainly was and has recently been renewed in the form of parades, rallies and other mass displays of revolutionary fervour. But sport and physical activity has not been used in this manner.

The Ideas of Revolution and Sport in Cuba

When Fidel Castro's forces succeeded in driving out the dictator Batista, much of the rest of the world was rather shocked. The idea that this 'new' revolution carried out by a band of a few badly shaven men who suddenly burst onto the world's political scene gave the appearance that the Cuban Revolution was an entirely novel situation. Within Cuba, however, nothing was further from the truth. Castro's success was a surprise to the middle classes in Havana and most of the political elite in the country, never mind the so-called experts in the USA, the Soviet Union and elsewhere in the world at that time, but the idea of revolution itself was nothing new. Revolution in Cuba is part of the historical national narrative inextricably tied to national sentiment and the efforts to form an independent Cuban nation.

Revolution in Cuba is inextricably tied to the colonial struggle for independence. Castro's success was not a sudden break with preceding historical national trajectory, but a culmination of a 200-year effort for national independence and sovereignty. Articulated as a process, the Cuban Revolution was a nationalist endeavour to assert the sovereign right of the people of Cuba to determine their own fate, whether that was against the Spanish in the nineteenth century or the Americans in the twentieth century.[13] The process was delayed and defeated, truncated and otherwise derailed throughout the nineteenth and twentieth centuries. Three particular armed struggles stand out, but are by no means the full extent of the history of revolution in Cuba. The first was the Ten Years' War fought from 1868 to 1878 against the Spanish by Revolutionary forces that ultimately led to the exile of numerous Cubans. The second was the War of Independence (1898–1901) that was eventually derailed by US interference and the annexation of Cuba by the USA. The outcome of this conflict resulted in Cuba becoming, in effect, a colony despite its own constitution; a constitution that American diplomats wrote, forced down Cuban politicians' throats at gunpoint and baldly declared that the USA could 'intervene' in Cuba's domestic affairs whenever the American government deemed it expedient to its own interests, a statement known as the Platt Amendment. The third moment was in 1933 when the Machado dictatorship was overthrown and for a brief moment it appeared that the Cubans would finally free themselves from the yoke of American hegemony only to find its tendrils more insidiously intertwined in national politics and political parties than originally had been imagined by Cubans.

When the Cuban Revolution triumphed in 1959, it was unclear at that time what the exact nature of this specific revolution was. Various historical positions have been taken as to whether the Cuban Revolution was communist from the very beginning or not. These debates began under the corrosive influence of Cold War ideologies, whatever their perspective, and that particular pernicious approach continues to permeate some analyses to this day, especially in political science scholarship in the USA. Essentially a barren debate, looking back in retrospect in this manner only serves to reinforce predetermined ideological positions of those who engage in such arguments. What is absolutely clear, however, is that a revolution was occurring.

However, the extent to which the Castro-led revolution would extend beyond a political revolution was not initially or readily apparent. By their very nature, revolutions are violent processes and create a great amount of unease and uncertainty among the populace in which they occur. They also are clear breaks with the past, while simultaneously effecting a rewriting of that same historical past in order to explain how the current situation came to become reality.[14] The Cuban Revolution faced this set of similar problems, and a principal means of articulating the new, the changes, the vitality, dynamism, 'progress' and revolutionary character of its political manifesto was through Revolutionary leaders' adoption of sport as a fundamental means of communicating these dramatic changes via embodied acts and discourses. The symbolism and practice of sport allowed Revolutionary leaders to demonstrate their 'natural' Cubanness as means of legitimating their usurpation of the existing order while also indicating the new order of things. At the same time, their reorganisation of sport and incorporation of it into the formation of a new Cuban society was a driving force of these monumental changes. Such drastic and dramatic changes also necessitated a further articulation of the reconceptualisation of society at its most basic – the definition of citizen and person. Sport provided one means of justifying and even legitimating the reshaping of individual persons, and through that recasting, of society.

Sporting Guerrillas

Sport, in general, and baseball, in particular, provided the Revolutionary leadership with a clear symbolic continuity of something wholly Cuban that was limited, at best, in its political associations with any of the previous regimes. Explicitly connected with the Revolution from its earliest triumphalist declarations, this twentieth-century discursive construction of the Cuban Revolution extended the struggle back to the 1800s against the Spanish. Drawing on this dormant and latent discourse, Fidel Castro blatantly linked sport with his leadership of the triumphant revolution: 'If I hadn't been a sportsman, I wouldn't have been a guerrilla, thus it was the continuous physical training that permitted me, after I conceived [of it], to make the revolutionary war'.[15] In particular, he connected sport-related practices to the knowledge of how to be guerrillas and revolutionaries:

> We learned to fight the war when we were young men like you all. Do you know how? Do you want me to tell you? Well, we learned to fight the war playing baseball, playing basketball, playing soccer; we played all sports, swam in the sea, swam in the rivers and climbed mountains.[16]

Castro's exhortations to packed plazas in early 1960s were not some new rhetorical invention. He was taking a cue from nineteenth-century Cuban revolutionaries. Even then, sport was portrayed as the training ground for the formation of potential revolutionaries. This was made apparent in the writings of late nineteenth-century Cuban ideologues who contrasted baseball with the bullfight and the civilised, modern Cuban with the barbarism of the colonial Spanish.[17] In fact, it was this long-standing connection in Cuban nationalist rhetoric that linked sport, and baseball in particular, with the preparations of soldiers for violent struggle against hated tyrannical rulers.[18]

The importance of sport to revolutionary leaders' legitimacy comprised more than nationalists' rhetorical flourishes, however. Sport also provided a theatre from which to exhibit Cuban leaders' vitality, athleticism and overall physical prowess. The construction of these 'sporting guerrillas' emerged from a series of games in which Revolutionary leaders played former military and police officers. The games, of course, were rife with symbolism. The Barbudos, made up of Revolutionary leaders including Fidel Castro, his brother, Raúl, Camilo Cienfuegos and others, played teams made up of soldiers or police officers; the same organisations who had been defending the Batista state and trying to snuff out the *Movimiento 26 de Julio*.[19] The exhibition games in which the Barbudos-defeated teams made up of former soldiers who had just months earlier been trying to kill the guerillas sent a clear message to all those who saw the media coverage of such spectacles. Those strategic, symbolic gestures reinforced both the Cubanness of the Revolution and alluded to the military superiority of the guerrillas over the Cuban armed forces, especially since baseball had been long associated with armed confrontation since the earliest days of baseball and Cuban nationalism. In defeating their opposition, the Revolutionary leaders, as the Barbudos, provided a not-so-subtle allegory.

These 'exhibition' games, however, were limited performances that occurred almost immediately after driving Batista out of Cuba. They dissipated until the crisis of the 1990s, when baseball was once again harnessed in a symbolic display of revolutionary ideology embraced by the Bolivarian Revolution of Venezuela and the Cuban Revolution. In an exhibition game between Venezuela and Cuba, in which Fidel Castro 'managed' the Cuban Team and Hugo Chavez not only 'managed' the Venezuelan contingent but also played first base and pitched in the game itself, the symbolism of the ties between the role model of the Cuban Revolution and the new-born Bolivarian one represented the nascent alliance between the two countries.[20] The 'friendship' between the two alleviated the Cuban economic crisis while solidifying the newly formed revolutionary regime in Venezuela. Chavez sent tons of barrels of oil at reduced cost while receiving highly trained professionals in numerous fields to augment and help build up Venezuela's socio-economic capacities and restructure Venezuelan society.

Praise for Chavez's skills on the diamond helped to legitimate the president's capacity to be a dynamic, active leader. This symbolism is as old as the state, in which the health and vitality of the monarch embodies the health of the state.[21] In modern politics, state leaders also demonstrate this embodied vital force through their practices at sport, even if apocryphal. From Mao's famous swim down the Yellow River, to President Obama's passion and skill at pickup basketball, political leaders use sport to symbolise their ability to be dynamic. The Cuban revolutionary leaders were no different. Castro's biographers make frequent mention of his baseball skills and as do some who repeat the totally false story that had US baseball scouts offered slightly more money, Castro would have signed as a pitcher thereby preventing his political actions.[22] Within Cuba as well, the sport-related prowess of the initial leaders of the Revolution were lauded. Fidel Castro, Camilo Cienfuegos and Che Guevara all played in the aforementioned exhibition baseball games.

Fidel Castro was a point guard on his high school basketball team.[23] Cienfuegos' baseball skills were noted throughout Cuba. Che Guevara played rugby as a youth in Argentina.[24] Castro and Guevara's apparent love of sport was made apparent with the numerous appearances they made at everything from chess tournaments and basketball games to the Havana Country Club golf course (before it was appropriated and closed). Sport provided a vital symbolic discourse for the establishment of a new state and Revolutionary society.

A Sporting State

Of greater lasting change was the investiture of sport as a revolutionary practice that was the inherent right of all persons. Almost immediately after Castro's victory, the newly formed Revolutionary state used sport as means of solidifying its claims for legitimacy with the Cuban population. It formalised sport's centrality by incorporating sport into its jurisprudence. The 1976 Cuban constitution, modelled on the earlier, short-lived 1933 revolutionary constitution, clearly enshrined sport into this reshaped Cuban society. Access to sport was guaranteed in three different places in the constitution. Article 8B declares that the government 'guarantees that no one will be left without access to studies, culture and sports'. Article 42 within the section entitled Equality states, 'The state consecrates the right achieved by the Revolution that all citizens regardless of race, color, or national origin enjoy the same resorts, beaches, parks, social centers of culture, sports, recreation and rest' More tellingly, sport receives its own stand-alone Article within the section on 'Fundamental Rights, Duties and Guarantees'. Article 51 reads:

> Everyone has the right to physical education, sports and recreation. Enjoyment of this right is assured by including the teaching and practice of physical education and sports in the curricula of the national education system and means placed at the service of the people, which makes possible the practice of sports and recreation on a mass basis.[25]

It is one thing to guarantee rights in a legal framework; it is entirely another thing to actually put those guarantees into practice. The legal framework of revolutionary law was essential yet laws and a legal system require more than declarative statements and intent.[26] It requires efforts of social transformation if it is truly a revolutionary system. Sport was to be one mechanism by which new revolutionary persons were to be formed.

Revolutionary Persons: Sport and the Forging of the 'New Man'

Because revolutions break with historically based social hierarchies, the peculiar forms of twentieth-century socialist states required other means of legitimating the reorganisation of social relations in the new power structure. Since, political revolutions are the usurpation of the supposed 'natural' order, an inherent component in the reordering of society is the necessity of making a new kind of person. A key component of the reshaping of Cuban persons was the reconstitution of various aspects of everyday life. Expressed in almost puritanical values in terms of the need to work diligently and make sacrifices, the reshaping of Cuban bodies was first and foremost an ideological mission.[27] The inculcation of new ethos, new definitions of personhood and, in effect, a different kind of social reality than had previously existed required direct forms of intervention.

Revolutionary authorities emphasised the power of sport as a motivating factor in social change. Sport became a vital aspect of the state's domestic legitimacy, not only through the elimination of segregated sports facilities and the construction of many new ones but also through the recalibration of social values, mores and norms. Cuba is not unique in this regard; the use of sport was vital for the remaking of persons in other socialist countries. In guaranteeing sport as a citizen's right, Revolutionary leaders pushed sport via a policy of mass participation in order to incorporate its citizenry in nationalist and socialist sentiment. Speaking before newly appointed sports administrators in 1961, Raúl Castro neatly summarised the position of sport.

> Sport, like everything, is a reflection of a country's social system. ... Sport under socialism is neither restricted nor commercialized. It is the mass sport with the participation of the people, all of the people, of all those who want to participate voluntarily. ... Under capitalism, sport, like almost everything, was an end, and the end was profit. Sport under a socialist regime is a means, before everything else, for the self-improvement of the citizen, for the betterment of his health. ... At the same time, it creates the conditions for and makes the citizens capable of increasing production, defending the country, and [providing] a healthy means of recreation.[28]

Obviously, Revolutionary leaders saw sport as a vital vehicle for the inculcation of revolutionary and socialist values. Flying in the face of the usual portrayal of socialist revolutions in which individualism is sacrificed for the greater good of society, the Cuban Revolution, impelled by the state, was not 'a standardizer of the collective will' as socialist societies are often portrayed; rather it was 'a liberator of man's individual capacity'.[29] In *Socialismo y el hombre en Cuba*, Guevara asserted the primacy of moral incentives over material incentives in the formation of the body, in effect proclaiming that the socialist body was an ideological construct made manifest in how an individual comported himself in relation to the rest of the world.[30] The supposedly inherent values of fairness, sacrifice and effort found in sport would prevail over the 'win at all costs' ethos of professional sport underpinned by capitalist values of competition, individual glory and wealth. Sport would provide a means for this transformation.

> Our country, our Revolution, our system, socialism, inculcates in humanity a special spirit of effort and struggle. Our athletes have to develop these characteristics of this high revolutionary spirit in themselves as well, which corresponds to a socialist athlete.[31]

Sport was a domestic, political instrument explicitly deployed in order to help develop the New Man. This is constantly repeated throughout the 1960s and 1970s when Fidel Castro spoke about sport. These speeches were made at the openings of youth centres, gymnasiums, schools and at the inaugural games of the Serie Nacional, the newly formed Cuban national baseball league organised on revolutionary ethos including the elimination of capitalist professionalism.[32] The overwhelming theme is the domestic agenda of developing sport for the building of the Revolutionary New Man and society both in terms of the sporting infrastructure and new forms of person. For example, at the opening of the Escuela de Iniciación Deportiva Escolar in Santiago de Cuba on September 2, 1977, Fidel Castro explained that:

> Sport is not only technical ability, nor is it physical conditions, it requires moral conditions, conditions of character, spiritual conditions, because between two athletes that have more or less the same physical skill, the one who wins will have more spirit, more character, more willingness for preparation, for the training, and is capable of making the supreme effort at the moment of competition.[33]

Sport, then, was a means of educating the body, and thus the person, of the requisite Revolutionary mores and values as well as a way of exhibiting one's own Revolutionary ethos. Tied to moral character, not the competition of capitalism in this instance but to the willingness to work on one's day off, the New Man would be a healthy individual with a new attitude towards work, would identify work with the pleasure of creation and social duty rather than a salary. One would become a generous person with a sense of collective social duties, capable of joining and empathising with all who suffer exploitation regardless of where they were born. An individual would arrive at these convictions through one's own reasoning, through self-discipline and be capable of defending one's beliefs at all costs and ready to fulfil every responsibility. The 'New Man' promoted the characteristics of individual struggle, discipline and sacrifice for the betterment of society that would coalesce in 'an impassioned spirit with a cold mind' and who could make painful decisions without flinching one muscle.[34] The idea of a revolutionary act became the core of Revolutionary consciousness that each individual was to develop with the assistance and guidance of the state in becoming a 'New Man'. Revolutionary sport was to play a vital role in the formation of these new moral persons.

The creation of new forms of human persons is never an immediate or easy transformation. The 'New Man' was not defined solely on how individuals comported themselves at work or in political meetings. The transformation required an all-encompassing effort that each person had to demonstrate in one's attitudes towards work, as well as how one related to one's fellow revolutionaries and others. These values and norms needed to be taught, consciously promoted, inculcated and reinforced as an explicit political transformation, and sport was a means of ensuring that the Revolutionary ethos would become embodied. Revolutionary leaders were not dealing with people without any histories, however. Specific ethos, definitions of what it meant to be Cuban and understandings of how the world worked and their basis in particular forms of social relations all had to be dismantled and then rebuilt.

The promotion and development of a domestic sports policy is embedded in a specific ethos that explicitly addresses who Cubans think they are. Of course, not just any version of *cubanidad* would do for the Revolutionary leadership in 1959 or even later. It had to be a specific kind of *cubanidad*, a revolutionary *cubanidad* that broke with the values, mores and ethos of the past that Louis Pérez documents so well in his masterful volume *On Becoming Cuban*,[35] while maintaining the continuity of the sense of being Cuban. The ethos of a collective *cubanidad*, instead of an individuated one, was a deliberately moral stance of how one person should relate to another and should find reasons and values that can be shared. For such a transformation to occur, a coherent collective conferring a stable, recognisable identity, salient in its ability to impart substantive and binding social relations rooted in mutual trust, had to be coalesced. Because this ethical stance on sport is irreducibly a sociopolitical one in which the cooperation of and social dependence on others is of prime importance, it is hardly surprising that any alternative models of sporting practice, such as that of professionalism, an ethos attenuated towards an individualistic ethical orientation, were to be abolished.

Sport was seen as an ideal implement for facilitating this transformation and therefore it was seen as a politically expedient practice to accelerate the elimination of a capitalist ethos from revolutionary Cuba. Whenever practiced, sport requires certain forms of discipline, a dedication to the act and the repetitive practice essential for the 'unthinking' bodily responses to the immediate moment. The leaders recognised that sport inculcates an accumulated sense of purpose that takes on bodily form, inscribed on bodily comportment, such that, through sport, the commonality of the mind becomes a commonality of the body that allows for greater harmonious, coordinated actions between people as they move and enact. For what is experienced in sport-related activities, even if one is 'merely' spectating, is 'a group of people finely attuned to the thoughts and actions of another, a group with a unity of purpose that defies an easy individuation'.[36] Thus, participation in sport became a process of inculcating the revolution and making the Revolution embodied in each individual via shared experience.

To facilitate such transformations, sport in Cuba needed dramatic development. That development was part of the *Instituto Nacional de Deporte, Educación Física, y Recreación's* (INDER) overarching programme of *masividad* that would build the necessary infrastructure while simultaneously transforming individuals' conceptions of themselves as humans and their roles and responsibilities in society:

> Sport in our country, or sports politics in our country, has two objectives: to promote the practice of sport for all the people, and fundamentally, the children and youth. But not only the children and the youth need sport but also the adults and people of greater age. ... We believe that, from our deliberate perspective, there are large possibilities.[37]

This agenda was abundantly apparent in the massive effort that nearly doubled participation in sport from 1977 to 1990. From the barely 170,000 Cubans involved in sport in the early days of the Revolution, participation rose to three million by 1977 and then continued its growth to nearly six million just before the collapse of the Soviet bloc and the onset of the Special Period in Times of Peace, a crisis that necessitated many changes in Cuban lives in which sport became ancillary to survival.[38]

Concluding Remarks

Sport became a principal mechanism for inculcating the revolutionary ethos and imagined Cuban revolutionary. For what is seen in athletic action is 'a group of people finely attuned to the thoughts and actions of another, a group with a unity of purpose that defies an easy individuation'.[39] What is also accumulated is a sense of purpose that takes on bodily form, inscribed on bodily comportment, such that the commonality of the mind becomes, through sport, a commonality of the body that then allows for greater harmonious, coordinated actions between people as they move and enact. Thus, sport, at both the grass-roots and at the world-class elite level, became part of a process of inculcating the Revolution and making the Revolution embodied in each individual via shared experience.

Revolutions are not singular events; they are processes. This point has been at the forefront of the rhetoric of Cuban revolutionary leaders since the guerrillas rode into Havana on New Year's Day, 1959. Revolutions are transformations of the accepted order of things and as a consequence do violence to social systems even if there is no actual physical violence. They cause uncertainty, anxiety and upheaval. They change the way people's worlds are formed and experienced. Revolutions thus appear at first glance to be antithetical to the purposes and roles of sport. However, it is abundantly clear from the various political revolutions of the twentieth century that sport does play some small part in these transformative processes. The Cuban case in particular illustrates the ways in which sport can be used as a means for effecting a change in social values instead of the readily accepted and much more common argument that sport is a reflection of society and therefore plays the more conservative role of reaffirming hegemonic social values. Although sport is most commonly associated with existing nation states, used as a tool of policy to maintain the *status quo* and reinforce a given world view, sport can and does, on occasion, play important roles in societies undergoing political revolutions, changing the course not only of that nation's history but also of the revolution itself. It may not be the instigating practice or embodied as a leading institution of revolutionary activity, but sport has played important roles as an agent of revolutionary change. Sport can be a revolutionary game changer.

Notes

1. Riordan, "Soviet-Style Sport," 38.
2. This is a modern conception of revolution. See Arendt, *On Revolution*, 21–58.
3. For the basics of Riordan's work, see Riordan, *Sport in Soviet Society* and *Soviet Sport*. Additional examples of his work can be found cited throughout this paper and elsewhere.
4. Krüger and Riordan, *The Story of Worker*.
5. I am using Joseph Nye's concept of soft power here. See Nye, *Soft Power*.
6. A phrase coined by Francis Fukuyama. Triumphalist when first proclaimed in the mid-1990s, it basically crowed that American hegemony was now the way of the world, a premature statement if ever there was one. See Fukuyama, *The End of History*.
7. Carter, *In Foreign Fields*, 97–107.
8. Carter, "The Olympics as Sovereign."
9. Brownell, *Beijing's Games*; Close, Askew and Xin, *The Beijing Olympiad*.
10. Brownell, *Training the Body for China*.
11. Riordan, *Sport, Politics and Communism*.
12. Macdonald, "Putting Bodies on the Line"; Roubal, "Politics of Gymnastics."
13. For generalised historical accounts of these armed conflicts and revolutionary processes in English, see the classics by Hugh Thomas and Louis Pérez (Thomas, *Cuba: A History*; Pérez, *Cuba: Between Reform*).
14. Arendt, *On Revolution*.
15. Ruiz Aguilera, *El Deporte de Hoy*, 93.
16. Ibid., 95.
17. Carter, "The Manifesto of a Baseball-Playing Country."
18. Carter, *The Quality of Home Runs*, 42–51.
19. The *Movimiento de Julio* was the name of the Castro-led guerrilla movement.
20. Carter, "New Rules to the Old Game," 208.
21. Hobbes, *Leviathan*.
22. A number of serious biographies chronicle Castro's sporting prowess, including Castro and Ramonet, *Fidel Castro: My Life*; Quirk, *Fidel Castro*; and Szulc, *Fidel: A Critical Portrait*. The apocryphal story that Castro was an outstanding baseball player who could have played professionally in the USA is reproduced in Balfour, *Castro*; Oppenheimer, *Castro's Final Hour*; and Price, *Pitching Around Fidel*, among others.
23. Szulc, *Fidel: A Critical Portrait*, 109, 115.
24. Anderson, *Che Guevara*, 27–8.
25. "Constitution of The Republic of Cuba," *Granma Weekly Review* (special supplement), March 7, 1976.
26. Zatz, *Producing Legality*.
27. Bunck, *Fidel Castro and the Quest*; Medin, *Cuba, the Shaping*.
28. Castro Ruz, *Discurso a la Primera*, 6.
29. Anderson, *Che Guevara*, 478–9.
30. Guevara, *Socialismo y el Hombre en Cuba*.
31. Ruiz Aguilera, *El Deporte de Hoy*, 134.
32. Ibid., see especially 95–108.
33. Ibid., 134, 139.
34. Anderson, *Che Guevara*, 636–7.
35. Pérez, *On Becoming Cuban*.
36. Morgan, *Why Sports Morally Matter*, 20.
37. Ruiz Aguilera, *El Deporte de Hoy*, 134.
38. Carranza Valdes, "La economía cubana"; Weinreb, *Cuba in the Shadow*.
39. Morgan, *Why Sports Morally Matter*, 20.

References

Anderson, Jon Lee. *Che Guevara: A Revolutionary Life*. New York: Grove Press, 1997.
Arendt, Hannah. *On Revolution*. London: Penguin Books, 1965.
Balfour, Sebastian. *Castro*. London: Longman, 1990.
Brownell, Susan. *Beijing's Games: What the Olympics Mean to China*. Lanham, MD: Rowman & Littlefield, 2008.

Brownell, Susan. *Training the Body for China: Sports in the Moral Order of the People's Republic*. Chicago, IL: University of Chicago Press, 1995.

Bunck, Julie Marie. *Fidel Castro and the Quest for a Revolutionary Culture in Cuba*. University Park: Pennsylvania State University Press, 1994.

Carranza Valdes, Julio. "La economía cubana: Balance breve de una década crítica." *Temas* 30 (2002): 30–41.

Carter, Thomas F. *In Foreign Fields: The Politics and Experiences of Transnational Sport Migration*. London: Pluto Press, 2011.

Carter, Thomas F. "The Manifesto of a Baseball-Playing Country: Cuba, Baseball, and Poetry in the Late Nineteenth Century." *International Journal of the History of Sport* 22, no. 2 (2005): 246–265.

Carter, Thomas F. "New Rules to the Old Game: Cuban Sport and State Legitimacy in the Post-Soviet Era." *Identities: Global Studies in Culture and Power* 15, no. 2 (2008): 194–215.

Carter, Thomas F. "The Olympics as Sovereign Subject Maker." In *Watching the Games: Politics, Power and Representation*, edited by J. Sugden, and A. Tomlinson, 55–68. London: Routledge, 2011.

Carter, Thomas F. *The Quality of Home Runs: The Passion, Politics, and Language of Cuban Baseball*. Durham, NC: Duke University Press, 2008.

Castro, Fidel, and Ignacio Ramonet. *Fidel Castro: My Life*. Translated by A. Hurley. London: Penguin, 2007.

Castro Ruz, Fidel. *Discurso a la Primera Plenaria Provincial de los Consejos Voluntarios Oriente (1 de octubre)*. La Habana: INDER, 1961.

Close, Paul, David Askew, and Xu Xin. *The Beijing Olympiad: The Political Economy of a Sporting Mega-Event*. London: Routledge, 2007.

Fukuyama, Francis. *The End of History and the Last Man*. New York: The Free Press, 2006.

Guevara, Ernesto. *Socialismo y el Hombre en Cuba*. Atlanta, GA: Pathfinder Press, [1965] 1992.

Hobbes, Thomas. *Leviathan*. Harmondsworth: Penguin, 1968.

Krüger, Arnd, and James Riordan. *The Story of Worker Sport*. Champaign, IL: Human Kinetics, 1996.

Macdonald, Charlotte. "Putting Bodies on the Line: Marching Spaces in Cold War Culture." In *Sites of Sport: Space, Place, Experience*, edited by Patricia Vertinsky, and John Bale, 85–100. London: Routledge, 2004.

Medin, Tzvi. *Cuba, the Shaping of Revolutionary Consciousness*. Boulder, CO: Lynne Rienner, 1990.

Morgan, William J. *Why Sports Morally Matter*. London: Routledge, 2006.

Nye, Joseph. *Soft Power: The Means to Success in World Politics*. New York: Perseus Books, 2005.

Oppenheimer, Andres. *Castro's Final Hour*. New York: Simon and Schuster, 1992.

Pérez, Louis A. *Cuba: Between Reform and Revolution*. Oxford: Oxford University Press, 1998.

Pérez, Louis A. *On Becoming Cuban: Identity, Nationality, Culture*. Chapel Hill: University of North Carolina Press, 1999.

Price, S. L. *Pitching Around Fidel*. New York: Harper Collins, 2000.

Quirk, Robert E. *Fidel Castro*. New York: W.W. Norton, 1992.

Riordan, James. *Soviet Sport: Background to the Olympics*. Oxford: Blackwell, 1980.

Riordan, James. *Sport in Soviet Society: Development of Sport and Physical Education in Russia and the USSR*. Cambridge: Cambridge University Press, 1977.

Riordan, James. *Sport, Politics and Communism*. Manchester: Manchester University Press, 1991.

Riordan, Jim. "Soviet-Style Sport in Eastern Europe: The End of an Era." In *The Changing Politics of Sport*, edited by Lincoln Allison, 37–58. Manchester: University of Manchester Press, 1993.

Roubal, Petr. "Politics of Gymnastics: Mass Gymnastics Displays Under Communism in Central and Eastern Europe." *Body & Society* 9, no. 2 (2003): 1–25.

Ruiz Aguilera, Raudol. *El Deporte de Hoy: Realidades y Perspectivas*. Ciudad de la Habana: Editorial Científico Ténica, 1991.

Szulc, Tad. *Fidel: A Critical Portrait*. New York: William & Morrow, 1986.

Thomas, Hugh. *Cuba: A History*. London: Penguin, [1971] 2010.

Weinreb, Amelia. *Cuba in the Shadow of Change: Daily Life in the Twilight of the Revolution*. Gainesville: University Press of Florida, 2009.

Zatz, Marjorie S. *Producing Legality: Law and Socialism in Cuba*. New York: Routledge, 1994.

Building Character and Socialising a Revolutionary: Sport and Leisure in the Life of Ernesto 'Che' Guevara

Charles Parrish

School of Recreation, Health, and Tourism, George Mason University, Fairfax, VA, USA

This essay focuses on the role sport and leisure played in the life of Ernesto 'Che' Guevara during childhood and adolescence. Specifically, the essay conceptualises how his sport and leisure experiences contributed to making Guevara the revolutionary and guerilla fighter. To be sure, a number of works on Guevara do recount his participation in sport but few specifically reflect on how these experiences may have influenced his later life. To accomplish this, I provide case examples of Guevara's engagement with sport and leisure during childhood and adolescence and link those experiences with the theoretical and philosophical foundations that position sport as a useful socialising agent and character-building tool. The goal of this work is to provide a paradigmatic lens that argues sport and leisure played a significant role in the development of a young Ernesto Guevara. These early experiences influenced and, in some cases, altered the path of the ambiguous adolescent who would later become the iconic twentieth-century Latin American revolutionary known around the world as Che.

In 1999 *Time* magazine compiled a list of the twentieth-century's most influential people from around the world. Certainly any list should be met with scepticism and this one is no exception given its inclusion of only two individuals from the Western Hemisphere south of the US border. Nevertheless, few would argue with two of the individuals the publication did include: Brazil's gift to world soccer, Pelé, and one of the world's most known revolutionaries of the twentieth century, Che Guevara. Interestingly, Ernesto 'Che'[1] Guevara was not selected for inclusion in the 'Leaders and Revolutionaries' category. Rather, *Time* listed him in the 'Heroes and Icons' list alongside the likes of Anne Frank, Marilyn Monroe, Mother Teresa and Princess Diana. At first glance this decision may seem peculiar, yet after reflecting on the magazine's categorical description it appears to be appropriate.[2] Guevara embodied most of the character traits ascribed to the Heroes and Icons personalities but much like Ariel Dorfman's biographical entry in the publication, the development of these traits is often overlooked.[3]

While the literature on Guevara does provide fleeting glimpses into his childhood, much of what is written focuses primarily on his experiences in Guatemala and Mexico, the Cuban Revolution, his subsequent diplomatic roles as part of Castro's new Cuban government, the revolution efforts in the Congo and Bolivia and ultimately his assassination in Bolivia. Beyond Guevara 'the revolutionary' and 'government diplomat', there has been a movement towards the study of Guevara as a popular icon. Indeed, the portrayal of Guevara as an icon has become the focus of doctoral dissertations and a number of books.[4] Most of these works focus on Alberto Korda's famous 1960 photograph of Guevara, known as *Guerrillero Heróico*, which depicts the revolutionary wearing a star-centred beret and staring into the distance. With the dispute over intellectual property rights of the *Guerrillero Heróico* photograph still unsettled, the most reproduced image in the history of photography ironically continues to serve as a source for lucrative amounts of capital exchange. Printed on posters, t-shirts, key chains, and rock band apparel (among many other objects), the enduring image of Guevara has been commodified as a popular symbol of resistance, protest, liberation and human rights movements around the world.[5]

Perhaps the works that provide the most revealing account of Guevara as a human being, rather than the mythical figure and iconic symbol constructed after his death, are the memoires written by friends and family members, Guevara's own published diaries, Alberto Granado's account of the motorcycle trip across South America and Walter Salles' 2004 cinematic depiction of the journey.[6] Specifically, the diaries and film offer unique insights into the evolving personality, beliefs and identity of a young Guevara before his transformation into a guerilla fighter. However, as Carte notes, analytical projects of this sort are prone to criticism.[7] Guevara, as an ambiguous adolescent being, clashes with critical prevailing notions of Guevara 'the political and cultural icon'. In short, the iconoclast image of Guevara the revolutionary serves as the dominant discourse on his life; thus, works that do not seem to fit within this accepted narrative are at risk of being marginalised for engaging in alternative and less critical discussions.

Nevertheless, analysis that ventures outside of the dominant 'Guevara the revolutionary icon' narrative can be constructive. Carte broke from such discourse by exploring the life of Guevara during his formative years and concluded that by focusing on 'Ernesto the boy', we are left with more questions than answers.

> ... before Ernesto Guevara was 'Che', he was an inexperienced young adult, flawed, like any other. Subsequently we may ask: Did Guevara make himself a trickster-bandit, or did society? What were the circumstances, personal or societal, that engendered a notorious guerilla, loved and revered, feared and hated? Does looking at this part of his life really blind us to later atrocities, as some critics claim? Or do they commit the same error by only focusing on his later life ... Or is it, when it is all said, that out of ten possible heads we have only seen one tail? Has our vision been incomplete, transient, not always well informed, uncompromising?[8]

We may never achieve a consensus on Carte's questions. However, by continuing to explore the formative years of 'Ernesto the boy' we can work towards a more holistic and balanced understanding of Guevara the revolutionary. Such accounts may also effectively offset the many posthumous works that, according to Fidel Castro, have sought to skew and discredit the truth.[9]

This essay seeks to build on Carte's exploration into 'Ernesto the boy' by focusing on the role sport and leisure played in his life during childhood and adolescence. Specifically, the essay conceptualises how his sport and leisure experiences contributed to making Guevara the revolutionary and guerilla fighter. To be sure, a number of works on Guevara do recount his participation in sport but few specifically reflect on how these experiences may have influenced his later life.[10] To accomplish this, I provide case examples of Guevara's engagement with sport and leisure during childhood and adolescence and link those experiences with the theoretical and philosophical foundations that position sport as a useful socialising agent and character-building tool. The goal of this work is to provide a paradigmatic lens that argues sport and leisure may have played a significant role in the development of a young Ernesto Guevara. These early experiences influenced and, in some cases, altered the path of the ambiguous adolescent who would later become the iconic twentieth-century Latin American revolutionary known around the world as Che.

Ernesto's Sport and Leisure Experiences

Swimming

Ernesto Guevara de La Serna was born in May of 1928 in Rosario, Argentina, and after relocating on several occasions over the next two years, his family temporarily settled in the northern Buenos Aires suburb of San Isidro. As biographer John Lee Anderson notes, the young family was initially financially privileged and spent much of their time at the beach of the San Isidro Nautical Club, which is located on the Rio de La Plata estuary.[11] Guevara's mother, Celia, was an avid swimmer and during the Argentine winter of 1930 she took her two-year-old son for a swim one day. That evening, young Ernesto suffered through an intense coughing episode and, despite medical intervention, the condition developed into chronic asthma. As a toddler, the future revolutionary hardly had a say in his mother's decision to include him as part of her leisure activities. Nevertheless, the asthma condition Guevara faced would remain with him for the rest of his life and significantly limit his mobility during the 'July 26 Movement' that overthrew Batista's forces in Cuba nearly 30 years later. Given the prevalence of asthma in the family, it would be far-reaching to attribute Che's chronic acute asthma to this isolated incident.[12] After all, heredity is known to be one of the major risk factors for asthma in children.[13] However, although this particular early leisure experience did not cause the asthma, it did trigger the initial severe asthmatic episode that would set the family in motion in search of treatment and relief.

Looking to stabilise young Guevara's asthma, the family moved to the dry mountain climate of the Córdoba province in central Argentina. The Guevara's were certainly not alone in their quest to seek a health cure in the *sierras* of Córdoba. Since the early decades of the twentieth century, Argentineans had sought out the many spas and resorts in this region that specialised in caring for individuals suffering from a range of respiratory ailments, including tuberculosis.[14] This phenomenon followed the Argentine state's strategic development of rural dispensaries and sanitariums to combat what they perceived to be social maladies threatening the government's own efforts to 'civilise' and 'modernise' the nation.[15]

While Guevara's asthma attacks became less frequent and intense in Córdoba, his condition continued to be a source of anxiety for the family. Initially, he did not attend school and his parents held him to a strict diet and physical activity regimen they thought helped control the severity of the asthma. Ironically, Guevara's asthma diminished after he swam, thus the family decided to join one of the local swim clubs.[16] During the summer months throughout his childhood, he swam three hours per day as a treatment to relax his chest muscles.[17] Ernesto was not content to limit his physical activity to swimming and with the support of his mother, Guevara began to engage in a variety of outdoor leisure pursuits.

He continued to swim for leisure as a young adult and his 'motorcycle diary' entries reveal that he frequently swam throughout his journey across Latin America. Beyond leisure, the diary also reveals Guevara leveraged his swimming prowess as a means to build rapport with some of the individuals he encountered on the journey. For example, the interns of the San Pablo (Peru) leper colony on the Amazon watched in awe as Guevara swam the width of the river. In total, the round trip feat lasted for more than two hours. The accomplishment made a profound impression on the patients at the colony and served as a source of respect and admiration for the aspiring doctor.

Golf

Guevara's father (Ernesto Guevara Lynch) was a shipbuilder by trade and he struggled to find stable work in the small town of Alta Gracia, Córdoba, during the 1940s. Also, the family's *yerba mate* plantation in Misiones province was suffering significant losses due to prolonged drought conditions and an acute drop in market value for the plant, which is used to make the popular *mate* (hot tea) of the River Plate region. Consequently, the family found itself in financial turmoil, but often attempted to disguise the reality of their situation by continuing to indulge in a lifestyle they could not afford. Guevara Lynch eventually garnered a contract to expand and upgrade the local Sierras Golf Course Hotel and it is here where young Guevara first became acquainted with the sport of golf. With the encouragement of his father, he began playing golf at the age of six and he practiced 'as much as he wished as he would do so at times when no one was playing'.[18] According to his father, Guevara loved golf and by age 15 he was a good player who enjoyed showing off his skills at the golf club near the family's weekend home in Villa Allende in the suburbs of the city of Córdoba.[19] Though no scorecards remain to validate the accuracy of his golfing legacy, Resnick notes Guevara became proficient enough to shoot scores below 90.[20]

Throughout his adolescence, Guevara intermittently worked as a golf caddy and as a result he developed strong bonds with the other caddies. Perhaps more important than his passion to play golf was the opportunity it provided for socialisation. Many of Guevara's friends growing up 'were the sons of miners, hired hands at the golf club, caddies or hotel waiters ... This is how Ernesto discovered, at a very young age, how the poor lived and what few prospects they had of improving their lot'.[21] While many scholars associate his desire to combat injustices of the poor and exploited with his motorcycle journey across Latin America in the early 1950s[22], Guevara's father suggests his empathy for the poor started a decade earlier and credits, at least in part, his golfing experiences as his introduction to social inequalities.[23] In short, the socialisation the golf club provided Guevara was not restricted to a cultural indoctrination of Córdoba's high society. On the contrary, the most meaningful relationships he developed at the golf club were with individuals of modest means whose purpose at the club was specifically related to labour.

Football (Soccer)

Interestingly, golf was one of the few sports Guevara Lynch condoned for his asthmatic son given the risks involved with strenuous physical activity. However, young Guevara longed to participate in the same childhood games and activities as his comrades. Fortunately for him, his mother Celia was supportive and insisted *Ernestito* be permitted to have a normal childhood. Ultimately, Guevara Lynch was unable to impose his will on his son, who was carried home by his friends on more than one occasion in the midst of a severe asthma attack brought on by his participation in one of the many physical activities they enjoyed. These experiences did not deter Guevara from engaging in such activities. Rather, they seemingly contributed towards his development of 'a fiercely competitive personality'.[24]

As a young boy in Alta Gracia, Guevara increasingly grew accustomed to the physical limitations associated with his health condition. He learned to cope with and persevere through the pain from participation in neighbourhood 'pick-up' football games and other physical activities. Furthermore, Guevara began to demonstrate a particular class affinity when organising the informal football matches. Growing up, he and his brother Roberto played football with 'teams of strays' and, as Resnick notes, Guevara and his golf caddie friends of modest means would test their virility on rudimentary grounds against boys from wealthy families.[25]

Reflecting on Guevara's indirect participation in football provides glimpses of early rebellious tendencies that in the end became a source of irony. Football has always been considered the most popular sport in Argentina and its popularity transcends the social classes (unlike golf, tennis and rugby). Consumption of the nation's professional football league dramatically increased following professionalisation (1931), while print and media coverage made the sport accessible in even the most remote corners of Argentina. During the 1940s River Plate's football team emerged as a dominant side and earned the admiration of many because of its attacking style and scoring efficiency. Guevara, realising he lacked an affinity for a particular club, decided to assert an allegiance for a particular team. While many across Argentina were drawn to the superior technical skills, scoring efficiency and success of River Plate, Guevara decided to support a hapless Rosario Central team. After all, Rosario was his birthplace and equally important for Ernesto, they were the clear underdog at the bottom of the standings. Supporting Rosario Central reaffirmed his *Rosarino* identity and set him apart from everyone else, most of whom either supported River Plate or Argentina's other popular club Boca Juniors.[26] However, at the time, Guevara could not have realised his affinity for 'Central' would eventually contradict his desire to help a particular marginalised sector of society.

As a medical student just a few short years later, Guevara and his motorcycle companion and lifelong friend Alberto Granado developed a mutual passion for studying and attempting to discover a cure for leprosy.[27] Both of their diaries chronicling the now famous 1952 motorcycle journey describe their time working at multiple leper colonies across Latin America, including the aforementioned San Pablo colony in Peru. Ironically, Rosario Central was bestowed their *Las Canallas* (Scoundrels) nickname for their unwillingness to participate in a charity football match with their cross town rivals Newell's Old Boys in the 1920s. The match was being organised by a group associated with Rosario's Hospital Carrasco to raise funds to support leprosy patients. Newell's Old Boys accepted the invitation and earned their nickname *Los Leprosos* (The Lepers) while Rosario Central declined and continues to be chastised as scoundrels for their lack of compassion for those affected by the disease.[28] The irony here is had Guevara been able to foresee his future efforts to care for leprosy patients when he decided to support one of the marginal football teams from Rosario (as opposed to one of Argentina's successful and popular clubs), he likely would have chosen Newell's over Rosario Central.

Finally, Guevara leveraged the football skills he developed on the 'rudimentary' open grass fields of Alta Gracia during his interactions with those he encountered while on his first journey across South America. Like swimming, football provided an opportunity to build rapport and gain the trust of those who looked upon the peculiar 'travelling doctors from Argentina' with scepticism. As outlined in the diaries, Guevara and Granado organised informal football matches to engage locals upon arrival at Machu Pichu, Lima and San Pablo in Peru and they both took part in a football tournament for the local side Independiente Sporting Football Club while at Leticia, Colombia, prior to departing for Bogotá on 1 July 1952.[29] On this occasion, like those that preceded it, Guevara performed well in goal, the one position suitable for him because of his asthma limitations. The football matches served as a means of escape for the leprosy patients and ultimately provided a means for Guevara and Granado to establish common ground with the many people they encountered and treated while touring the continent.

Chess

Physically demanding activities were not the only leisure pursuits that contributed to Guevara's maturation process as a young boy. Confined to home due to his medical condition, Guevara's father instilled in him a love for reading and a passion for the cerebral game of chess. Once he had the rules mastered, young Guevara frequently played chess with neighbours, further developing the advanced skills of strategic planning and tactful response he would later call upon on as *Comadante* Che Guevara in Cuba during the revolution. Former international chess master and Argentine champion Miguel Najdorf played against Guevara later on in life, once in Mar del Plata and again at an event in post-revolution Cuba. On the latter occasion, Guevara earned a draw with the chess legend. Najdorf later described Guevara as a 'first class player' who, like a guerilla fighter, preferred 'an aggressive style and respected sacrifices'.[30]

Equally important, chess offered young Guevara additional exposure to 'leftist' ideology. Guevara's parents were politically active with an overt disdain for the capitalist tenet of the Argentine Republic, which they perceived to be imposed from the outside by British and American imperialist interests. Together, their strong political position 'had a decisive influence on the boy who was to become Che Guevara'.[31] Their political position was further reinforced by the influx of Spanish Republican refugees seeking safe haven from Franco's Nationalists during the Spanish Civil War. In Alta Gracia, as well as across Córdoba province and Argentina, a committee was set up for the purpose of coordinating assistance for Republican political refugees fleeing the fascist advances in Spain. Throughout the 1930s and 1940s central Argentina received a significant influx of Spanish exiles and Guevara would soon become captivated by the first-hand accounts of the conflict.[32]

The González Aguilar family arrived in Alta Gracia from Spain at the onset of hostilities. The patriarch of the family, Juan González Aguilar, was a doctor who served as head of naval health for the Republic. After initially seeking exile in France, he joined his family and many friends in Alta Gracia. Sharing the same disdain for fascist rule the Guevara's befriended the exiles and young Ernesto soon became 'inseparable' from the eldest of the González Aguilar children. As Resnick notes, Guevara spent much time honing his chess skills at the González Aguilar family home in Alta Gracia.[33] Consequently, he was exposed to countless first-hand stories of the atrocities committed by the fascists in Spain as told by the Republican exiles who made the González Aguilar home a social centre.[34] Perhaps the most important exile befriended by the Guevara family through the González Aguilar social network was General Jurado, a former Spanish Republic general and war hero. According to Guevara Lynch, the war stories of General Jurado and the demeanour in which they were told provided young Guevara 'the model for a military man … he (Ernesto) was full of admiration for him … I have often asked myself if the stories of this Spanish general turned out to be valuable lessons for Ernesto in his revolutionary struggles'.[35]

Rugby

Of the sport and leisure pursuits young Ernesto Guevara practiced, rugby was his favourite. After the family left Alta Gracia for the larger urban city of Córdoba, Guevara became acquainted with the Granado brothers (Gregorio, Tomás and Alberto). Though Guevara was in classes with Tomás at the Deán Funes school, it was his relationship with the older Alberto that evolved into a lifetime friendship. Indeed, this friendship would lead the two across South America on Granado's now famous 500cc motorcycle[36] and eventually to Cuba where Granado would join Guevara post-revolution and later become instrumental in developing the Cuban Rugby Union in the 1990s.

The Granado brothers, with Alberto being the rugby enthusiast, spearheaded an effort to put together a proper rugby team called Platense in lower Córdoba, but 'rarely managed to get together the fourteen players required to form a rugby team'.[37] Alberto later organised and coached the *Estudiantes* rugby team and was openly reluctant to allow the asthmatic and frail 14-year-old Guevara to participate. Alberto eventually relented and in 1943 Guevara began practicing with the team twice per week, earning 'a reputation as a fearless attacker on the pitch'.[38] Guevara's passion for rugby blossomed and his practice of the sport spilled over into his daily life at home. As Guevara Lynch recalls, Guevara and his younger brother Roberto would practice on the paved patio at home 'where they took some serious knocks on the hard ground'.[39] Guevara developed into a gifted rugby player and his aggressive physical approach to the game prompted Alberto Granado to bestow the 'Fúser' nickname on him. The name, aside from being original, was shorthand for the combination of the words 'Furibundo [Furious]' and 'Serna' (Guevara's surname). Due to his fearless tackling ability, Fúser played in the back, though the scrum cap he wore on the field was likely the brunt of many jokes.

After his family moved back to Buenos Aires in 1947 Guevara, who had finished high school and was now working for the Córdoba Provincial Roads Directorate, received word that his grandmother had fallen gravely ill. He immediately resigned from his post and joined his family to be closer to his grandmother, where he would carefully watch over her until she passed away. According to his family, Guevara was emotionally moved by his caretaking experience. He decided to remain in Buenos Aires and enrol at the Faculty of Medicine at the University of Buenos Aires. It is here where Guevara received training in medicine and later his licensure as a doctor.

Though his studies were demanding and time-consuming, Guevara managed his time wisely and continued to play rugby against his doctor's wishes. Guevara Lynch enrolled both Guevara and his younger brother Roberto as members of the San Isidro Club (SIC), of which Guevara Lynch himself was a founding member. At SIC, Guevara began to play rugby with more regularity and at a higher level than he had previously with Alberto Granado's *Estudiantes* team in Córdoba. Playing with the reserve team, he found creative ways to mitigate the limitations brought on by his asthma. 'During matches, he always managed to recruit a friend, who would run along the line with his inhaler and hand it over to Ernesto ... If he felt seriously out of breath, he would ask the referee's permission to stop for a moment and use the inhaler, and then carry on playing'.[40]

Realising his son was putting himself needlessly in danger Guevara Lynch pleaded with him to abandon rugby yet his efforts only prompted the young Guevara to pledge that he would continue playing 'even if it kills me'.[41] Guevara Lynch then talked his brother-in-law (Martín) Martínez Castro, who was the club's president, into removing Guevara from the team. Perhaps offering a glimpse into the resolve and rebellious nature that would give rise to the Che legend a decade later, Guevara continued playing rugby for the Atalaya Polo Club.

Guevara's enthusiasm for rugby soon intersected with his passion for literature. As a teenager in Córdoba, Guevara had already become versed in a number of classic pieces of literature, including works by Freud, Dumas, Mallarmé, Baudelaire, Zola, Marx, Stalin, Faulkner, Steinbeck and, of course, Sarmiento, among many others. He also enjoyed writing poetry and on occasion penned short stories throughout his youth. Frequently using his father's rented studio on Paraguay Street in Buenos Aires as a study, Guevara also briefly used the space as an editorial office for the rugby magazine *Tackle*. The publication began as an in-depth review of select rugby matches from the previous week and Guevara, along with his brother Roberto and 10 of his friends, provided the content under pseudonym names. Guevara had deservedly earned the nickname *el Chancho* (The Pig) back in Córdoba for his notoriously sloppy appearance and unclean attire. He used to say, for instance, 'It's been twenty-five weeks since I washed this rugby shirt'.[42] He used a variant of that nickname, *Chang Cho*, for his magazine contributions.

The weekly magazine lasted for 11 issues, spanning the Argentine fall and winter months from May to July of 1951. Guevara's contempt for the class divisions that exist in Argentinean rugby soon spilled out into its pages.[43] He chastised the exclusive nature and bourgeoisie make-up of its practitioners and the Anglophile nature of the sport's demographics.[44] After the police paid him a visit and accused the young medical student of spreading communist propaganda, which was punishable in Perón's Argentina, and due to a lack of funds the magazine was abandoned.[45] Few (if any) remaining copies of the publication exist today. Most references to the publication, like this one, are descriptive and are based on second-hand accounts. It is possible the copies Guevara may have saved were either destroyed after a torrential rain flooded his father's Buenos Aires Arenales Street apartment basement in 1972 or they were simply discarded by an aunt with a reputation for purging seemingly unwanted items from the family home. If not for the astuteness of Manolo, a building concierge, Guevara's now famous diaries would have met a similar fate following the 1972 flood.

Nevertheless, Guevara's early involvement in rugby further made apparent the class divisions that exist in society at a crucial point in his maturation process. This buttressed his evolving philosophical and ideological position that scorned the societal structures that created class divisions. Perhaps equally important, his participation in rugby provided an opportunity to channel his aggression and a practical learning experience that emphasised the importance of teamwork, discipline and respecting the opponent while cultivating a sense of courage and perseverance. Paraphrasing Castañeda, rugby had two lasting implications for Guevara. On the one hand it entailed an exceptional physical challenge that resulted in the development of willpower. On the other hand, rugby's cerebral component offered 'him the opportunity to develop his skills as a leader and strategist'.[46] Both of these implications proved paramount during the Cuban Revolution and contributed towards his enduring legacy.

Discussion: Developing Character and Socialising a Revolutionary

The enduring belief that participation in sport and leisure potentially develops such positive character traits as self-discipline, perseverance, leadership, respect for authority and cooperation among other benefits is grounded in the *British Amateur Sporting Ideal*, or simply *Athleticism*. Much work has been done to both trace the origins of the ideology and its integral role in forging modern societies.[47] Indeed, the influence of the ideology can be found in all corners of the globe, particularly where the British have a historical legacy. In the USA, the early pioneers who fought for the institutionalisation of physical education in schools, as well as a place for organised sporting competition and informal play for children in everyday life, borrowed heavily from this ideology and, like the British, they placed additional emphasis on the health benefits associated with physical activity.[48]

In Argentina, a similar discourse took place and this is not surprising given European philosophy and cultural practices, both directly and indirectly, contributed towards the construction of modern Argentina.[49] After the fall of the conservative caudillo Juan Manuel de Rosas in 1852, Argentina, led by liberal politicians and intellectuals such as Alberdi,

Mitre and Sarmiento, embarked on a modernisation project that held Northern European culture, particularly that of the British, in high regard.[50] In fact, the extent of British cultural, commercial and capital influence in Argentina at the end of the nineteenth century and well into the twentieth century was significant enough to prompt ongoing scholarly debates about the appropriateness of referring to Argentina during this era as part of an 'informal empire'.[51] Although the education system in Argentina diverged from earlier models that incorporated British approaches, certain elements remained.[52] Specifically, the efforts of Argentina's physical education pioneer Enrique Romero Brest considered, among other systems, the benefits (and perils) of the English system and its emphasis on sport when he developed the Argentine system in the first decade of the twentieth century. Although the Argentine system evolved over time, it continued to emphasise the health, psychological and social benefits associated with sport and team games.[53]

With respect to formal athletic clubs and organised sporting competitions, the British influence in Argentina is conspicuous. The first football clubs established in the country were set up by British railway workers in the last quarter of the nineteenth century. As the clubs increased in number and size, so too did the network of British private schools. As Archetti explains, football was initially practiced within the structured setting of the British schools and athletic clubs. It was to be played in certain manner and was an exercise to instil the 'games ethic' with an emphasis on sportsmanship, teamwork and fair play. Winning in the absence of these ideals was to undermine its purpose.[54] By the first decade of the twentieth century, the masses began practicing football in large numbers and it soon became more organised and professional in nature while also serving as a mode of identity construction for the various heterogeneous barrios.[55] Many English sports and team games, such as rugby and field hockey, did not undergo this transformation. Consequently, they remained cultural activities reserved for middle-class Argentineans seeking to conserve the ideals of *Athleticism* and a signifier of social class status.

This is very much the context in which young Guevara engaged sport and leisure in Argentina during the 1940s and early 1950s. The prevailing philosophical perspective that organised physical activities can, under the right conditions, develop 'good character' and serve as a socialising agent remains at the fore of contemporary thought.[56] Assuming this philosophy is sound, we can conceptualise how sport and leisure activities may have afforded young Guevara the opportunity to develop self-discipline, perseverance and willpower, leadership, an appreciation for teamwork and cooperation, respect for the opponent, loyalty, courage, as well the ability to strategise and cope with adversity. The development of these character traits during his childhood would prove significant during the successful campaign that overthrew Cuban dictator Fulgencio Batista in 1959. For Costañeda, willpower was the key attribute and guiding principle in the making of Guevara and this trait evolved directly from his battle with asthma during physical activity throughout his adolescent years. 'From his youthful rugby days in Córdoba to his execution in the jungles of Bolivia, he always started off from the premise that it was enough to want or will something for it to happen. There was no obstacle too great for willpower'.[57]

Furthermore, as I have noted in this essay, sport and leisure served as a key socialising agent for the future revolutionary. Through these experiences, including chess at the González Aguilar family home and neighbourhood football matches with 'teams of strays' of all social classes, Guevara was routinely in touch with the realities associated with the oppressed and poor at a young age. While some seemingly attribute the beginning of his fight for social justice to his motorcycle trip with Alberto Granado in isolation of the context of his childhood, this position unjustly marginalises the influence his childhood sport and leisure experiences likely had on the future revolutionary.

Finally, Guevara leveraged his sport and leisure background during his trips across South America. By organising football matches and demonstrating his swimming prowess, he was able to build rapport and establish a sense of solidarity with those he and Alberto Granado met on their journey, particularly the patients at the various leprosariums they visited along the way. As Granado himself expressed years later, Guevara insisted that the stigmatised lepers be treated in a more humane and friendly way.[58] Engaging them through sport and leisure was one effective strategy to accomplish this end.

The enduring legacy of Ernesto Guevara is firmly grounded in his revolutionary efforts, as it should be. These are certainly his enduring contributions and claim to fame (or infamy). What I have attempted to convey in this essay is Guevara's sport and leisure experiences, more than simply 'forming a bitter sense of humor'[59], significantly contributed towards his development and revolutionary accomplishments. Through swimming, golf, soccer, rugby and even chess, young Guevara developed important character traits, mainly a will to persevere. Furthermore, the opportunity for socialisation through some of these activities shaped his political position and passion for social justice.

Notes

1. Perhaps it is useful to explain that *che* is a colloquial term often used as an interjection to gain someone's attention in Argentina. It closely resembles the English use of the word 'hey', or more directly, 'hey you'. Being Argentinean and due to his frequent use of the term, Ernesto's Cuban comrades referred to him as simply *El Che* and the nickname stuck. Guevara embraced the name and eventually began formally signing bank notes as *Che* as Cuba's Governor of the National Bank.
2. The Leaders and Revolutionary category is described as being 'People who helped define the century's political and social fabric'. Heroes and Icons are 'People who exemplify courage, selflessness, exuberance, superhuman ability, and amazing grace'.
3. Dorfman, Ariel. "Che Guevara: The Guerilla," *Time*, June 14, 1999.
4. Casey, *Che's Afterlife*.
5. Ziff, *Che Guevara*. See also the 2008 documentary *Chevolution* (directed by Luiz Lopez and Trisha Ziff).
6. See Castro, *Che: A Memoir*; Ferrer, *Becoming Che*; Gadea, *Ernesto*; Granado, *Traveling with Che Guevara;* Guevara, *The African Dream*; Guevara, *Back on the Road*; Guevara, *The Motorcycle Diaries*; Guevara, *The Bolivian Diary*; Rojo, *My Friend Che*; and Salles, *The Motorcycle Diaries*.
7. Carte, "Trickster, Traveler, Cultural Hero," 167–83.
8. Ibid., 180.
9. Castro, *Che: A Memoir*, 26–34, 75–81.
10. An exception to this statement are the reflections of Ernesto Guevara Lynch, Che's father, who specifically explores young Ernesto's childhood in search for clues and reasons as to how his

sickly and frail son developed into a strong guerilla revolutionary. See Guevara Lynch, *Young Che*, 103–54. See also Castañeda, *Compañero*, 16–17. The author also briefly mentions sport as a potential significant factor in the development of 'Che the revolutionary', particularly the sport of rugby.

11. Anderson, *Che Guevara*, 12.
12. Celia was also asthmatic and several of Che's siblings later developed mild asthma.
13. For recent studies that investigate risk factors for asthma in children see Klinnert et al., "Onset and Persistence of Childhood Asthma"; and Chen, Tsai, and Lee, "Early-Life Indoor Environmental Exposures," 19–25.
14. Armus, *The Ailing City*. See also Ablard, *Madness in Buenos Aires*.
15. Rodriguez, *Civilizing Argentina*.
16. Anderson, *Che Guevara*, 16–17.
17. Resnick, *The Black Beret*.
18. Guevara Lynch, *Young Che*, 140.
19. Ibid.
20. Resnick, *The Black Beret*, 1970.
21. Guevara Lynch, *Young Che*, 108.
22. For example, Kate Havelin dedicates a chapter entitled 'Becoming Che' that coincides with the completion of the motorcycle trip around Latin America with Alberto Granado. See Havelin, *Che Guevara*.
23. Guevara Lynch, *Mi hijo el Che*.
24. Anderson, *Che Guevara*, 19.
25. Resnick, *The Black Beret*.
26. Scher, *La Patria Deportista*.
27. In fact, by this time Granado was already practicing medicine as a biochemist at a leprosarium in Córdoba province.
28. Fabbri, *El Nacimiento de Una Pasión*, 104–11. Also, it is important to point out this is the dominant version of the origin of the nicknames and that others do exist. For example, some suggest Rosario Central's *canallas* nickname was an insult directed at the club's fans by supporters of Belgrano.
29. Ernesto and Alberto also served as contracted coaches for the Independiente Sporting side while in Leticia, though it is unclear how much (if any) money actually changed hands. See Granado, *Traveling with Che Guevara*, 167–74.
30. Guevara Lynch, *Young Che*, 154.
31. Ibid., 60.
32. Castañeda, *Compañero*, 13–15.
33. Resnick, *The Black Beret*.
34. Guevara Lynch, *Young Che*, 118-123.
35. Ibid., 122–3.
36. Alberto's La Poderosa II (The Strong One) was named after his first La Poderosa, a bicycle.
37. Guevara Lynch, *Young Che*, 138.
38. Anderson, *Che Guevara*, 28.
39. Guevara Lynch, *Young Che*, 142.
40. Ibid.
41. Ibid.
42. Anderson, *Che Guevara*, 36.
43. Then, and now, rugby remains a leisure practice associated with Argentina's middle class, who have maintained an expansive network of British private schools and athletic clubs sponsoring a combination of sports such as rugby, field hockey, cricket, and polo.
44. Gálvez, *Che Deportista*.
45. After re-election Perón's administration instituted oppressive measures to thwart any threats deemed communist, socialist, or otherwise in opposition to *peronism*. For an in-depth look at the essence, foundation, limits, and interaction of *peronism* with oppositional political positions see Finchelstein, *Transatlantic Fascism*; Healey, *The Ruins of the New Argentina*; James, *Resistance and Integration*; and Karush and Chamosa, *The New Cultural History of Peronism*.
46. Castañeda, *Compañero*, 17.

47. See Mangan, *Athleticism in the Victorian and Edwardian Public School*; *The Games Ethic and Imperialism*.
48. For a thorough analysis see Green, *Fit for America*; Guttmann, *From Ritual to Record*; and Mangan and Walvin, *Manliness and Morality*.
49. See Armus, *The Ailing City*, 276–306; and Scharagrodsky, "La educación física escolar Argentina," 63–92.
50. Scobie, *Argentina*; See also Edwards, *Argentina: A Global Studies Handbook*; Hedges, *Argentina: A Modern History*; and Jakubs, "A Community of Interests."
51. Brown, *Informal Empire in Latin America*.
52. The Lancastrian model of pedagogy was imported into Argentina from England by James Thomas in 1818. Both the post-revolution conservative government and subsequent liberal intellectual leaders and governments at the end of the nineteenth century retained some of the key elements of the model, such as instilling nationalism and subordination in the nation's youth through education. See Szuchman, *Order, Family, and Community*.
53. Aguero, Iglesias, and del Valle Milanino, "Enrique Romero Brest y los inicios de la educación física escolar," 1–38.
54. Archetti, *Masculinities*, 48–72.
55. Frydenburg, *Historia social del fútbol*.
56. For a contemporary overview of this topic see Delaney and Madigan, "The Sociology of Sports," 96–115; and Weiss, Smith, and Stuntz, "Moral Development in Sport and Physical Activity," 187–210.
57. Castañeda, *Compañero*, XV.
58. Granado Jiménez, *Con el Che Guevara*.
59. James, *Che Guevara*, 38.

References

Ablard, Jonathan. *Madness in Buenos Aires: Patients, Psychiatrists, and the Argentine State, 1880–1983*. Athens, OH: Ohio University Press, 2008.

Aguero, Abel L., Silvia B. Iglesias, and Ana E. del Valle Milanino. "Enrique Romero Brest y los inicios de la educación física escolar: Su tiempo, su vida, su pensamiento, y su obra." *ea-journal* 1, no. 1 (2009): 1–38. ISSN 1852-4680.

Anderson, John Lee. *Che Guevara: A Revolutionary Life*. New York: Grove Press, 1997.

Archetti, E. P. *Masculinities: Football, Polo, and the Tango in Argentina*. New York: Berg, 1999.

Armus, Diego. *The Ailing City: Health, Tuberculosis, and Culture in Buenos Aires, 1870–1950*. Durham, NC: Duke University Press, 2011.

Brown, Matthew, ed. *Informal Empire in Latin America: Culture, Commerce and Capital*. Malden, MA: Blackwell, 2008.

Carte, Rebecca. "Trickster, Traveler, Cultural Hero: Ernesto 'Che' Guevara." *Studies in Latin American Popular Culture* 27 (2008): 167–183.

Casey, Michael. *Che's Afterlife: The Legacy of an Image*. New York: Vintage Books, 2009.

Castañeda, Jorge G. *Compañero: The Life and Death of Che Guevara*. New York: Alfred A. Knopf, 1998.

Castro, Fidel. *Che: A Memoir by Fidel Castro*, edited by David Deutschman. Melbourne: Ocean Press, 2006.

Chen, Y. C., C. H. Tsai, and Y. L. Lee. "Early-Life Indoor Environmental Exposures Increase the Risk of Childhood Asthma." *International Journal of Hygiene and Environmental Health* 21 (2011): 19–25.

Delaney, Tim, and Tim Madigan. *The Sociology of Sports: An Introduction*. Jefferson, NC: McFarland, 2009.

Edwards, Todd L. *Argentina: A Global Studies Handbook*. Santa Barbara, CA: ABC-Clio, 2008.

Fabbri, Alejandro. *El Nacimiento de Una Pasión: Historia de los clubes de fútbol*. Buenos Aires: Capital Intelectual Ediciones, 2006.

Ferrer, Carlos 'Calica'. *Becoming Che*. Buenos Aires: Editorial Marea, 2006.

Finchelstein, Federico. *Transatlantic Fascism: Ideology, Violence, and the Sacred in Argentina and Italy, 1919–1945*. Durham, NC: Duke University Press, 2010.

Frydenburg, Julio. *Historia social del fútbol: del amateurismo a la profesionalización*. Buenos Aires: Siglo XXI, 2011.

Gadea, Hilda. *Ernesto: A Memoir of Che Guevara*. Translated by Carmen Molina and Walter I. New York: Doubleday, 1972.

Gálvez, William. *Che Deportista*. La Habana: Editora Política, 1995.

Granado, Alberto. *Traveling With Che Guevara: The Making of a Revolutionary*. New York: New Market Press, 2004.

Granado Jiménez, Alberto. *Con el Che Guevara de Córdoba a la Habana*. Córdoba: Op Oloop Ediciones, 1995.

Green, Harvey. *Fit for America: Health, Fitness, Sport and American Society*. New York: Pantheon, 1986.

Guevara, Ernesto 'Che'. *The African Dream: The Diaries of the Revolutionary War in the Congo*. New York: Grove Press, 2000.

Guevara, Ernesto. *Back on the Road: A Journey through Latin America*. New York: Grove Press, 2001.

Guevara, Ernesto Che. *The Bolivian Diary*. Melbourne: Ocean Press, 2006.

Guevara, Ernesto Che. *The Motorcycle Diaries: Notes on a Latin American Journey*. Melbourne: Ocean Press, 2003.

Guevara Lynch, Ernesto. *Mi hijo el Che*. Barcelona: Editorial Planeta, 1981.

Guevara Lynch, Ernesto. *Young Che: Memories Of Che Guevara By His Father*. Translated and edited by Lucía Álvarez de Toledo. New York: Vintage Books, 2007.

Guttmann, Allen. *From Ritual to Record: The Nature of Modern Sport*. New York: Columbia University Press, 1978.

Havelin, Kate. *Che Guevara*. Minneapolis, MN: Twenty-First Century Books, 2007.

Healey, Mark. *The Ruins of the New Argentina: Peronism and the Remaking of San Juan after the 1944 Earthquake*. Durham, NC: Duke University Press, 2011.

Hedges, Jill. *Argentina: A Modern History*. New York: I.B. Taurus, 2011.

Jakubs, Deborah L. "A Community of Interests: A Social History of the British in Buenos Aires, 1860–1914." PhD diss., Stanford University 1986.

James, Daniel. *Che Guevara: A Biography*. New York: Stein and Day, 1969.

James, Daniel. *Resistance and Integration: Peronism and the Argentine Working Class, 1946–1976*. New York: Cambridge University Press, 1988.

Karush, Matt, and Oscar Chamosa, eds. *The New Cultural History of Peronism: Power and Identity in Mid-Twentieth-Century Argentina*. Durham, NC: Duke University Press, 2010.

Klinnert, M. D., H. S. Nelson, M. R. Price, A. D. Adinoff, D. Y. Leung, and D. A. Mrazek. "Onset and Persistence of Childhood Asthma: Predictors from Infancy." *Pediatrics* 108, no. 4 (2001): E69.

Mangan, J. A. *Athleticism in the Victorian and Edwardian Public School: The Emergence and Consolidation of an Educational Ideology*. London: Frank Cass, 2000 (originally published 1981).

Mangan, J. A. *The Games Ethic and Imperialism: Aspects of the Diffusion of an Ideal*. London: Frank Cass, 1998 (originally published 1986).

Mangan, J. A., and James Walvin. *Manliness and Morality: Middle-Class Masculinity in Britain and America, 1800–1940*. New York: St. Martin's, 1987.

Resnick, Marvin. *The Black Beret: The Life and Meaning of Che Guevara*. New York: Ballantine Books, 1970.

Rodriguez, Julia. *Civilizing Argentina: Science, Medicine, and the Modern State*. Chapel Hill: University of North Carolina Press, 2006.

Rojo, Ricardo. *My Friend Che*. New York: Dial Press, 1968.

Salles, Walter, dir. *The Motorcycle Diaries*. Park City, UT: Sundance Films, 2004.

Scharagrodsky, Pablo. "La educación física escolar Argentina (1940–1990): De la fraternidad a la complementariedad." *Anthropoligica* 22, no. 22 (2004): 63–92.

Scher, Ariel. *La Patria Deportista*. Buenos Aires: Editorial Planeta, 1996.

Scobie, J. R. *Argentina: A City and a Nation*. New York: Oxford University Press, 1964.

Szuchman, Mark D. *Order, Family, and Community in Buenos Aires: 1810–1860*. Stanford, CA: Stanford University Press, 1988.

Weiss, Maureen R., Alan L. Smith, and Cheryl P. Stuntz. "Moral Development in Sport and Physical Activity." In *Advances in Sport Psychology*, edited by Thelma S. Horn, 187–210. Champaign, IL: Human Kinetics.

Ziff, Trisha, ed. *Che Guevara: Revolutionary and Icon*. New York: Abrams Image, 2006.

'The Struggle That Must Be': Harry Edwards, Sport and the Fight for Racial Equality

David K. Wiggins

School of Recreation, Health, and Tourism, George Mason University, Manassas, VA, USA

This essay assesses the contributions of Harry Edwards to the Civil Rights Movement and the quest for racial equality in the USA. Through the utilisation of Edwards' own writings and a number of other primary and secondary sources, it examines how Edwards attempted to secure equality of opportunities for Black athletes and how he used sport in the battle for racial justice and fairness. It is evident that Edwards is a revolutionary who has altered the way that sport is viewed, making individuals aware that sport is an institution that encompasses similar forms of inequality prevalent in other societal institutions, and is not the great saviour for Blacks in the USA. Demonised by some for much of his career, Edwards has been honoured multiple times recently in an assortment of different ways for his many accomplishments both within and outside the sports world.

Harry Edwards is, by whatever definition employed, a revolutionary. Intelligent, physically imposing, highly determined, extremely confident and always courageous, Edwards has fought for almost his entire adult life to ensure that African Americans are treated fairly in sport and that the USA lives up to its democratic principles. He also has pushed, both individually and in concert with other revolutionaries, for a fundamental change in how we think about sport and what policies need to be implemented to make it better. Like many revolutionaries, Edwards has always been a lightening rod, beloved and admired by many while at the same time being loathed and disrespected by others. Like many revolutionaries, Edwards undertook a number of approaches in his efforts to effect change, including scholarly writings, lectures, protests and boycotts. And like many revolutionaries, Edwards, in the latter stages of his career, worked more often within the system, a result of progress and positive changes in sport rather than any fundamental alterations in his basic principles and philosophical approach to the world. Seemingly out of the realm of possibility many years ago, Edwards has been recently acknowledged for his many accomplishments. He has been invited to deliver plenary addresses and has received other tributes. Perhaps more than anything else, this recognition has come from a new-found respect people have for the man who has served for so long as the conscience of sport.[1]

Educational Attainments and Leader of Protests

Born November 22, 1942, into squalid conditions in East St Louis, Edwards grew up in a household that saw his mother abandon him and his seven siblings. Edwards' father worked as a labourer. Yet, in spite of these circumstances, Edwards would go on to become a scholarship athlete and an outstanding student, earning a Bachelor's degree from San Jose State College in 1964, a Master's in 1966 and a doctorate from Cornell University in 1973. From 1967 to 1969, he was an instructor of sociology at San Jose State College, and an Assistant Professor and then Professor of Sociology at the University of California, Berkeley, from 1970 until his retirement from the school in 2000. He complemented his academic work by serving as an assistant to the commissioner of Major League Baseball and as a consultant to both the San Francisco 49ers and Golden State Warriors.[2]

Edwards first garnered national attention in 1967 when he led a protest of Black students at San Jose State who threatened to 'physically interfere' with the college's opening football game against the University of Texas at El Paso.[3] The Black students, organised into a group called United Black Students for Action, put forth nine specific demands, ranging from the elimination of discrimination in housing to the mistreatment of African American athletes on campus. University administrators eventually addressed the demands, but not before racial tension became so inflamed that the football game had to be cancelled. The cancellation of the game resulted in Edwards receiving a sharp rebuke from the then California Governor Ronald Reagan, who called him 'unfit to teach'. Not to be outdone, Edwards responded by declaring that Reagan was 'a petrified pig, unfit to govern'.[4]

The confrontation at San Jose State demonstrated the increasing involvement of African American athletes in the Civil Rights Movement and Edwards' controversial practice of using sport to achieve racial equality. Assuming a public persona that was all fire and brimstone, Edwards confronted the white establishment head on, and sport became one of his most powerful tools. As a former athlete, Edwards appreciated the many sporting successes of Black athletes and the symbolic importance of these achievements for the African American community. But it was precisely because of his past athletic experience that he understood widespread media attention could be gained if a sporting event was disrupted. Moreover, as a university-trained sociologist with a critical understanding of sport and race relations, he knew perhaps as well as anyone that the success of African American athletes alone would never eliminate racism in sport and American society. Far more effective, he believed, was to have Black athletes, along with sympathetic white athletes, speak out more forcefully against racial inequality and place demands on a white power structure infatuated with and financially dependent on sport. As Edwards noted regarding the San Jose State affair:

> What activity is of more relevance to a student body than the first football game of the season? What activity is of more relevance to a college town after a long and economically drought-stricken summer than the first big game? And what is of more immediate importance to a college administration than the threat of stopping a game that had been contracted for under a $12,000 breach of contract clause and the cancellation of all future competition commitments if the game were not played?[5]

Encouraged by the outcome at San Jose State College, and after having many conversations with young African American athletes, Edwards in 1967 organised the Olympic Project for Human Rights (OPHR), a group that would eventually include nationally known African American athletes such as Lew Alcindor, Mike Warren, Tommie Smith and John Carlos, and whose primary purpose was to organise a boycott of the 1968 Olympic Games in Mexico City. Such a proposal was not new. As Edwards has always been quick to point out, African Americans had discussed the possibility of boycotting the Olympic Games years before the OPHR was founded. In 1960, for example, Black activists asked decathlete Rafer Johnson to boycott the Games in Rome to protest police brutality of African Americans in the South. Johnson refused and went on to capture the gold medal in

Rome (he was also the flag bearer and team captain). In 1964, Dick Gregory, an African American comedian and Civil Rights activist, advocated a boycott of the Tokyo Olympics to bring attention to racial inequality.[6] Mal Whitfield, three-time Olympic Gold Medalist in track and field, also urged a boycott of the 1964 Games. Whitfield's was an extraordinary proposal, considering his official duties as a goodwill ambassador for the USA. Yet, Whitfield argued that a boycott would call attention to the racial injustice in 'a nation where the color of one's skin takes precedence over the quality of one's mind and character'. Most importantly, Whitfield noted that African American athletes had 'been conspicuous by their absence from the numerous Civil Rights battles around the country', and urged them to become more involved. 'What prestige would the United States have if every single Negro athlete, after qualifying for the U.S. Team, simply decided to stay at home and not compete because adequate Civil Rights legislation had not been passed by Congress?' he asked in an article he wrote for *Ebony* in 1964. 'For one thing, such action would seriously dampen American foreign policy during a crucial period in history'.[7]

After seeking advice from prominent Civil Rights leaders such as Martin Luther King, Jr, Floyd McKissick and Louis Lomax, and after staging a Black youth conference in Los Angeles and another meeting at The Americana Hotel in New York City in late 1967, the OPHR issued a list of six demands. Conceived largely by Edwards, the list demanded the restoration of Muhammad Ali's heavyweight championship; the inclusion of at least two African American coaches to the men's US track-and-field team; the desegregation of the New York Athletic Club; the appointment of at least two African Americans to positions on the US Olympic Committee; the exclusion of white-supremacist nations South Africa and Southern Rhodesia from the 1968 Olympics; and the removal of Avery Brundage as President of the International Olympic Committee because of his racist views.[8]

However, Edwards and OPHR leadership soon realised that there were decided philosophical differences among former and current Black athletes, the Black community more generally and the larger American public regarding the benefits of an Olympic boycott. Part of these differences, as Jesse Owens' biographer William J. Baker notes, was generational. Former great Olympic champions such as Owens and Rafer Johnson adamantly opposed a boycott of the Mexico City games.[9] These two legendary Black Olympians could not understand the value of a boycott, rehashing the age-old argument that sport served as the great leveller in society and that athletic success would lead to racial acceptance and freedom of opportunities.[10] Importantly, some Black athletes who would most likely compete in Mexico City, as well as large segments of the Black and white communities, agreed. For instance, Ralph Boston, one of the most successful long jumpers in the history of track and field, opposed the boycott, contending that the best way to further the cause of Black Americans was through athletic success and Olympic competition, though he did say that if a boycott were 'strongly supported by the great majority of Negro athletes, I would have to go along with it'. Still, he 'believed Negroes can do more good for themselves and their race by going to the Olympics and doing well than they can by staying home'.[11]

Those who opposed the boycott often incurred Edward's wrath. No one was immune, especially those legendary Black athletes whom he believed could contribute to the cause but naively maintained that sport was the great saviour for African Americans and that it would eventually lead to racial understanding, and possibly even a colour-blind society. Of all athletes, perhaps the one targeted the most was Jesse Owens, the famous Black Olympian who symbolically shattered the Nazis belief of Aryan superiority by capturing four gold medals in the 1936 Olympic Games in Berlin. Edwards spared Owens no insult, calling him 'gullible', 'misinformed' and an 'Uncle Tom'. To Edwards, Owens was naïve to think that sport brought Blacks and whites closer together, and a dupe to believe in the sanctity of the Olympic Games.[12]

Edwards received as much as, or even more than, he meted out. He was castigated and called an ingrate, a radical bent on destroying the hallowed institution of sport for his own selfish purposes. Like so many other supposed Black radicals of the period, he was seen as a dangerous man whose every move needed to be watched and monitored. This task fell to the Federal Bureau of Investigation (FBI). 'Considerable publicity has been given Edwards, an instructor at San Jose State College, San Jose, California, in connection with the boycotting of an athletic event by Negro athletes', wrote the Director of the FBI, in one directive to the regional headquarters in San Francisco. 'Promptly review the information in your files concerning Edwards and submit a recommendation to include him on the Rabble Rouser Index if justified'.[13]

The attacks on his character and the FBI surveillance only stiffened Edwards' resolve to make visible racial discrimination by disrupting the sporting world's normal way of doing things. In February 1968, the OPHR organised a successful boycott of the New York Athletic Club's (NYAC) indoor track meet at Madison Square Garden to protest the discriminatory policies of the club (it did not allow Blacks or Jews as members). Because of the boycott, NYAC officials were forced to cancel the meet's high-school competitions, and entire college teams, even the Soviet national squad, withdrew. In addition, Edwards and the OPHR contributed to the protests of Black athletes on predominantly white university campuses.[14] No longer willing to accept the *status quo*, Black athletes, sometimes in cooperation with sympathetic white teammates, protested the discriminatory treatment from white coaches, fought for the inclusion of Black studies in university curriculums and pushed for better housing and more Black administrators, among other things. These protests, which first appeared on the campuses of the University of California, Berkeley, the University of Texas at El Paso and the University of Washington sometimes cost Black athletes their starting spots and, in the most extreme cases, their careers.[15]

On the surface, the success of the NYAC boycott and the various Black athletic revolts on predominantly white university campuses boded well for the ultimate goal of the OPHR, which was to boycott the 1968 Mexico City Olympic Games. The boycott, however, never took place. Unable to foster unanimity of opinion among members of the OPHR, Black athletes, with Edwards' blessing, decided to compete in Mexico City, but not in any victory-podium celebrations. In this way, they could maintain a semblance of unity. Asking Black athletes, particularly those from sports in which the Olympics represented the peak of athletic competition, to forego the Mexico City Games was asking them to commit the ultimate act of selflessness. But for other athletes, like UCLA standout Lew Alcindor, whose ultimate goal was to play in the National Basketball Association, the decision not to participate in the Olympics was less complicated. Many of these athletes, Alcindor included, never went to Mexico City.[16]

OPHR athletes ultimately decided not to boycott the medal ceremonies. However, they did agree that individual athletes could show their own form of protest. The most famous was Black Power salutes of Tommie Smith and John Carlos on the victory stand following their respective first- and third-place finishes in the 200-meter dash. As the National Anthem played, Smith and Carlos solemnly bowed their heads and raised their Black-gloved fists high in the air (Smith wore his glove on his right hand, Carlos on his left). For their actions, Smith and Carlos were kicked out of the Olympic village and sent home.[17] In contrast, after capturing the gold medal in heavyweight boxing, George Foreman paraded around the ring waving a small American flag. Foreman's patriotic display and Smith and Carlos' defiant gesture illustrated the philosophical differences among Black athletes.[18]

The lasting influence of the OPHR on sport, race relations and the larger Civil Rights Movement has long been debated. Edwards offered his own assessment of the OPHR's influence 10 years after its dissolution, claiming that the OPHR had played a valuable role in the hiring of more Black coaches and administrators at the intercollegiate and Olympic levels of competition. Most importantly, the activities of the OPHR had 'shattered for all time' the 'illusion of sports inherently insular and apolitical character'. The cancellation of the San Jose State–UTEP football game, the boycott of the NYAC track-and-field meet, the Black athletic revolts on predominantly white university campuses and the protests lodged at the Mexico City Olympic Games left no 'doubt that sport was far removed from the "toy department" of human affairs'. All of these activities made clear, wrote Edwards, that not only was sport' a 'serious business (in both a figurative and a literal sense), but also an important component in this nation's domestic social control machinery and in its international political propaganda program'.[19]

An Activist Scholar Taking Sport Seriously

In 1970, just two years after leading the OPHR, Edwards took a position as an assistant professor of sociology at the University of California, Berkeley. He seemed to settle into his new position with relative ease, teaching courses in his academic discipline, including a course in the sociology of sport, which routinely drew standing room-only crowds, and assuming the standard responsibilities of service and research expected of a tenure-track faculty member. From a quantifiable standpoint, Edwards got off to a quick start, even at an institution with such lofty scholarly responsibilities and expectations as Berkeley. He had already published his account of the OPHR in his *The Revolt of the Black Athlete* (1969).[20] Published by The Free Press, the book provides details about the inner workings of the OPHR and Edwards role in it. The same year as his appointment at the University of California, Berkeley, Edwards published *Black Students* (1970), a book examining the difficulties and experiences of Black college students.[21] In 1973, Edwards published the *Sociology of Sport*, the first monograph to seriously analyse the role of sport in America, and sports' interconnection and influence on other societal institutions.[22] In addition to these books, Edwards would later publish his memoir, *The Struggle That Must Be: An Autobiography* (1980), and numerous essays in magazines and academic journals such as the *Black Scholar*, *Society*, *Psychology Today*, *Ebony*, *Crisis* and *Journal of Sport and Social Issues*.[23]

Edwards' writings were used as ammunition in the fight for racial equality in sport and American society. His words were meant to sting, to elicit responses from what he viewed as a largely naïve American public unaware of the racism present in sport. Although rather formulaic and repetitive in nature, his publications pricked the consciousness of individuals through a critical assessment of the interconnection among race, sport and American culture. He eschewed any notion of neutrality in his publications, writing boldly and seemingly without fear about racial issues and what measures should be taken to correct them, thus creating an environment free of prejudice and discriminatory practices. Edwards' writings make clear the complexity of a man who was part academician, part radical, part activist and part social critic.[24]

The one publication that encapsulates much of Edwards' thinking is his memoir.[25] Although *The Revolt of the Black Athlete* is perhaps his most famous work, *The Struggle That Must Be*, published when Edwards was only 38, provides detailed information about his upbringing, the people who were most influential in his life and the forces that shaped the man he had become. In the tradition of great Black autobiographies written by such important figures as James Weldon Johnson, Maya Angelou, Langston Hughes and Richard Wright, Edwards' memoir is honest, straightforward, smart, bittersweet and sometimes poignant. He traces his life from his impoverished childhood in East St Louis to his early years at Berkeley. Among the more interesting aspects of the memoir is Edwards' disclosure of being trailed by the FBI. To the agency, Edwards was an enigma. Why a man with a PhD from Cornell would assume a life of radicalism and political protest was beyond even the FBI's vast realm of comprehension. As one G-man puts it: 'I don't understand why Edwards with his athletic ability, education, and background would become so angry, militant and outspoken'.[26]

Whether the FBI knew it or not, Edwards' radicalism resulted in large part from the influences of Paul Robeson and Louis Lomax, two men who have individual chapters devoted to them in *The Struggle That Must Be*. In the chapter 'Brother Lomax', Edwards recounts his close friendship with Lomax and the profound ways in which the well-known Black author, journalist and television personality impacted his life. It was Lomax who suggested that Edwards discard the 'suit and tie' and adopt a more radicalised persona, wholly distinct from 'another middle-class Negro with something to say about Civil Rights'. As Edwards notes:

> [S]lowly and quite deliberately I broke down to pseudorevolutionary rags and began to develop that separate identity Lomax thought so necessary in gaining critical access to and the attention of the media. At times it was as much as I could do to keep a straight face, standing before crowded auditoriums, under blazing television lights, delivering a lecture developed for my race relations class from a rostrum, festooned with reporters microphones, or bombarding white America with rhetoric calculated to outrage[27]

If Lomax persuaded Edwards to change his public image, Paul Robeson served as Edwards' inspiration and role model. In a chapter titled 'Declaration and Disengagement: A Refuge', Edwards, who possessed a near-encyclopaedic knowledge of the history of African American participation in sport, wrote that his understanding of the struggles experienced by Robeson in athletics 'enhanced my understanding of the forces that had molded my own life and activities'. To Edwards, Robeson, the outstanding student-athlete, singer actor and civil rights activist from Rutgers University, was the 'great forerunner' whose life and numerous achievements made clear the 'need for more than just protest demonstrations'. 'Dramatic revelation is one thing', noted Edwards:

> delineating through systematic investigation the precise dynamics of sports' relationship to society – and to the Black community in particular – is quite another. And if the sacrifices made and the insights gained were to be of any lasting consequence, the latter had to be accomplished.[28]

The call for a systematic approach to the study of sport was taken up most fully by Edwards in *Sociology of Sport*.[29] Based on his dissertation from Cornell University, 'Sport in America: Its Myths and Realities', and obviously a response to his own call for the 'need for more than just protest demonstrations', *Sociology of Sport* was the first textbook of its kind written in the USA, preceding the publication of several other survey texts on the sociology of sport that came out during the 1970s.[30] Edwards also wrote a large number of articles for popular periodicals and scholarly journals, gave numerous interviews, appeared frequently on television and delivered a host of presentations and plenary addresses.[31] He was also perhaps the most-quoted man in the USA regarding issues related to race and sport. During this period, Edwards continued to be highly critical of sport, publicly declaring that in spite of the rhetoric about it being free from prejudice and discrimination, it was yet one more institution that reflected power relations and the systematic exploitation of Blacks in a racist America.[32]

Trouble With Tenure at Berkeley

Edwards' blistering assault on sport in America made him a lightning rod of sorts, a divisive force, liked by some hated by others. No one seemed to take a neutral position on the man writer Ronald Glover called a 'change agent'.[33] Edwards seemed to relish this fact, but at times it caused him serious problems. One famous incident occurred in 1977. In January of that year, Edwards received notice from the sociology department at the University of California, Berkeley, that he had been denied tenure by a 10-8 vote with one abstention. The reason given for the denial was that 'he needed one or two more articles in established journals'.[34]

Edwards received unofficial word that senior members of his department had rationalised their negative votes on the basis that sport and race relations were not worthy of sociological study. 'Race Relations', wrote Edwards, 'was held to be a minor subarea of stratification, and sports were regarded simply as the legitimate subject matter of physical educators-not sociologists'.[35] Although impossible to confirm how much this attitude impacted the decision, there is no question that during this time the sociological study of sport had yet to realise legitimate status as a subfield in either physical education or the parent discipline of sociology. As made clear by noted sport sociologists such as John Loy and Jay Coakley, the sociological study of sport has been a low priority in departments of physical education where the sciences reign supreme and in departments of sociology where sport attracts relatively little interest to researchers and scholars.[36] This is part of a larger discussion taken up most notably by historians Elliott Gorn and Michael Oriard, who point out in their well-known essay, 'Taking Sports Seriously', that the study of sport has always been at the 'margins' of most academic disciplines, including history, sociology, philosophy, English, psychology and anthropology.[37]

Be that as it may, Edwards was angered by the decision and, in customary fashion, announced to the world that he had been denied tenure, and went on to vehemently protest it. One of his first actions was to send a telegram to President Jimmy Carter complaining of the 'rampaging racism in the institutions of higher education and other realms of minority life in this nation'. Without mentioning the issue, Edwards wrote, '[B]y deliberate intent and systematic design, the bureaucratic and administrative lynching of minorities in American higher education has emerged as a frightening but undeniable patterned reality'.[38] Edwards and his followers later held a protest rally on campus in which Edwards read the aforementioned telegram to President Carter in its entirety.[39] Edwards also discussed the ordeal in an article titled, 'Edwards vs The University of California', which was published in the May 1977 issue of *The Black Scholar*.[40] In the piece, Edwards cited a 1974 NAACP (National Association for the Advancement of Colored People) study that compared Berkeley to the University of Alabama and University of Mississippi in regards to the recruitment of Black students and 'its hiring, retention and promotion of Black faculty and staff personnel'.[41]

Why someone is denied tenure is extraordinarily difficult to assess. But Edwards was convinced that the vote to deny him a lifetime contract at Berkeley was racist and political. He claimed that Berkeley never intended for him to get tenure, and that the university did everything it could to ensure that his stay was a short one. He received a notice early in his career that his contract would not be renewed if he had not completed his dissertation by the prescribed time (customary now in academia). He suggested that he had been denied an opportunity to move from the department of sociology to the department of Afro-American studies because, as he stated, being in the latter programme 'would be the most difficult position from which to dislodge me'. He was denied university research support to participate in a project dealing with the People's Republic of China. Moreover, he believed, faculty and staff had regularly provided information to intelligence agencies regarding his campus activities and the 'personal conversations' he had had 'with other scholars and gentlemen'.[42] In spite of these constraints, Edwards pointed out that in six years he had established an exemplary career at Berkeley, having already published three books and more than 50 articles. He also taught some of the largest and most popular courses on campus, served on committees at the departmental, university and professional levels, and had lectured at over 300 colleges and universities worldwide.[43]

Edwards' tenure denial quickly became a cause célèbre. Thousands of Berkeley students signed a petition demanding that the tenure decision be overturned. The large majority of the 63 graduate students in the sociology department signed their own petition condemning the tenure decision. The Black graduate student caucus publicly denounced the decision, as did all 13 tenured Black faculty members at Berkeley. Civil Rights activists, professional groups and associations, and student organisations and faculty from universities in the USA and abroad expressed concerns about Edwards' case. Chancellor Albert Bowker received hundreds of letters and other forms of communication denouncing the decision and the negative impact it was having on the reputation of the university.[44]

Ultimately, the level of negative publicity became so great that Bowker created a 'special panel' to investigate the incident.[45] After consulting with this group, Bowker reversed the decision and granted Edwards tenure. Bowker, though, in a 1991 interview conducted by Harriett Nathan as part of the 'University History Series', could not resist getting in one last jab, saying that Edwards' 'scholarship was, in fact, adequate or satisfactory'. In a statement that could be interpreted in a number of ways, Bowker followed-up by noting, 'There was a feeling of equity involved, that he [Edwards] had been hired to fill a certain role on the campus and had done that. There was never any misrepresentation about who he was'. Later in the interview, Bowker was much more explicit about why he had overturned the tenure decision. Edwards, he said, 'had been a useful role model for the Black athletes, and in several particular instances had been quite useful … He always told them when they were off on the wrong track'.[46]

Irrespective of what Bowker believed, Edwards was ecstatic about finally being granted tenure. Any thoughts, however, that the decision would soften his views or render him less outspoken or courageous, were quickly dispelled in the fall of 1978 when he confirmed a previous statement he had made to a writer for *Black Thoughts Journal*, a Black student publication on campus. 'I am going to turn out the lights at Berkeley', he said. 'I am going to be the last one to leave'. In fact, continued Edwards:

> I was so serious about being the last one to leave U.C. Berkeley that I had made it a provision of my last will and testament that my ashes are to be secretly spread on the Berkeley campus so that I literally wouldn't leave until the place was bulldozed.[47]

Academic Reform, Black Athletes, and the Continuing Allure of Sport

If anything, getting past the tenure ordeal had given him a new lease on life, and he continued to write in a prolific fashion and speak out with great fervour about the various issues regarding race, sport and American culture. Although various issues would continue to draw Edwards' attention, the two that perhaps defined him the most were the education of Black athletes and the African American community's overemphasis on sport. Always interested in the education of Black athletes, Edwards in 1983 became embroiled in the debate over the passage of the National Collegiate Athletic Association's (NCAA) academic reform measure known as Proposition 48.[48] Intended to encourage and improve the academic performance of student athletes, Proposition 48, which did not go into effect until 1986 and dictated that incoming freshmen had to demonstrate minimum academic competencies (700 on the SAT or 15 on the ACT, and a 2.0 GPA in 11 core courses in high school) before being granted eligibility, drew much criticism from a large number of African Americans.[49] Prominent African Americans, including perhaps most famously basketball coaches John Cheney of Temple and John Thompson of Georgetown, were opposed to the new legislation, and to successive Propositions 42 and 16. Both Cheney and Thompson believed these propositions were based on racially biased standardised tests and therefore would most negatively impact Black athletes. In fact, Cheney and Thompson were correct. Blacks did score lower than whites on standardised tests, and it was they who would be the ones most negatively affected by the academic reform measures implemented by the NCAA.[50]

Like tennis great Arthur Ashe and other influential African American leaders, Edwards initially favoured the new legislation.[51] Even though the requirements were relatively low and established without the involvement of presidents from Historically Black Colleges and Universities (HBCUs), and even though colleges were more concerned about eligibility than education, Edwards supported the new legislation 'because it sent the message to young people that we did expect some semblance of academic achievement as well as their athletic proficiency. We expected them to do something intellectually as well as athletically'.[52] Gradually, however, Edwards changed his opinion. In a well-known 2000 essay, titled 'Crisis of Black Athletes on the Eve of the 21st Century', Edwards declared that 'it is now clear that the greatest consequence of Proposition 42, and similar regulations has been to limit the opportunities – both educational and athletic – that would otherwise be available to Black youths'. Although he conceded that some improvements had been made in the graduation rates of Black athletes (speculating that these improvements were perhaps more a result of improved academic support services than anything else), Edwards felt that the overall results of the NCAA's academic reform efforts had fallen woefully short because they 'were neither conceived nor instituted with due consideration of Black youths' circumstances beyond the academy and the sports arena'.[53]

Edwards' changing view of academic reform was intertwined with his shifting position on the role and meaning of sport for African Americans. For much of his career, he had warned African Americans of the dangers and harmful effects resulting from an overemphasis on sport. In one memorable essay, 'The Single-Minded Pursuit of Sports, Fame and Fortune is Approaching an Institutionalized Triple Tragedy in Black Society', Edwards argued that Black youth had become so obsessed in their pursuit of athletic glory that more appropriate and realistic career choices such as education, medicine, law, economics and politics were not even being considered. Black families, said Edwards, were partly to blame for this obsessive behaviour. Imbued with the belief in innate Black athletic superiority, influenced by the media regarding sport and economic mobility and unaware of visible and influential role models outside the world of sport, Black families had become much more aggressive than their white counterparts in encouraging their children to aspire to careers in sport.[54]

More recently, Edwards has spent far less time cautioning African Americans about their overemphasis on sport. In fact, on at least two occasions he actually praised African Americans for continuing to place such an inordinate amount of attention on sport. In a 2000 interview in *Colorlines*, titled 'The Decline of the Black Athlete: An Interview with Harry Edwards', and in an article in *Society*, titled 'Crisis of Black Athletes on the Eve of the 21st Century', Edwards pointed out that the USA was experiencing a decline in the number of outstanding African American athletes, a result of a number of societal factors and constraints.[55] Much of the Black athletic talent pool, like that for Black lawyers, doctors, educators, businessmen and other professionals, was being greatly diminished, a consequence of racial discrimination, 'erosion or elimination of Civil Rights gains', 'exit of the Black middle-class from the traditional Black community', deterioration of the Black family and 'political infrastructure' and 'structural economical shifts in the broader society'.[56]

Faced with this reality, Edwards softened some of his earlier arguments and contended that rather than 'de-emphasizing or abandoning sport, or simply allowing our involvement to wane, Black people must now more than ever intelligently, constructively, and proactively pursue sports involvement'.[57] Sounding like an early twentieth-century progressive reformer as much as a radical sport sociologist, Edwards stressed that Black youth must be encouraged to participate in all levels of sport so they can better learn lessons of life and the discipline required. Playing sports also put them 'in contact with the clergy, mentors, health workers, counselors, government workers, with people from the economic and corporate sector'.[58] In essence, sport was to serve as the 'last hook and handle', a means of keeping Black youth, particularly Black males, out of the criminal justice system or hospital emergency room or funeral parlour.[59] Importantly, Edwards' push for involvement in sport was not done naively. He fully recognised that the ultimate solution to the myriad problems faced by Black youth would require substantive changes in almost every area of American life. He was also fully aware that while he was advocating the notion of the 'last hook and handle', the privatisation of children's athletic programmes, cutbacks in educational funding and the deterioration of playgrounds and other recreational sites was reducing economically disadvantaged minority groups' access to sport.[60]

The Establishment Takes Notice

Edwards' theoretical understanding of race and sport was put to the test in a more practical way in the 1980s when he was hired as a consultant with the Golden State Warriors of the National Basketball Association and the San Francisco 49ers of the National Football League, and as a Special Assistant to Commissioner Peter Ueberroth of Major League Baseball.[61] These positions, when combined with his salary at Berkeley and the royalties from his various books and lectures, augmented what was already a substantial income. The new positions also brought forth a new legion of critics. His detractors questioned his commitment to reform and efforts to secure more opportunities for African American athletes, now that he was an insider employed by the very embodiment of the white power structure he had so roundly criticised for much of his career.[62] In typical fashion, though, Edwards was seemingly unfazed. In 1988, he told the *New York Times* sportswriter Robert Lipsyte, 'The establishment has changed to the extent that they decided to invite me in but I'm like a Statue of Liberty, I've been in the same position since day one'.[63]

Of the three positions Edwards took in professional sport, the historical record provides far more details about his responsibilities with the 49ers and Major League Baseball. He began his consulting work with the 49ers in 1985. His responsibilities included travelling with the team, providing assessments of potential draft choices and advising players on such issues as drug use, financial investments and post-athletic career opportunities. Like Jack Scott, Dave Meggyesy and many of the other radical thinkers associated with the earlier 'athletic revolution', Edwards had always viewed performance-enhancing drugs and inadequate preparation for life after sport as two of the biggest concerns for professional athletes. Much of his time with the 49ers was spent talking to players about the two topics.[64]

Two years after assuming the position with the 49ers, Edwards was hired as a special assistant to baseball Commissioner Peter Ueberroth. The position was an outgrowth of the infamous remarks by Los Angeles Dodgers General Manager Al Campanis that Blacks lacked the 'necessities' to manage a Major League Baseball team. Edwards was tapped to help identify and prepare Blacks for managerial and upper-level administrative positions in America's National Pastime.[65] It was a painstakingly slow process, in no small part because baseball was losing its appeal among African Americans. Nevertheless, Edwards designed strategies to increase the pool of Black candidates. His ultimate goal was to rid baseball of 'the good old boy network of mediocre white men who keep recycling each other'.[66]

But almost from the moment he took the position, Edwards was rebuked by the Frank Robinson-led Baseball Network, Inc., and other critics, for being an outsider who lacked institutional knowledge of the game. He was additionally criticised for acting too slowly, for effecting far too little change.[67] Recently, however, Major League Baseball has shown itself to be much more racially sensitive. The league has hired several minority candidates for managerial and upper-level administrative positions. Richard Lapchick, Director of the Institute for Diversity and Ethics in Sport, gave the league an 'A' for its racial hiring practices in his 2012 Major League Baseball Racial and Gender Report Card.[68] How much Edwards contributed to this grade is impossible to determine. The high mark may have had more to do with Commissioner Bud Selig's 1999 directive that requires teams to compile lists of potential minority candidates for manager, general manager and other executive positions. Still, Edwards' efforts cannot be totally discredited.[69]

In 2000, Edwards retired from Cal Berkeley.[70] Upon leaving the university (he is now professor emeritus), Edwards became Director of the Oakland Department of Parks and Recreation, a position probably incongruous with his skills and temperament.[71] Therefore, it was not surprising that after three less-than-harmonious years he resigned. Since then, he has continued to write and travel the country, discussing issues of race and sport in interviews, panel discussions and plenary addresses.[72] Ironically, he has become somewhat of a media darling, the go-to man whenever reporters, journal editors, television heads and academicians need a quote, analysis or interpretation on matters of race and sport.[73] He is almost always willing to talk about controversial issues in sport with anyone, anywhere. And he seldom disappoints. He is engaging, thought-provoking and serious.[74]

One interesting phenomenon is that Edwards is now occasionally offered speaking engagements that would never have been tendered earlier in his career. In 2011, for instance, Edwards was asked to deliver a plenary address by the NCAA Scholarly Colloquium at its pre-NCAA conference symposium in San Antonio, Texas.[75] Notwithstanding the fact that he was extended the invitation by a group of academicians with no official ties to the NCAA, the mere fact that Edwards presented the keynote speech at a conference sponsored by an organisation he had so severely criticized was a monumental and culturally significant event. In an address, titled 'Transformational Developments at the Interface of Race, Sport, and the Collegiate Athletic Arms Race in the Age of Globalization', Edwards revisited some of his earlier arguments, including the reasons for the slow pace of racial integration in sport and decline in number of African American athletes.[76]

Preserving the Legacy of the Man

Another interesting phenomenon of late is the outpouring of appreciation for Edwards' life and career, and the interest in preserving his legacy. Part of the reassessment and memorialising of the Black athletic revolt now some 45 years old, Edwards' many activities and accomplishments, along with the protests of Smith, Carlos and other African American athletes, have captured the imagination of scholars from a variety of disciplinary areas. His career has gone through a reclamation project of sorts.[77] Why it has happened is open to speculation. Perhaps it has to do with the continued fascination people have with the interconnection of race, sport and American culture. Although this is undoubtedly part of the answer, ultimately the reasons for such renewed attention now being paid to Edwards seems far more complicated. Maybe the interest stems from an effort, as Maureen Smith explains in her work on the meaning of the statue erected of Tommie Smith and John Carlos at San Jose State to make amends for the 'racial transgressions' and the 'historical baggage of racism' so prevalent in the USA. Other plausible reasons are the same ones historian Dan Nathan has used to explain the recent fascination with Negro League baseball. To Nathan, the new-found attraction of Negro League baseball for whites is perhaps 'a way of denoting one's liberalism and racial awareness and sensitivity'. On the other hand, such interest might be 'related to the yearnings for a more coherent sense of community and racial solidarity'.[78] In the post-Civil Rights era, is the interest in Edwards explained by a desire among African Americans for a sense of racial solidarity that was found in the Black athletic revolts and the larger Black Power movement of the late 1960s?

All of the new-found interest in Edwards by academicians is perhaps best represented by the 2009 special issue of the *Journal for the Study of Sports and Athletes in Education*, titled 'The Legacies of Harry Edwards for Sport Sociology', and the 2012 book, *Sport, Race, Activism, and Social Change: The Impact of Dr. Harry Edwards' Scholarship and Service*.[79] The special issue of the *Journal for the Study of Sports and Athletes in Education*, co-edited by David J. Leonard and C. Richard King, includes essays ranging from a re-evaluation of Edwards involvement in the 1968 Olympic boycott to the Black athletic revolts on predominantly white university campuses. Although all the pieces in the special issue are nicely done and interesting, the three that seem especially insightful and thought-provoking are Douglas Hartmann's essay 'Activism, Organizing, and the Symbolic Power of Sport: Reassessing Harry Edwards' Contributions to the 1968 Olympic Protest Movement', Leonard and King's article 'Revolting Black Athletes: Sport, New Racism, and the Politics of Dis/identification' and an interview conducted by Jay Johnson and Matthew A. Masucci with Edwards titled 'No Final Victories: Forty Years on the Frontlines of Race, Sport, and Culture: An Interview with Scholar/Activist Dr. Harry Edwards'.[80]

Hartmann's essay, based to a large extent on his well-known book, *Race, Culture, and the Revolt of the Black Athlete* (2003), argues persuasively that the most significant contributions made by Edwards to the 1968 Olympic protest movement were 'in the areas of education, organization and leadership, and media communications'.[81] Edwards' rhetorical skills, his understanding of the symbolic power of sport, organisational skills and acumen, and media savvy, helped mobilise Black athletes in the fight for racial justice and equality.[82] In their article, Leonard and King argue that Black athletes involved in the revolts of the 1960s have been memorialised and celebrated in an effort to demonise modern Black athletes while simultaneously 'legitimizing national projects of meritocracy, colorblindness, and American racial progress'.[83] In the interview conducted by Johnson and Masucci, Edwards' comments are reminiscent of W.E.B. DuBois famously prescient statement in the *Souls of Black Folk* (1903) that 'the problem of the Twentieth Century is the problem of the color-line'.[84] Edwards, instead, reminded Johnson and Masucci of one of his previously published essays from the *Civil Rights Journal* in which he wrote 'that the problem of the 21st Century is going to be the problem of diversity in all its tremendous variations'.[85] Edwards claimed that what he had learned from working as a consultant with professional sports teams 'is that it is precisely because of the differences that we have that gives value to our diverse input'. He continued:

> People are sick of the 'us versus them.' There is no them, there is only us, not just in this country but on this planet, and if we don't learn that lesson, it's not going to be 'us' for very long because the situation is just that dire and dangerous.[86]

Just three years after the appearance of the special issue in the *Journal for the Study of Sports and Athletes in Education*, Fritz G. Polite and Billy Hawkins published their co-edited book, *Sport, Race, Activism, and Social Change: The Impact of Dr. Harry Edwards' Scholarship and Service* (2012).[87] The book includes 11 chapters, along with an introduction by Polite, a conclusion (which probably would have been better as an introduction) by Hawkins and an epilogue by Edwards. Two of the 11 chapters, Michael Lomax's 'Revisiting the Revolt of the Black Athlete: Dr. Harry Edwards and the Making of (the New) African American Sport Studies' and Polite, Steven N. Waller, Stephanie Hill and Dawn Norwood's 'Fostering Dr. Harry Edwards's Legacy: Black Athletes Taking Responsibility in an Age of Sport Reform' are reprinted essays.[88] The most original chapter that deals directly with Edwards is perhaps Linda Greene's 'The Impact of Dr. Harry Edward's Work on Legal Scholarship'. Extraordinarily well-documented, Greene explains how legal scholars who have dealt with sport have depended on Edwards many publications.[89]

The special issue of the *Journal for the Study of Sport and Athletes in Education* and Polite and Hawkins co-edited book are just two of the latest publications providing insights into the life and career of Edwards and the many contributions he has made in the struggle for racial equality. These works, combined with Edwards' own writings and many other accomplishments, make clear he is a complex man whose singleness of purpose is only matched by his energy, foresight, intelligence and rhetorical skills. Like all revolutionaries, Edwards is extraordinarily independent. He is willing to share his ideas. He freely expresses his opinions. And he aggressively confronts injustices wherever he finds them. How he became this man is better left to the psychologist to determine. But there seems to be little question that he learned a great deal from many Black intellectuals and activists who preceded him. In fact, he seems to be an amalgamation of several historically important African Americans: His writing style is reminiscent of W.E.B. DuBois', his organisational skills recall Booker T. Washington's, his courage seems hewed from that of Paul Robeson, his gift for oratory reminds many of Malcolm X and his understanding of the media suggests Louis Lomax. Although some prefer to categorise him as a reformer, Edwards has clearly revolutionised how we conceive of sport, and how it both reflects societal values and can be used to fight racial justice. Through it all, he has never harboured any illusion that there would come a day in America where there was complete racial harmony. As he noted to me in a signed copy of the *Journal for the Study of Sports and Athletes in Education* devoted to his career: 'The challenge of achieving America is diverse and dynamic; the struggle, therefore, is multi-faceted and perpetual; and there are *no* final victories'.[90]

Notes

1. Edwards, *The Struggle That Must Be*; Mark Kram, "Gale Contemporary Black Biography: Harry Edwards," http://www.answers.com/topic/harry-edwards
2. Ibid.; Robert Lipsyte, "An Outsider Joins the Team," *The New York Times*, May 22, 1988.
3. Edwards, *The Revolt of the Black Athlete*; Edwards, *The Struggle That Must Be*; and Kram, "Gale Contemporary Black Biography."
4. Ibid. Quote is taken from Kram, "Gale Contemporary Black Biography."
5. Edwards, *The Revolt of the Black Athlete*.
6. Ibid.
7. Mal Whitfield, "Let's Boycott the Olympics," *Ebony*, March 1964, 95–6, 98–100.
8. Edwards, *The Revolt of the Black Athlete*. For very nice interpretations of the 1968 Olympic boycott, see Bass, *Not the Triumph But the Struggle* and Hartmann, *Race, Culture, and the Revolt of the Black Athlete*.
9. Baker, *Jesse Owens*.
10. Edwards, *The Revolt of the Black Athlete*.
11. For Boston's views, see Wiggins and Miller, *The Unlevel Playing Field*.
12. Edwards, *The Revolt of the Black Athlete*. For a Black Olympic athlete who was highly critical of Owens, see Matthews, *My Race Be Won*.
13. Edwards, *The Revolt of the Black Athlete*. For other FBI reports, see Edwards, *The Struggle That Must Be*.
14. Edwards, *The Revolt of the Black Athlete*; *The Struggle That Must Be*.
15. Ibid.; Wiggins, "The Year of Awakening"; Wiggins, "The Future of College Athletics is at Stake," 188–208; and Brooks and Althouse, "Revolt of the Black Athlete."
16. Edwards, *The Revolt of the Black Athlete*; Edwards, *The Struggle That Must Be*; Bass, *Not the Triumph But the Struggle*; Hartmann, *Race, Culture, and the Revolt of the Black Athlete*; and Smith, "'It's Not Really My Country'."
17. Edwards, *The Revolt of the Black Athlete*; Edwards, *The Struggle That Must Be*; Bass, *Not the Triumph But the Struggle*; Hartmann, *Race, Culture, and the Revolt of the Black Athlete*; Wiggins, "The Year of Awakening"; Smith, *Silent Gesture*; Carlos and Zirin, *The John Carlos Story*; and Brooks and Althouse, "Revolt of the Black Athlete."
18. Edwards, *The Revolt of the Black Athlete*; Hartmann, *Race, Culture, and the Revolt of the Black Athlete*; and Bass, *Not the Triumph But the Struggle*.
19. Edwards, "The Olympic Project."
20. Edwards, *The Revolt of the Black Athlete*.
21. Edwards, *Black Students*.
22. Edwards, *Sociology of Sport*.
23. Edwards, *The Struggle That Must Be*; "Change and Crisis in Modern Sport"; "Crisis of Black Athletes"; "The Black Athletes"; "The Single-Minded Pursuit," 138, 140; "The Collegiate Athletic Arms Race"; and "Beyond Symptoms."
24. Ibid.
25. Edwards, *The Struggle That Must Be*.
26. Ibid.
27. Ibid.
28. Ibid.
29. Edwards, *Sociology of Sport*.
30. Edwards, "Sport in America"; *Sociology of Sport*.
31. For a nice listing of Edwards' various publications, see Greene, "The Impact of Dr. Harry Edwards's Work."
32. Edwards first lays out most fully his conception of the relationship among race, sport and American culture, in his *Sociology of Sport*.
33. Ronald Glover, "Change Agent: Dr. Harry Edwards," The Black Sports Network, July 16, 2006, http://blacksportsnetwork.com/articles/features/Dr.E_071606.asp
34. Edwards, "Edwards vs The University of California"; *The Struggle That Must Be*.
35. Edwards, *The Struggle That Must Be*.
36. Loy, "The Emergence and Development"; Coakley, "Sociology of Sport in the United States."
37. Gorn and Oriard, "Taking Sports Seriously."
38. Edwards, *The Struggle That Must Be*.
39. Ibid.

40. Edwards, "Edwards vs The University of California."
41. Ibid.
42. Edwards, *The Struggle That Must Be*.
43. Ibid.; Edwards, "Edwards vs The University of California."
44. Ibid.
45. Ibid.
46. Nathan's interview with Bowker, September 6, 1991, content.cdlib.org/view?docld=hb1p 3001gg&doc.view = entire_text
47. Edwards, *The Struggle That Must Be*.
48. Edwards, "The Collegiate Athletic Arms Race"; Edwards, "The Black 'Dumb Jack'"; Edwards, "Educating Black Athletes"; Edwards, "Beyond Symptoms," 3–13; and Smith, *Pay for Play*.
49. Ibid.
50. Ibid.
51. Ibid.
52. *New Pittsburgh Courier*, December 27, 1986.
53. Edwards, "Crisis of Black Athletes."
54. Edwards, "The Single-Minded Pursuit," 138, 140.
55. Leonard "The Decline of the Black Athlete"; Edwards, "Crisis of Black Athletes."
56. Edwards, "Crisis of Black Athletes."
57. Ibid.
58. Leonard, "The Decline of the Black Athlete."
59. Ibid.
60. Ibid.
61. Lipsyte, "An Outsider Joins the Team"; Kram, "Gale Contemporary Black Biography"; Glover, "Change Agent: Dr. Harry Edwards"; and William D. Murray, "Edwards to Assist Ueberroth in Effort to Find 'Creditable' Minorities to Fill Variety of Posts," *New Pittsburgh Courier*, June 27, 1987.
62. Eddie Jefferies, "Edwards Under Fire, But He Can Handle It," *New Pittsburgh Courier*, September 19, 1987; Mary Hyman, "Some Black Players are Critical of Edwards," *Baltimore Sun*, October 19, 1987; and "Black Group Blasts 'Failing' Edwards," *The Washington Post*, August 19, 1987.
63. Lipsyte, "An Outsider Joins the Team." See also, Mike Well, "Edwards Silent After Being Called a 'Puppet'," *New Pittsburgh Courier*, September 5, 1987.
64. Lipsyte, "An Outsider Joins the Team"; Kram, "Gale Contemporary Black Biography." See also, Scott, *The Athletic Revolution*; Meggyesy, *Out of Their League*.
65. See Hoose, *Necessities*; Peter Gammons, "The Campanis Affair," *Sports Illustrated*, April 20, 1987; Steve Springer, "April 6, 1987: The Nightline That Rocked Baseball," *Los Angeles Times*, April 6, 1997; Reggie Jackson, "We Have a Serious Problem That Isn't Going Away," *Sports Illustrated*, May 11, 1987; and Ruck, *Raceball*.
66. Quoted in Lipsyte, "An Outsider Joins the Team."
67. Ibid.
68. "Major League Baseball Earns Top Grade for Racial Hiring Practices," http://www.spokes man-recorder.com/2012/10/17/major-league-baseball-earns-top-grade-for-racial-hiring-practices.
69. Ibid.
70. Lipsyte, "An Outsider Joins the Team"; Kram, "Gale Contemporary Black Biography."
71. Janine DeFao, "Harry Edwards to Head Oakland Parks-Rec/Expert on Sports and Race is Major Jerry Brown's Pick," *San Francisco Chronicle*, May 13, 2000, http://www.sfgate.com/p olitics/article/Harry-Edwards-to-head-Oakland-Parks-Rec-Expert-2779937; Ellen Griffin, "Time Out With Harry Edwards: Oakland's New Director of Parks and Rec," *MacArthur Metro*, November 2000, http://macarthurmetro.org/pdfs/metoo-11pdf; and Sandra Gonzales, "Oakland Activist Takes on New Career," September 23, 2000, http://lists.village.virginia.edu/ lists_archive/sixties-l/1798.html
72. For Edwards' resignation as Director of the Oakland Department of Parks and Recreation, see J. Douglas Allen-Taylor, "The Oakland City Hall Shakeup," July 4, 2003, www.berkeleydail yplanet.com. Some of the best insights regarding Edwards' thinking can be gleaned from his many interviews. See for example, Leonard, "The Decline of the Black Athlete"; Johnson and Masucci, "No Final Victories."

73. Lipsyte, "An Outsider Joins the Team"; Kram, "Gale Contemporary Black Biography."
74. Ibid.
75. The NCAA Scholarly Colloquium was the brainchild of Myles Brand, former university administrator and NCAA president. In 2013, the NCAA decided to stop funding the colloquium. See Ellen Staurowsky, "NCAA's Decision to Withdraw Funding for Scholarly Colloquium is an Attack on Academic Freedom," *College Sports Business News*, June 21, 2013, http://collegesportsbusinessnews.com/issue/January-2013/article/what-does-the-ncaas-decision-to; Paul Steinbach, "Scholars React to Cancellation of NCAA Colloquium," *Athletic Business*, April 2013, http://upload.athleticbusiness.com/articles/keyword.aspx?keyword=athletics
76. See Edwards, "Transformational Developments."
77. See the *Journal for The Study of Sports and Athletes in Education* (Summer 2009) and Polite and Hawkins, *Sport, Race, Activism, and Social Change*. At the time of this writing, the Association for the Study of African American Life and History was putting together a session, "45 years since the Black power fists protest at the 1968 Olympics" at its 2013 conference. See http://www.h-net.org/announce/show.cgiID=202401.
78. Smith, "Frozen Fists in Speed City"; Nathan, "Bearing Witness to Blackball."
79. See the *Journal for The Study of Sports and Athletes in Education* (Summer 2009) and Polite and Hawkins, *Sport, Race, Activism, and Social Change*.
80. Hartmann, "Activism, Organizing, and the Symbolic Power of Sport"; Leonard and King, "Revolting Black Athletes; and Johnson and Masucci, "No Final Victories."
81. Hartmann, "Activism, Organizing, and the Symbolic Power of Sport."
82. Ibid.
83. Leonard and King, "Revolting Black Athletes."
84. Johnson and Masucci, "No Final Victories"; DuBois, *The Souls of Black Folk*.
85. Edwards, "An End of The Golden Age."
86. Johnson and Masucci, "No Final Victories."
87. Polite and Hawkins, *Sport, Race, Activism, and Social Change*.
88. Lomax's essay ("Revisiting The Revolt of the Black Athlete") was previously published in the *Journal of Sport History* and Polite et al.'s essay ("Fostering Dr. Harry Edwards Legacy") was previously published in the *Journal for the Study of Sports and Athletes in Education*.
89. Greene, "The Impact of Dr. Harry Edwards's Work."
90. See *Journal for The Study of Sports and Athletes in Education*.

References

Baker, William J. *Jesse Owens: An American Life*. New York: Free Press, 1986.

Bass, Amy. *Not the Triumph But the Struggle: The 1968 Olympics and the Making of the Black Athlete*. Minneapolis: University of Minnesota Press, 2002.

Brooks, Dana D., and Ronald Althouse. "Revolt of the Black Athlete: From Global Arena to the College Campus." *Journal for the Study of Sports and Athletics in Education* 3 (Summer 2009): 195–214.

Carlos, John, and Dave Zirin. *The John Carlos Story: The Sports Moment That Changed the World*. Chicago, IL: Haymarket Books, 2011.

Coakley, Jay. "Sociology of Sport in the United States." *International Review for Sociology of Sport* 22 (1987): 63–77.

DuBois, W. E. B. *The Souls of Black Folk*. New York: Fawcett, 1961.

Edwards, Harry. *The Revolt of the Black Athlete*. New York: The Free Press, 1969.

Edwards, Harry. *Black Students*. New York: Free Press, 1970.

Edwards, Harry. "The Black Athletes: 20th Century Gladiators for White America." *Psychology Today* 7 (November 1973): 43–48.

Edwards, Harry. *Sociology of Sport*. Homewood, IL: The Dorsey Press, 1973.

Edwards, Harry. "Sport in America: Its Myths and Realities." PhD diss., Cornell University, 1973.

Edwards, Harry. "Change and Crisis in Modern Sport." *The Black Scholar* 8 (October–November 1976): 60 65.

Edwards, Harry. "Edwards vs The University of California." *The Black Scholar* 8 (May 1977): 32–33.

Edwards, Harry. "The Olympic Project for Human Rights: An Assessment Ten Years Later." *The Black Scholar* 10 (Mar.–Apr. 1979): 2–8.

Edwards, Harry. *The Struggle That Must Be: An Autobiography*. New York: Macmillan, 1980.

Edwards, Harry. "Educating Black Athletes." *The Atlantic Monthly*, August 1983, 31–38.

Edwards, Harry. "The Black 'Dumb Jock': An American Sports Tragedy." *The College Board Review* 131 (Spring 1984): 8–13.

Edwards, Harry. "The Collegiate Athletic Arms Race: Origins and Implications of the 'Rule 48' Controversy." *Journal of Sport and Social Issues* 8 (Winter–Spring 1984): 4–22.

Edwards, Harry. "Beyond Symptoms: Unethical Behavior in American Collegiate Sport and the Problem of the Color Line." *Journal of Sport and Social Issues* 9 (Summer/Fall 1985): 3–13.

Edwards, Harry. "The Single-Minded Pursuit of Sports Fame and Fortune is Approaching an Institutionalized Triple Tragedy in Black Society." *Ebony* 43 (Aug. 1988): 138–140.

Edwards, Harry. "An End of the Golden Age of Black Participation in Sport." *Civil Rights Journal* 3 (Fall 1998): 19–24.

Edwards, Harry. "Crisis of Black Athletes on the Eve of the 21st Century." *Society* 37 (Mar.–Apr. 2000): 9–13.

Edwards, Harry. "Transformational Developments at the Interface of Race, Sport, and the Collegiate Athletic Arms Race in the Age of Globalization." *Journal of Intercollegiate Sport* 4 (Jun. 2011): 18–31.

Gorn, Elliott J., and Michael Oriard. "Taking Sports Seriously." *Chronicle of Higher Education*, March 24, 1995, A52.

Greene, Linda. "The Impact of Dr. Harry Edwards's Work on Legal Scholarship." In *Sport, Race, Activism, and Social Change: The Impact of Dr. Harry Edwards' Scholarship and Service*, edited by Fritz G. Polite, and Billy Hawkins, 144–166. San Diego, CA: Cognella, 2012.

Hartmann, Douglas. "Activism, Organizing, and the Symbolic Power of Sport: Reassessing Harry Edwards Contributions to the 1968 Olympic Protest Movement." *Journal for the Study of Sports and Athletes in Education* 3 (Summer 2009): 181–194.

Hartmann, Douglas. *Race, Culture, and the Revolt of the Black Athlete: The 1968 Olympic Protests and Their Aftermath*. Chicago, IL: University of Chicago Press, 2003.

Hoose, Philip M. *Necessities: Racial Barriers in American Sports*. New York: Random House, 1989.

Johnson, Jay, and Matthew A. Masucci. "No Final Victories: Forty Years on the Frontlines of Race, Sport, and Culture An Interview with Scholar/Activist Dr. Harry Edwards." *Journal for the Study of Sports and Athletes in Education* 3 (Summer 2009): 233–251.

Leonard, Dave. "The Decline of the Black Athlete: An Interview with Harry Edwards." *Colorlines* 30 (Apr. 2000): 20–24.

Leonard, David J., and C. Richard King. "Revolting Black Athletes: Sport, New Racism, and the Politics of Dis/identification." *Journal for the Study of Sports and Athletes in Education* 3 (Summer 2009): 215–232.

Lomax, Michael. "Revisiting The Revolt of the Black Athlete: Harry Edwards and the Making of the New African-American Studies." *Journal of Sport History* 29 (Fall 2002): 469–479.

Loy, John. "The Emergence and Development of the Sociology of Sport as an Academic Specialty." *Research Quarterly for Exercise and Sport* 51 (1980): 91–119.

Matthews, Vincent (with Neil Amdur). *My Race Be Won*. New York: Charterhouse, 1974.

Meggyesy, Dave. *Out of Their League*. Berkeley, CA: Ramparts, 1970.

Nathan, Daniel A. "Bearing Witness to Blackball: Buck O'Neil, the Negro Leagues, and the Politics of the Past." *Journal of American Studies* 35 (2001): 453–469.

Polite, Fritz G., and Bill Hawkins, eds. *Sports, Race, Activism, and Social Change: The Impact of Dr. Harry Edwards' Scholarship and Service*. San Diego, CA: Cognella, 2012.

Polite, Fritz G., Steven N. Waller, Stephanie Hill, and Dawn Norwood. "Fostering Dr. Harry Edwards Legacy: Black Athletes Taking Responsibility in an Age of Sport Reform." *Journal for the Study of Sports and Athletes in Education* 3 (Summer 2009): 143–158.

Ruck, Rob. *Raceball: How the Major Leagues Colonized the Black and Latin Game*. Boston: Beacon Press, 2011.

Scott, Jack. *The Athletic Revolution*. New York: Free Press, 1971.

Smith, John Matthew. "'It's Not Really My Country': Lew Alcindor and the Revolt of the Black Athlete." *Journal of Sport History* 36 (Summer 2009): 223–244.

Smith, Maureen Margaret. "Frozen Fists in Speed City: The Statue as Twenty-First-Century Reparations." *Journal of Sport History* 36 (Fall 2009): 393–414.

Smith, Ronald A. *Pay for Play: A History of Big-Time College Athletic Reform.* Urbana: University of Illinois Press, 2011.

Smith, Tommie (with David Steele). *Silent Gesture: The Autobiography of Tommie Smith.* Philadelphia, PA: Temple University Press, 2007.

Wiggins, David K. "The Future of College Athletics Is At Stake: Black Athletes and Racial Turmoil on Three Predominantly White University Campuses, 1968–1972." *Journal of Sport History* 15 (Winter 1988): 304–333.

Wiggins, David K. "The Year of Awakening: Black Athletes, Racial Unrest, and the Civil Rights Movement of 1968." *The International Journal of the History of Sport* 9 (Aug. 1992): 188–208.

Wiggins, David K., and Patrick B. Miller. *The Unlevel Playing Field: A Documentary History of the African American Experience in Sport.* Urbana: University of Illinois Press, 2003.

Kwementyaye (Charles) Perkins: Indigenous Soccer Player and Australian Political Activist

Daryl Adair and Megan Stronach

University of Technology, Sydney, Australia

Aboriginal and Torres Strait Islander peoples, the two main Indigenous groups in Australia, have fought protracted battles for physical and cultural survival in the wake of European colonisation. During the 1960s, drawing upon the example of the American civil rights movement, a small but disproportionately influential number of Aboriginal activists argued for voting rights, recognition by the Federal government, and – by the 1980s – land rights for traditional custodians. During the 40-year period from 1960 to 2000, the life and times of Indigenous icon Charles Perkins provide powerful insights into the challenge of negotiating or demanding Aboriginal rights in a dominant non-Indigenous society. As this paper shows, Perkins's engagement in soccer provided a pathway for him into wider society; it allowed him opportunities to meet with non-English-speaking migrants who also felt on the margins of mainstream culture. Although a professional athlete, Perkins also developed a passion for education, and, with assistance of non-Indigenous mentors, learned how to undertake political campaigns, 'work' the media, and intimidate opponents. Whereas he began political life as a reformer, he soon became a radical. Perkins was the consummate Aboriginal activist in a period when 'blackfellas' were not expected to speak up. This paper takes a biographical approach, pinpointing key experiences and influences in Perkins' life and his journey in sport, education and politics. There is an emphasis on how sport shaped his thinking about society, and, particularly in his later years, his assertion that sport should not simply reflect the *status quo*, it should be used by those on the margins to agitate for change. Thus, Perkins was deemed especially controversial; this is because the presumed sanctity of sport and its 'separation' from political influence was cherished in twentieth-century Australian culture. Perkins was not only an activist for Aboriginal causes, he had the temerity – most notably on occasions in which the international media spotlight was on Australia – to pursue them in the context of sport.

From Alice Springs to Adelaide

The late Kwementyaye (Charles) Perkins[1] was a profoundly influential Aboriginal leader and one of the greatest Australians of the twentieth century. Born in the central Australian town of Alice Springs, Perkins spent much of his childhood away from his mother, not by choice but at the behest of state authorities.[2] The 1930s and 1940s were a period in which the policy of forced separation – known today as the Stolen Generations – was in full effect, especially in rural and remote regions where many Aboriginal families were located.[3] In his autobiography, *A Bastard Like Me*,[4] Perkins spoke powerfully against this practice and his experience of it:

> Welfare officers took the child away by force from the tribal mother and put the child in Welfare or Church homes, in dormitories and on reserves. That is where I was brought up, in a

dormitory. There was a dormitory for all the young blokes. These were the dormitories where they brought children up. This was to keep them away from the tribal people. It was cruel and unnatural.

Perkins[5] emphasised the systematic way in which Aboriginal families were forcibly broken up:

> If tribal people were living around the towns, on cattle stations or near settled places, permanently resident there, the police would just whip them off, no trouble. Children were the main victims of this division of families. The troopers would ride up and say, 'All right, get the half-caste kids!' Like rounding up the lambs from the rest of the sheep, they would separate them, put them in a truck and off they would go. These kids were brought up in institutions across the Territory. That is why a lot of us have hang-ups. How else could it be? You miss the love of a mother and all the other things that go with it, the family circle. As a young kid, four or five years old, dumped with a lot of strangers, you can be emotionally scarred for life.

At the age of 10 years, Perkins was sent from Alice Springs to Adelaide, the capital city of South Australia, a distance of some 1300 km.[6] The Anglican church wanted to provide education for a small group of Aboriginal boys in dormitories, something that was best done in a major city. Perkins became one of 23 Indigenous boys relocated to St Francis House during the 1940s, where they were inculcated with Christian teaching, the three R's of schooling and (from the perspective of the clergy) a stable and disciplined environment.[7] Herein lay a cruel paradox: Aboriginal people were required to 'assimilate' into wider society, but they were expected to do so while being deemed unequal. Consistent with the punitive objectives underlying the Stolen Generations, this represented an effort by policy-makers, whether in governments, churches or state institutions, to expunge Indigenous culture and erode Aboriginal society, and by this process assert the presumed 'right' to dominance of European Australians.[8]

Perkins' years at school in Adelaide were, as he recalls, disastrous. Charlie, as he was commonly known, was expected to be enthusiastic about the 'opportunity' given to him by education, but there was a lack of understanding about his needs as a new student and indeed a paucity of support. Perkins[9] later wrote:

> There was no person to sit down with us and say, 'Now listen, this is how you do this,' or 'Why don't you try this?' I failed so miserably that they said I had no future. I never had a real friend at school amongst the white children or teachers. Within myself I felt an outcast. I was a kind of loner. My only friends were fellow Aborigines. What united us as well was the common struggle to exist and find some happiness. The only happiness I found came through sports. This was generally the case with all of us [Aboriginal boys].

Like so many young boys of colour on the margins of a white-dominated society, whether in Australia,[10] New Zealand[11] or the USA,[12] sport provided something of a refuge from many of the struggles they were facing at school or in the wider community. Sport was hardly a safe house, for it was also a site of discrimination and marginalisation.[13] But at least here Aboriginal boys, much like Māori and African-American youth abroad, had an opportunity to showcase their sense of physical capital in an environment where the 'rules of the game'[14] were more familiar to them than the seemingly cryptic European obsessions with writing cursive and figuring out long division. Although there are risks in overstating physical acumen among Aboriginal youth – in the sense of it being something they 'possess' rather than develop[15] – Perkins[16] described with joy the confidence he exuded when taking to the playing field:

> Sport was natural to us. It was a means of self-expression and satisfaction. At school we played Aussie Rules, Rugby Union and Rugby League football – the lot. Aboriginals are good at sport, every sport. The boys' home supplied all the best sportsmen in the district, at the Le

Fevre Boys' Technical School we used to win everything: races, the high-jump, the hop-step, anything. We bowled faster, hit harder than anybody. We were the best fighters, so nobody ever fought with us too often because they knew they would be beaten up. The only difficulties we had were academic, and there, nobody seemed willing to help us.[17]

The Importance of Soccer

While a student in Adelaide, Perkins first saw the game of soccer but had no idea about it – presuming that someone was kicking a basketball. He recalls that at the age of 14 some lads from what he described as the under 18 State Intermediate Team invited Perkins and a few of his Aboriginal mates to an impromptu game. Despite never having played soccer, needing to have the rules explained to the them, and running around in bare feet rather than in boots, Perkins recounts that 'They [the opposition] never got a kick … We beat them ten goals to nil!'.[18] Whether one takes this story literally or believes that Perkins wove the tale with a twinkle in his eye, the game of soccer was now firmly on this young man's radar. Later in that year (1950), at age 14, Perkins connected with a local soccer club, Port Thistle, which was near where he resided in Semaphore, a beachside suburb in working-class Port Adelaide. He recalls: 'I could play soccer better than most people and was improving all the time. I played one year junior, then senior at fifteen, and after that I played first division'.[19] Just as important, though, was his sense of connection with the Port Thistle club and its supporters, who were a combination of Scottish migrants and docks labourers.

> I got on well with the club crowd. They treated me like a human being. That was where I first felt free, when I began to play soccer. The team would talk roughly to me and I would know where I stood … The Soccer Club became my home and I found a new security in my ability to play well. I found some friends in soccer. Most of all, I found a place where I could be somebody.

In choosing soccer, rather than the dominant local brand of football, Australian Rules, Perkins identified with the struggles of ethnic groups to establish a migrant culture and indeed a place in a new society; Adelaide was new to Perkins too. He met his first girlfriend at Port Thistle; no surprise she was a Scottish-born lass. As the relationship blossomed, Perkins' beau introduced him to people in soccer from other clubs, and so he began to understand migrant stories from various parts of Europe. He recalls:

> I learnt to relax as a part of this 'international set', proud that I was the only Australian [locally born] in it. They accepted me for what I was and were never paternalistic or embarrassed by my presence. I felt free amongst these various national groups.[20]

Perkins could also straddle cultures: notwithstanding his love for soccer and affinity with working-class migrants, he was also fond of the wider Port Adelaide community:

> Once you're in the Port you grow up in the Port, you stay with the Port, you know, the Port area, and Port Adelaide. It's a tough area, very tough, you know, but we sort of made a lot of good friends there, you know, in amongst the white people and all the people we went to school with.[21]

He also understood the passion for Australian Rules football in Port Adelaide, and, by choosing soccer, that he stood out from others: 'I was good at Aussie Rules. I could have played for Port Adelaide [Magpies]. I could have been a good Aussie Rules player. My nephews and my cousins … played for the top teams'.[22] Perkins explained why he identified with two football codes: 'I grew up in the Port you see, in that sense, and that's why I'm a Port Adelaide Aussie Rules supporter, and I still am today, after all these years'.[23] But it was soccer Perkins played and where his sporting, cultural and social future lay.

As will become apparent from this article, Perkins not only evolved into a very capable soccer player, but also became a renowned advocate of Aboriginal needs and concerns in

Australian society. The skills needed to achieve the latter did not seem obvious at first, either to Perkins' teachers or himself. He received the following advice from one of his school teachers: "'Look, you're pretty dumb" ... "You're not very good at school. You're [sic] marks are very poor because you haven't got much brains". "You ... ought to do some trade"'.[24] Perkins accepted that this sort of advice was meted out to many of his classmates, whatever their background, and that he was in no position to argue given his grades: 'I thought well he must know, he's a teacher, I'm not'.[25] Between the teacher and a priest at St Francis, Perkins then left school and was presented with a job prospect as an apprentice fitter and turner with British Tube Mills between 1952 and 1957 (the year in which he became fully qualified). But he had no interest in this line of work and, in his words, 'hated every minute of that trade'.[26] For Perkins, playing soccer gave him purpose and joy away from an occupation he detested. In 1957, he was 21 years old and had emerged as a star on the football pitch:

> By then I was one of the highest-paid soccer players in South Australia. I was playing in the best team in the State, Budapest. We won all the awards. One year I won the award for the best and fairest soccer player in the State. I was in the best team and I was one of the best players. I felt really good. Soccer was the only thing going for me that really mattered. My work did not matter at all. It was an inconvenience to my soccer career. The worst days of the week were the days I had to go to work. It was like a horrible nightmare.[27]

Perkins was, like all types of 'professional' footballers of his era in Australia, a part-time player. Budapest FC paid him eight pounds per week, which certainly bolstered his overall income, and for the first time in Perkins' life he had discretionary money – as well as abundant food on the table.[28] Of course, the big money in soccer was not in Australia, but in Europe. Out of the blue, Perkins received an invitation to trial with the prominent English team, Everton FC, complete with passage by boat to Britain. However, after an acrimonious on-field experience at training, and despite being offered a part-time position at Everton, Perkins left the club telling them in no uncertain terms, 'I don't like your attitude'.[29] Where he was going was very unclear. This land was more foreign to Perkins than going to Adelaide from Alice Springs as a boy. After a stint working in North England coal mines and playing soccer locally for Wigan FC, Perkins was given an offer to try out with Bishop Auckland FC, near Newcastle, a leading amateur team that, despite its status, was paying its players. Perkins joined their clandestine payroll. He had a strong season, earning the interest of talent scouts from some of the better known professional clubs.[30]

However, Perkins also had an offer to captain and coach the Adelaide Croatia Soccer Club. Ultimately, despite the fact that he was happy in England and had grown very fond of its people, he felt that this was the right opportunity to return to Australia.[31] Back in Adelaide, Perkins excelled in his new soccer roles, leading the Adelaide Croatia Soccer team in 1958–1959, and helping them to claim the regional Ampol Cup in 1961. Perkins also had representative honours, playing numerous times for South Australia. Two other Aboriginal soccer stars played alongside him for the state: Gordon Briscoe (his cousin) and John Moriarty, with whom he had lived at St Francis. Perkins' future in football now seemed assured: he had trusted people around him and a wealth of experience from living abroad.[32] No one could have predicted that Perkins was about to take a very different life path, one that gradually took him away from his 'comfort zone' in soccer and towards three great unknowns – politics, education and marriage.

Life-Changing Decisions

Perkins was on the cusp of some life-changing decisions. Since returning from Britain he had developed a concerted interest in the politics and policy issues affecting Aboriginal people. With growing self-confidence as a result of his stature as a sporting figure, Perkins was now increasingly prepared to speak out.[33] The institutionalised racism that he and other Aboriginal people confronted was also faced, in various ways, by black and coloured people in apartheid South Africa and in the deep south of the USA. Read[34] provides a deft summary of the Australian experience in the 1960s:

> Aborigines ... could be kept forcibly on any [outback] reserve, which could be created, altered or abolished without warning. They could be removed from any town or fringe-camp, or anywhere else the chief protector declared prohibited. Drinking, gambling and disobeying a manager's instructions were prohibited. All Aboriginal children under [the age of] 16 were declared to be in the [parliamentary] minister's care and liable to be institutionalised. It was an offence for Aborigines to 'consort with' or have sexual relations with non-Aborigines.

For Perkins, the worlds of sport and politics occasionally coincided. Notably, his great friend John Moriarty found out that when the South Australian soccer team travelled interstate 'the soccer authorities had to gain permission from the Protector of Aborigines'[35] for Indigenous players to travel. He and Perkins were hardly unfamiliar with the aforementioned exemption passes: as kids they frequently told police that they had left them at St Francis House. And when Perkins worked as a fitter and turner, 'he was not allowed [being non-exempted] to join the Australian Workers' Union'.[36] But for Moriarty, Perkins and Briscoe, the honour of representing their state at soccer was sullied by the fact that their participation was subject to assent from the Protector of Aborigines. It was a racially charged kick in the guts for sportsmen who, by and large, had not suffered the same degree of discrimination or economic disadvantage as 'ordinary' Aboriginal people.

Around the same time, the South Australian branches of the Federal Council for the Advancement of Aborigines (FCAA) and the Aborigines Advancement League (AAL) were lobbying public opinion to alter the South Australian Aborigines Act. Perkins, Moriarty and Briscoe took an active role by distributing a petition to the migrant communities they were familiar with through their role in soccer.[37] Perkins was soon elected vice-president of FCAA, working alongside a progressively minded white politician, Don Dunstan. Both men spoke at public meetings and rallies, but Perkins – as an Aboriginal activist – was more of a novelty, and to the media a very captivating personality. He was interviewed on the Adelaide television programme 'Meet the Press', and was forthright in his argument that 'assimilation could never be achieved until Aborigines were equal under the law'. What was more, he insisted, education 'with a purpose' was needed to allow 'natives' to be properly equipped to be part of the white world.[38]

Kerrin[39] has argued that the goals of white leaders of the FCAA and AAL were reform of existing legislation, which therefore overlooked commitment to self-determination for Aboriginal people. Perkins, at least in this early phase of his political life, had what might be described as a pragmatic view of Indigenous progress. Like his Aboriginal colleagues Moriarty and Briscoe, Perkins imagined a society wherein Aboriginal people were given the opportunity to acquire skills, achieve respected status and integrate successfully into mainstream society.[40] Given what we know about Perkins' experiences of white education and his disdain for a vocation in a factory setting, his harping about Aboriginal 'opportunity' seems to be a remarkable departure from a few years back. On the other hand, as Read has averred, Perkins most likely advocated assimilation because, in 1961, he 'was scarcely aware of the meaning of the word ... and knew no other policy'.[41] Perkins' focus was on ending discrimination against Aboriginal people; self-determination had yet to enter his consciousness.

In September 1961, in Malvern Lutheran Church, Perkins married Eileen Munchenberg. Notwithstanding her German ancestry, she was described by Perkins as a white 'Australian' girl who had grown up in Adelaide. The latter distinction was important, because up until that time Perkins had a poor opinion of local white girls – other than those whom he considered to be of migrant background. Perkins was well accepted by Munchenberg's family, something he found difficult to accept at first given that, for most of his life, he had felt (or been made feel) inferior in a white-dominated society. Ironically, it was Perkins' own family that found the matrimony disagreeable, in that they were upset that he had married outside of the Aboriginal community.[42] This was an intriguing position given that Perkins' mother and father each had an Aboriginal and a non-Aboriginal parent.[43] Munchenberg, like so many other women of her time, would fulfil the role of dutiful wife, supporting her husband in his endeavours.[44] At that time, Perkins' focus was soccer, which provided financial support for him and his wife:

'Croatia was paying me very good money. All the money I wanted I could get. I would eat at their restaurants for free as well. Every time I scored a goal I would get ten pounds for myself. Every time we won a match I would get another bonus'.[45]

However, a twist of fate was imminent: 'It was during this time I became conscious of the fact that I was physically ill. I did not know this illness was to have a major bearing on my life'.[46] Perkins had contracted nephritis, a problem with his kidneys, and required hospitalisation. He recovered, but remained predisposed to that condition. He did his best to ignore it. So by the early 1960s Perkins was a renowned soccer player, an emerging figure in Aboriginal politics, had an awareness that he was prone to kidney trouble and had married.

As mentioned previously, Perkins had a poor scholastic experience at school and, for the most part, seemed to accept his teachers' view that he had little aptitude for academics. However, there must have been a kernel of doubt in his mind about their prognosis because, while in England, Perkins had what might be described as an epiphany. When Bishop Auckland played a match against Oxford University, he found the academic environment alluring. Perkins later recalled:

That day it started going through my mind that I would like to go to university one day. There on that Oxford soccer field I began to think, 'Geez, it's lovely around here. These blokes here are going to university. I wonder if I could go to university?' I had thought about it before but on that particular day it came home to me with force because of these surroundings, the atmosphere and the people I met there. One's life turns about unexpected events. At that stage it was the quality of life at university that appealed to me rather than any educational motivation.[47]

After marrying Munchenberg, Perkins flirted with the idea of going to school to study for matriculation, the entry standard to be eligible for university. He had heard that Sydney University was the best place to earn a degree,[48] so it was in Sydney he proposed to complete secondary school. It was, as he recalled, 'a leap in the dark'.[49] He did not know anyone in Sydney, and would need to work, as would Munchenberg, to put a roof over their heads.[50] The plan was for Perkins to secure a position playing professional soccer with one of the Sydney clubs. He eventually found his place with the Pan Hellenic team. Perkins later recalled:

There were some very good players in the team. I was the only Australian and I was captain. Everybody else spoke Greek or Yugoslav or Hebrew, or something else. I was the one they all used to turn to, often because I was the one who could speak English the best, especially to the referee.[51]

Although Perkins loved soccer, there was now a vision for what might come after his playing days:

Football served a three-fold purpose. The first was to provide me with finance for my study. Second, it enabled me to keep fit because I needed to study for such long hours. Third, it was a means whereby I could mix socially and enjoy myself comfortably. However, the end objective of it all was the university degree. That was my main reason for playing soccer at a high level consistently and being so determined to do it, so I could get my degree and speak and work on Aboriginal affairs. Those four years in Sydney were devoted to educating myself to operate in Aboriginal affairs effectively. There was no other reason for this.[52]

University and Radical Politics

In order to qualify for university, Perkins attended Metropolitan Business College in Sydney. He defied the predictions of his teachers in Adelaide; he was off to university. Like many mature-aged students, Perkins was highly motivated and keen to succeed. He later recalled:

> Everything I did in the university course was just like pouring water on to a dry sponge, as far as learning was concerned. The more I learnt, the more my interest developed, and everything I learnt I sort of hung on the Aboriginal peg. I would think to myself: 'I have to learn this because that will be necessary in Aboriginal affairs. I have to do sociology to give me a broad outlook, and psychology, and political science in case I get involved in government and so on'.[53]

While Perkins' studies at university were critical, so too was his education from another source. He was persuaded, reluctantly, to meet with the Reverend Ted Noffs, a Methodist preacher at Wayside Chapel in Sydney. Perkins was not too thrilled about linking up with a white clergyman, for the 'church really exploited Aboriginal people and ... and dispossessed us'.[54] However, with Noffs, he later recalled, 'I just found a man who set me alight'.[55] Perkins looked up to Noffs as a mentor, the latter encouraging Perkins to speak up and speak out on issues of social justice for Aboriginal people. Receiving two types of education, Perkins' mind was percolating with ideas and causes – all of which revolved around the condition of Indigenous Australians. Over time, Perkins' belief that assimilation would provide the same opportunities for Aboriginal and non-Aboriginal people was supplanted with a more radical notion: that Indigenous Australians needed to be politically assertive in order to realise what was entitled to them – full civil rights.[56]

Perkins was one of the very few Aboriginal students at University of Sydney, but by 1965 he was one of its best known. There is not space here to do justice to his various endeavours and achievements, which are covered in depth by other sources.[57] But his political initiatives were characterised by radicalism, courage, candour, imagination and ingenuity. Perkins was elected President of the lobby group, Student Action for Aborigines (SAFA), which had been formed at the University of Sydney in 1964. Most famously, this group – which comprised white- and black-skinned activists – planned a 'freedom ride' into rural New South Wales, inspired by the tactics of the Civil Rights Movement in the American south.[58] The objective was to undertake 'a fact-finding trip to remote western New South Wales towns so students could see for themselves the conditions of life for Aboriginal people'.[59]

What they discovered was no secret to locals: Aboriginal people were widely deprived of the same liberties as whites, and they faced systematic discrimination in many walks of life. A segregationist culture either excluded or marginalised Aboriginal people in country towns, a fact that Perkins and his colleagues sought to expose. The very fact that they travelled in a bus with a large sign on the side – SAFA – created attention as they arrived in country towns. But more than that, the 'temerity' of the students to question the racially divisive *status quo* in such places was an affront to many whites. In Walgett, SAFA protested against the fact that Aboriginal ex-servicemen were not welcome on the premises of a local Returned and Services League. Perkins was shown the door under a threat of police intervention, which he welcomed for personal safety. SAFA subsequently set up a peaceful protest outside the club, which attracted not only hostility from many locals but also plenty of media attention in the town and back in Sydney.[60] Perkins and his fellow students also caused a stir at Moree by campaigning against a Council edict, instituted in 1955, that 'No person, being a full-blooded or half-caste aboriginal native of Australia, or being a person apparently having an admixture of aboriginal blood'[61] was allowed to use the local swimming baths. According to proponents of the Council resolution, white tourists were more likely to come to Moree and use the baths if they were restricted to people of their 'own kind'. There were also alarmist suggestions that whites were at risk of disease – particularly sexually transmitted infection – by sharing the same water as Aboriginal people. A SAFA-organised protest again made the papers in Sydney, and so the activists were not going to be dismissed easily, notwithstanding heated opposition by threatened locals. The stand-off was not in vain: the Mayor of Moree and leading aldermen approached SAFA and promised them that the racially biased 1955 statute would be withdrawn.[62] The Freedom Riders had a win; Moree's Indigenous community was now able to swim and play in the local baths. It was a small but welcome gain in a period when Aboriginal people were slowly gaining rights that non-Aboriginal people had already assumed, such as being granted the right to vote from 1962.

Profile and Influence

In Adelaide, Perkins' performances in soccer gave him public profile when voicing an opinion; he was not easily ignored. Concurrently, his time with Don Dunstan and FCAA had provided Perkins with the confidence to address a white audience. Now, after further education from Noffs and the experience of being both a student and an activist, Perkins had become a well-known public figure. His priorities had thus changed: 'When I came to Sydney my deep interest in sport was transferred more to Aboriginal affairs. I realized that Sydney was the centre of the mass media and this was where I could get an opinion across to people in Australia'.[63] Perkins was not only a political activist, he was also interested in practical solutions for Indigenous people. In 1964, for example, Perkins, Noffs and two colleagues formed the Foundation for Aboriginal Affairs; its goal was 'to assist Aboriginal people migrating to Sydney to find jobs and housing'.[64] The Foundation tried to empower Indigenous patrons; this was critical at a time when assimilation was central to Australian public policy. However, although Perkins believed in media activism and local engagement, he also understood that the federal government wielded political power over the whole country. He wanted to influence public discourse around policies affecting Aboriginal people, and so Canberra – the national capital – was the best place to do that.[65] In 1969, Perkins secured a position as a Research Officer in the newly formed Office of Aboriginal Affairs, Department of Prime Minister and Cabinet, which was set up in 1967 in the wake of a successful referendum that empowered the Commonwealth (rather than the states and territories) to assume responsibility for Aboriginal welfare. This new role was just the start of what became for Perkins a three decades career as a bureaucrat in Aboriginal Affairs and a political lobbyist on Indigenous issues to governments. He was also a key member of numerous Aboriginal organisations, in areas such as housing, the arts and sport.[66]

In the early 1970s, soon after Perkins assumed his role with Aboriginal Affairs, his health deteriorated rapidly. His already weak kidneys were malfunctioning and he relied inordinately on machines to detoxify his blood. It was extremely debilitating and very depressing for him. Perkins was convinced that he would die, so set about returning to his birthplace, Alice Springs, in order to pass on. He paused in Adelaide for treatment at the

Queen Elizabeth (public) Hospital and stayed nearby to recuperate before moving to Alice. Good fortune was with him: the death of a local woman, who donated her organs, gave Perkins the opportunity for a state-funded operation. He could not believe his luck and, during a recovery phase, felt a surge of energy to make the most of the rest of his life.[67] There is not scope in this brief paper to do justice to Perkins' subsequent accomplishments and disappointments in Aboriginal affairs, but his politically active roles during two international sport events provide fascinating snippets into both his radicalism and pragmatism.

Brisbane Commonwealth Games, 1982

The 1982 Games were staged one year after South Africa's Springbok rugby team toured New Zealand, playing against the All Blacks. This was in violation of the 1977 Gleneagles Agreement, in which Commonwealth nations agreed to discourage sporting contacts with South Africa as a protest against apartheid in society and sport.[68] Historians have recently been given access (under the 30-year rule) to Australian Government Cabinet Papers on this issue. Messenger[69] reports that

'Barring New Zealand from taking part in the 1982 Brisbane Commonwealth Games was one of the options considered by the Australian government'. This related, in large part to fear of 'an African boycott ... which might additionally highlight Australian [and particularly Queensland] government policies toward Aborigines'.

In Australia, various Aboriginal organisations approached African Commonwealth nations, urging them not to send teams to Australia. While these Indigenous activists had sympathy for the anti-apartheid cause, their principal concern was the poverty and destitution of their own people. They asked the African teams to boycott the Games as a protest against the maltreatment of Australia's Indigenous people. This had no impact. Instead, the African consensus was that Australia had done much to counter apartheid and so should be rewarded by the presence of teams from the African continent – expect, of course, South Africa.[70]

With an absence of support from abroad, Aboriginal activists rallied around a key issue in 1980s Queensland – the state government's efforts to block the purchase of land by Commonwealth agencies, which was to be handed over to Indigenous people. The conservative state premier, Joh Bjelke-Petersen, complained that this would give special privileges to blacks, who should 'live exactly as we do'.[71] He neglected to mention that a mere 3% of Aboriginal housing was anything like the standard of accommodation that white Australians were accustomed to, and the fact that although Indigenous Australians constituted less than 2.5% of the national population, they comprised 35% of those in prisons.[72] Black and white were worlds apart in Queensland. And Brisbane was about to showcase itself to the world via the Commonwealth Games. For Aboriginal activists, this presented an opportunity to voice their grievances to national and global audiences.

The Bjelke-Petersen government, sensing reputational risk to Queensland from Indigenous protestors and their supporters, 'rushed through a bill giving police the right to search and detain any person suspected of intending to disrupt the Games'.[73] Among the new powers, police were able to 'refuse access to the Games area, and search any place on a major route' to the event.[74] Although 'marches and demonstrations without a permit were already banned under existing legislation', Aboriginal activists were not intimidated by these rules, old or new. In January 1982, a Black Protest Committee was formed. Perkins, one its key spokespersons, told the press that 'the Commonwealth Games would not take place unless genuine land rights were granted'.[75] His position was not unexpected: in late 1981, he had sensationally told *The Bulletin*, a widely read national magazine, that 'The Brisbane Games will be Australia's Battle of Wounded Knee'.[76]

Although a radical, Perkins was also a pragmatist. He wanted to see blacks and whites live together in harmony, and was inspired by the peaceful activism of Martin Luther King. His fiery rhetoric was intended to capture attention, but he then sought to manage protest so that it did not alienate Aborigines from their non-Aboriginal supporters. He was walking a tightrope. On September 25, just a few days before the Games, Perkins called on Indigenous people 'to march with or without a permit' through the streets of Brisbane.[77] However, the Black Protest Committee broadcast its own rules. In Perkins' own words:

> no drunk Blacks marching and no armed Blacks marching. No knuckle-dusters, no knives … Anyone who brings a gun … is going to be ordered out of the march … You don't have to resort to shooting in a democracy … demonstrations, sit-ins, marches, all good stuff … so long as nobody gets hurt in the process.[78]

Some 2000–3000 people marched along an unapproved route, yet obeyed the law in terms of keeping the peace. The police sensibly kept their distance, and the event concluded with leading Aboriginal spokespersons outlining their grievances. Perkins focused on the failure of land rights for Indigenous Queenslanders and the meekness of the media in not supporting protests to improve the conditions of Aboriginal Australians.[79]

Although dissent during the Commonwealth Games did not bring about immediate reforms, it certainly provided Aboriginal activists with a platform in which to air their concerns to an international audience. Perkins, as ingenious as ever, conspired to present the Australian Head of State, Queen Elizabeth II, with a wide-ranging petition (focusing on land rights, legal reforms, etc.) during her visit to Brisbane to open the Games. Perkins, by virtue of his leadership role in the Federal Government's Aboriginal Development Commission, was an invited guest at a Parliament House reception in Canberra for Her Majesty. To avoid controversy, he cleverly arranged for the queen to receive the petition before the event.[80] Perkins later recalled:

> The queen came along, we shook hands. I never bow to my head to any queen or monarch. 'How are you going your Excellency? Welcome to my country. On behalf of the Aboriginal people I'd like to welcome you here'. We started to talk – 'I'm glad you got our petition. I didn't want to embarrass you, I just wanted to make sure you got it. Have your read it?'. 'Yes I have'. 'Well it's all in there about Aboriginal affairs in this country. Things are not very good, and we were just hoping that you would take more interest in it'.[81]

Perkins, by sending the petition and engaging with the queen in this way, risked the wrath of the Federal Government. However, astute as always, Perkins deflected calls for him to resign, pointing out that 'his appointment was legally protected by the Governor-General', who was the queen's representative in Australia, and that his counsel 'had been entirely appropriate'.[82]

Sydney Olympic Games, 2000

The Olympic Games provided another opportunity for Perkins to use a global sport event to lobby for the Aboriginal cause. His involvement began much earlier than the event itself. Perkins was appointed to the Sydney Olympic Bid Committee (SOBC) in 1991. This stemmed from his high-profile and sporting connections, but most of all his capacity to add 'Aboriginality' to the bid.[83] After all, the Olympic Games were expected to coincide with a 10-year reconciliation process that was due to 'end' in December 2000. However, according to Indigenous academic Langton,[84] Perkins' recruitment was tokenistic in the sense that he was expected to be complicit rather than outspoken about Indigenous issues. However, it was not long before Perkins declined to 'toe the Committee line'. Meeting with IOC Committee members in Lausanne in 1993, Perkins broke ranks by publicly criticising China's human rights record; this was in direct breach of the bid process and without the authority of SOBC. However, Perkins had a wider agenda; he was not simply spin doctoring in favour of Sydney by criticising Beijing. Instead, Perkins' comments were much more strategic in the sense that he coupled this condemnation of China by also emphasising human rights abuses against Indigenous Australians. This was a radical departure from what SOBC had expected of Perkins; it had misunderstood his prime commitment – the condition of Aboriginal peoples in Australia. The Olympic bid was thus cleverly used by Perkins as a way of leveraging political capital for the Indigenous cause back home.

The NSW Minister for Transport, and Chairman of the Sydney Bid Committee, Bruce Baird, initially claimed that any talk of a split between the Committee and Perkins as a result of his remarks was 'mischievous'. Later, he conceded that Perkins' comments had not been 'helpful' to the Olympic Games' bid. Soon after, Baird was shown on television carrying Perkins' bags out of the team's hotel in Lausanne at which point he hurriedly left for the airport to catch a plane back to Australia. Perkins' actions were said to have 'snubbed' the Bid Committee — his response was that the Committee had 'snubbed' him.[85] Perkins denied he had been reprimanded for his comments and said he was returning home to take up a position as Chief Executive of the Aboriginal and Islander Legal Service. Nevertheless, he made no more contributions to the Olympic bid. While that incident may have been the end of Perkins' connections to the Sydney Olympics, the political situation in Australia during the lead-up to the Games was such that Perkins simply could not remain gagged and languishing on the sidelines.[86]

A formal process of reconciliation began in Australia in 1991 when the *Council for Aboriginal Reconciliation Act 1991* (Cth) was passed unanimously by the Federal Government. It was considered 'desirable'[87] that reconciliation between Indigenous and non-Indigenous Australian be achieved by January 1, 2001, the centenary of Australian Federation. The Sydney Olympic Games would thus be staged as reconciliation was realised.[88] However, Indigenous groups indicated that talk of reconciliation was tokenistic without genuine changes to the condition of Aboriginal people; as such several of them indicated that they would use the exposure afforded by the Games to focus world attention on human rights abuses and racism against Indigenous Australians. At the time, Bruce Baird warned, 'anyone who threatens Sydney's Olympic bid had better watch out'.[89] Early talk of lobbying for the disqualification of Sydney's bid and then of boycotting the Games was abandoned by mid-1999 as Indigenous groups began planning a highly visible campaign of 'shaming' governments through public protests and extensive media activity.[90] However, they stressed that any protest would be peaceful. Adding fuel to the simmering discontent was Prime Minister John Howard's refusal to apologise on behalf of the nation for the stolen generations and their legacy.[91] Perkins joined in the debate saying that 'if such protests gave Australia a negative image it served the country right'.[92]

In the late 1990s, a number of legislative provisions dealing with public order and the Olympics had been passed, with police gaining far-reaching powers, including the power to remove people causing 'inconvenience' or 'affront' from public spaces at Olympic Park and the Sydney Harbor foreshore. The *Olympic Arrangements Act 2000 No 1* (NSW) was proposed in April 2000.[93] This Act would extend regulatory powers throughout the CBD and many other key places in Sydney.[94] In the same week, the Federal Minister for Aboriginal Affairs, John Herron, made his infamous denial that there was never a generation of stolen Aboriginal children, claiming that the removal of only 10% of Aboriginal children from their families did not amount to a 'stolen generation'.[95]

Bitter feelings erupted and in an interview with BBC radio (and a potential audience of 200 million listeners around the world), Perkins used rhetorical tactics similar to that of 1982, warning that 'Anything can happen', and that the Sydney Olympics would erupt in 'burning cars, burning buildings'. He claimed that the row over the stolen children definition 'would force direct conflict between white and black Australians'.[96]

> Perkins: We didn't want to complicate the Games. We wanted the Games to go on. All the Aboriginal people, we said let's have peaceful protests here and there. Now it's turned very nasty, ugly. It is going to be violent, and we're telling all the British people: 'Please don't come over. If you want to see burning cars and burning buildings, then come over. Enjoy yourself. But if you want to come to the Games, come to the Games and go straight home again. BBC reporter: This is strong language, Mr. Perkins – burning cars, burning buildings. Perkins: Yes. What else can we do, brother? Two hundred years the white people have taken everything from us, and we stood up to it and we said: 'Right, do things peacefully, according to the law of the land, everything in a proper manner, administration and all the rest of it.' What has that got us? Nowhere![97]

Perkins was ridiculed as a threat to Australian national pride at a critical moment in its history; there were even calls for him to be arrested.[98] Criticism like this never bothered Perkins. Although the Sydney Olympics did not feature significant public protests by Aboriginal groups, their message was made evident in the opening ceremony, where prominent Australian rock artists performed while wearing T-shirts with the word 'sorry' emblazoned at the front. There was also an importance place for an Aboriginal icon at the Games: world champion 400-m runner, Cathy Freeman, was given the honour of lighting the Olympic flame, and, in one of the most emotional moments in Australian sport history went on to win a gold medal. Unlike at Brisbane in 1982, the Sydney Games had afforded Aboriginal people respect in the opening and closing ceremonies, while several Indigenous athletes represented both Australia and their own people with distinction. Prime Minister John Howard still refused to apologise for the Stolen Generations, but in the wake of the Games his defiance seemed out of step with an increasing number of Australians.[99]

On October 18, 2000, less than three weeks after the Sydney Olympic Games, Perkins died of kidney failure, The New South Wales Government acknowledged his passing, with Deputy Premier and Minister for Aboriginal Affairs Dr Andrew Refshauge moving a Motion of Condolence. In an Obituary speech, Parliamentary Secretary Colin Markham commented on Perkins' actions prior to the Games:

> I know that Charlie was outspoken, and that in some quarters people believed he was outrageous, but Charlie spoke from his heart; Charlie spoke about what he believed in; he spoke for Aboriginal people in this country and for people with a real moral conscience. I can assure honourable members that his passing will leave a great void in the social conscience of white Australia. Some people have referred to the comment 'Burn, baby, burn' that Charlie Perkins made prior to the Olympic Games. But that was Charlie. He grabbed the attention of the media. If he had said anything else, the media probably would not have bothered writing anything about him. He grabbed the attention of the media because that is what Charlie was like.

> I recall that on the morning after he made that comment I received a phone call from a media outlet in Wollongong, asking me if I thought that what he had said was outrageous. I said, 'No, I do not think what he said was outrageous. If Charlie had said anything different to that I would have been utterly surprised. Charlie said that to grab your attention. You have phoned me to find out what is going on. If he had said anything else he probably would not have got a run'. Charlie brought the attention of the international media to the fact that there was a real issue in Australia so far as Indigenous Australians were concerned. He intended to highlight that right up to and during the Olympic Games. His ill health and subsequent demise prevented him from doing so. I do not believe that Charlie would have wanted anything to happen, but that is what he said and that is how he grabbed the attention of the media.[100]

The Motion was passed unanimously, with Honourable Members and officers of the House standing in their places to show their respect. Perkins was afforded the honour of a state funeral.

Since his passing, the Charles Perkins name has adorned numerous roads, buildings and educational centres. Among them, ironically enough, is the Charles Perkins Centre for Aboriginal Studies at Lefevre High School in Adelaide,[101] a place where his teachers had concluded he was intellectually weak. The most recent, and arguably most impressive accolade to Perkins is the University of Sydney's $220m medical research facility, named the Charles Perkins Centre, which is committed to preventing a range of debilitating non-communicable diseases, such as diabetes and coronary disease. These are significant problems in Australian society but are particular risk factors within Aboriginal communities. Perkins, the beneficiary of medical help to prolong his life by 28 years, would surely approve.

Conclusion

Perkins is now widely revered as an iconic Aboriginal and great Australian. It took him great courage to achieve this status. He was radical by way of oratory but his revolutionary vision was never one of separatism; blacks and whites needed to learn to live together. Perkins' violent talk was never matched by violent actions, which he discouraged. His proficiency at sport provided pathways into wider society that very few Aboriginal people experienced. But he never rested on his laurels; when sport was no longer an option, then education and its skill sets took centre stage. It was through this combination of physical and intellectual capital that Perkins was eventually able to contribute to public life. As he once recalled: 'Aboriginal Affairs and soccer have been my passions and where I could work out my problems through both of those two things … Soccer was where I got my satisfaction, my fulfilment'.[102] To Perkins, sport offered the prospect of being treated as an equal, though given the reality of racism at the time, he endured on-field taunts and heckling from crowds about his Aboriginality. In multiethnic soccer, though, this was rarer than in many other sports.

As this chapter has shown, Perkins was never sentimental about drawing a line between sport and political activism. He sensed that sport, as one of Australia's 'sacred cows', was an environment within which political causes could attract plenty of interest – even if most reactions were negative. According to Pilger, Perkins regarded the Sydney Olympics as a lost opportunity for the Aboriginal cause: 'I spoke to him in hospital the day after the Sydney Olympics ended, and he was cursing, typically, the muting of a 'shaming campaign' in which he had hoped to participate'.[103] He was undoubtedly right: 13 years after the Games little has changed in terms of the condition of Aboriginal people in Australia.

Notes

1. The convention within Aboriginal Australia is not to use the first name of a deceased Indigenous person wherever possible. There are profound complexities associated with this;

as non-Indigenous authors, we have sought to respect the deceased by acknowledging at the outset the substitute name ascribed to Perkins upon his death – Kwementyaye.

2. Perkins did not meet his father until the age of 33 years. His mother, Hetti Perkins, was the daughter of Harry Perkins, a white man from Broken Hill, and Nellie Errerreke, an Aboriginal woman from the Arrernte people of Central Australia. Hetti identified as an Eastern Arrernte Aboriginal woman. She had a total of 11 children from two relationships, the second of which produced Charles and Ernest. Their father was Martin Connelly, whose mother was a Kalkadoon Aboriginal and father Irish (Read, *Charles Perkins: A Biography*, 149; Read, "Perkins, Hetty (1895–1979)"; and The University of Sydney in Collaboration with the Koori Centre, "Dr Charles Perkins AO Program").

3. Read, "The Stolen Generations."

4. Perkins, *A Bastard Like Me*, 14.

5. Ibid., 14–15.

6. Perkins was accompanied to Adelaide by his brother Ernest. However, Perkins' autobiography *A Bastard Like Me* (1975) mentions Ernest only once – in a photograph on page 34. It is an intriguing omission. Peter Read wrote later that Charlie and 'kid-brother' Ernie had not bonded closely: 'The institutionalised life of St Francis House had not allowed true brotherly feelings to develop' (Read, *Charles Perkins: A Biography*, 198). Not an altogether adequate explanation.

7. Perkins, *A Bastard Like Me*; Read, *Charles Perkins: A Biography*.

8. Rowley, *The Destruction of Aboriginal Society*.

9. Perkins, *A Bastard Like Me*, 30.

10. Tatz, "Aborigines, Sport and Suicide."

11. Hokowhitu, "'Physical Beings'."

12. Hoberman, *Darwin's Athletes*.

13. Tatz, *Obstacle Race*.

14. Bourdieu, *In Other Words*.

15. Godwell, "Aboriginality and Rugby League in Australia"; Godwell, "Playing the Game"; and Adair and Stronach, "Natural-Born Athletes?"

16. Perkins, *A Bastard Like Me*, 39.

17. For a similar discussion by Perkins about Aboriginal youth and proficiency at sport, this time 23 years after his autobiography, see Hughes, "Charles Perkins."

18. Perkins, *A Bastard Like Me*, 40.

19. Ibid., 40.

20. Ibid., 41.

21. Hughes, "Charles Perkins," Interview 2.

22. Ibid.

23. Ibid.

24. Ibid.

25. Ibid.

26. Ibid.

27. Perkins, *A Bastard Like Me*, 40–1.

28. Ibid., 41.

29. Hughes, "Charles Perkins," Interview 2.

30. Maynard, *The Aboriginal Soccer Tribe*, 58.

31. Perkins, *A Bastard Like Me*, 51.

32. Maynard, *The Aboriginal Soccer Tribe*, 58.

33. Read, *Charles Perkins: A Biography*.

34. Ibid., 55–6.

35. Maynard, *The Aboriginal Soccer Tribe*, 56.

36. Read, *Charles Perkins: A Biography*, 57.

37. Ibid., 57.

38. Ibid., 58.

39. Kerrin, "Charles Duguid and Aboriginal Assimilation in Adelaide, 1950–1960."

40. Ibid.

41. Read, *Charles Perkins: A Biography*, 61

42. Perkins, *A Bastard Like Me*, 56–9.

43. See note 2.

44. Read, *Charles Perkins: A Biography*, 63.
45. Perkins, *A Bastard Like Me*, 53.
46. Ibid., 59.
47. Ibid., 50.
48. Hughes, "Charles Perkins," Interview 3.
49. Perkins, *A Bastard Like Me*, 64.
50. Hughes, "Charles Perkins," Interview 3.
51. Perkins, *A Bastard Like Me*, 69.
52. Ibid., 69–70.
53. Ibid., 70.
54. Hughes, "Charles Perkins," Interview 3.
55. Ibid.
56. Farquharson, 2000.
57. Perkins, *A Bastard Like Me*; Read, *Charles Perkins: A Biography*; and Hughes, "Charles Perkins," Interviews 4–7.
58. Arsenault, *Freedom Riders*.
59. National Museum of Australia, "Freedom ride, 1965."
60. Curthoys, *Freedom Ride*.
61. Ibid., 118.
62. Ibid., 118–9.
63. Perkins, *A Bastard Like Me*, 68.
64. Pollock, "Foundation for Aboriginal Affairs."
65. Perkins, *A Bastard Like Me*.
66. Read, *Charles Perkins: A Biography*; The Charlie Perkins Trust, accessed November 23, 2013. http://www.perkinstrust.com.au/timeline.html
67. Hughes, "Charles Perkins," Interviews 6–7.
68. Tatz, "Race, Politics and Sport."
69. Messenger, "Tackling Serious Issues in History."
70. Tatz, "Race, Politics and Sport."
71. Read, *Charles Perkins: A Biography*, 234.
72. Ibid.
73. Ibid., 234.
74. Ibid., 34.
75. Ibid., 234.
76. *The Bulletin*, September 15, 1981, p. 24.
77. Read, *Charles Perkins: A Biography*, 239.
78. Ibid., 239–40.
79. Ibid.
80. Ibid.
81. Ibid., 243.
82. Ibid., 244.
83. Elder, Pratt and Ellis, "Running Race Reconciliation."
84. Langton, *Well I Heard It on the Radio and I Saw It on the Television*.
85. Mason, *Sydney 2000*.
86. Ibid.
87. Council for Aboriginal Reconciliation, "Reconciliation: Australia's Challenge."
88. Elder, Pratt and Ellis, "Running Race Reconciliation."
89. Australian Broadcasting Commission, "Radio Interview."
90. Martin, "Public Assembly and Dissent in Sydney."
91. Reporter, "Ministers Up in Arms."
92. Ibid., 6.
93. The *Olympic Arrangements Act 2000 No 1* (NSW) was enacted on May 1, 2000.
94. Martin, "Public Assembly and Dissent in Sydney."
95. Willacy, "Senator Herron Repeats Claim."
96. "Aborigines Target Olympics," *BBC News*, April 2, 2000, accessed September 27, 2013. http://news.bbc.co.uk/2/hi/asia-pacific/698730.stm
97. Farr and Ludlow, "Burn Baby Burn."
98. Elder, Pratt and Ellis, "Running Race Reconciliation"; Gardiner, "Running for Country."

99. White, "Cathy Freeman and Australia's Indigenous Heritage."
100. Hansard, "Proceedings of the Parliament of NSW," November 1, 2000.
101. Lefevre High School, Adelaide, accessed September 9, 2013 http://www.lefevrehs.sa.edu.au/index.php?page=2107
102. Perkins, "Video Interview, 5 May. Personal possession Eileen Perkins, Australian Biography VII (cameraroll2), cited in Maynard, 44."
103. Pilger, "Charles Perkins: A Tribute."

References

Adair, Daryl, and M. Stronach. "Natural-Born Athletes? Australian Aboriginal People and the Double-Edged Lure of Professional Sport." In *Sport and Challenges to Racism*, edited by J. Long and K. Spracklen, 117–134. Basingstoke: Palgrave Macmillan, 2011.

Arsenault, Raymond. *Freedom Riders: 1961 and the Struggle for Racial Justice*. Oxford: Oxford University Press, 2006.

Australian Broadcasting Commission, "Radio Interview, Cited by Booth, D. and Tatz, C. (1994). Sydney 2000: The Games People Play." *Current Affairs Bulletin* 70, no. 7 (1993): 4–11.

Bourdieu, Pierre. *In Other Words: Essays Toward a Reflexive Sociology*. Stanford, CA: Stanford University Press, 1990.

Council for Aboriginal Reconciliation. *Reconciliation: Australia's Challenge*. Final Report of the Council for Aboriginal Reconciliation to the Prime Minister and the Commonwealth Parliament. 2000. Accessed March 3, 2013. http://www.austlii.edu.au/au/other/IndigLRes/car/2000/16/text02

Curthoys, Ann. *Freedom Ride: A Freedom Rider Remembers*. Crows Nest: Allen & Unwin, 2002.

Elder, Catriona, A. Pratt, and C. Ellis. "Running Race Reconciliation, Nationalism and the Sydney 2000 Olympic Games." *International Review for the Sociology of Sport* 41, no. 2 (2006): 181–200.

Farquharson, J. "Obituary - Charles Nelson (Charlie) Perkins". Obituaries Australia. 2000. Accessed May 7, 2014. http://oa.anu.edu.au/obituary/perkins-charles-nelson-charlie-810

Farr, Malcom, and M. Ludlow. "Burn Baby Burn, How Charles Perkins Incinerated Sympathy for Stolen Generation." *Daily Telegraph*, 4 April 2000.

Gardiner, Greg. "Running for Country: Australian Print Media Representation of Indigenous Athletes in the 27th Olympiad." *Journal of Sport and Social Issues* 27, no. 3 (2003): 233–260.

Godwell, Darren. "Aboriginality and Rugby League in Australia: An Exploratory Study of Identity Construction and Professional Sport." Unpublished Masters thesis, Department of Kinesiology, University of Windsor, Canada 1997.

Godwell, Darren. "Playing the Game: Is Sport as Good for Race Relations as We'd Like to Think?" *Australian Aboriginal Studies* 1 (2000): 12–19.

Hoberman, John M. *Darwin's Athletes: How Sport has Damaged Black America and Preserved the Myth of Race*. Boston, MA: Houghton Mifflin, 1997.

Hokowhitu, Brendan. "'Physical Beings': Stereotypes, Sport and the 'Physical Education' of New Zealand Māori." *Culture, Sport, Society* 6, no. 2–3 (2003): 192–218.

Hughes, Robin. "Charles Perkins." *Australian Biography Project*. Full Interview Transcript (12 pages), 1998. Accessed March 15, 2013. http://www.australianbiography.gov.au/subjects/perkins/ interview1.html through to http://www.australianbiography.gov.au/subjects/perkins/interview12.html

Kerrin, Rani. "Charles Duguid and Aboriginal Assimilation in Adelaide, 1950–1960: The Nebulous 'Assimilation' Goal." *History Australia* 2, no. 3 (2011): 85.1–85.17.

Langton, Marcia. *Well I Heard It on the Radio and I Saw It on the Television: An Essay for the Australian Film Commission on the Politics and Aesthetics of Filmmaking by and about Aboriginal People and Things*. Sydney: Australian Film Commission, 1993.

Martin, Christopher. "Public Assembly and Dissent in Sydney: One Year on from the Olympic Games." *Alternative Law Journal* 271 (2002): 32–36.

Mason, David. "Sydney 2000: How We Won the Games: *Videocassette*." *Seven Nightly News*, A. Sanders (pros.) 1993

Maynard, John. *The Aboriginal Soccer Tribe: A History of Aboriginal Involvement with the World Game*. Broome: Magabala Books, 2011.

Messenger, Robert. "Tackling Serious Issues in History." *Canberra Times*, February 17, 2012.

National Museum of Australia. "Freedom Ride, 1965." Accessed March 15, 2013. http://indigenous rights.net.au/section.asp?sID=33

Perkins, Charles. *A Bastard Like Me*. Sydney: Ure Smith, 1975.

Pilger, John. "Charles Perkins: A Tribute." Accessed September 9, 2013. http://johnpilger.com/articl es/charles-perkins-a-tribute

Pollock, Zoe. "Foundation for Aboriginal Affairs." *Dictionary of Sydney*, 2008. Accessed March 15, 2013. http://dictionaryofsydney.org/entry/foundation_for_aboriginal_affairs

Read, Peter. *Charles Perkins: A Biography*. Ringwood: Viking, 1990.

Read, Peter. "Perkins, Hetty (1895–1979)." Australian Dictionary of Biography, National Centre of Biography, Australian National University. 2000. Accessed April 20, 2013. http://adb.anu.edu. au/biography/perkins-hetty-11371/text20315

Read, Peter. *The Stolen Generations: The Removal of Aboriginal Children in New South Wales, 1883 to 1969*, NSW Department of Aboriginal Affairs 2007.

Reporter. "Ministers Up in Arms Over Protest Warning" *The Courier-Mail*, January 28, p. 6, 2000.

Rowley, Charles D. *The Destruction of Aboriginal Society*. Ringwood: Penguin Books Australia, 1972.

Tatz, Colin. "Aborigines, Sport and Suicide." *Sport in Society* 15, no. 7 (2012): 922–935. doi:10. 1080/17430437.2012.723352

Tatz, Colin. *Obstacle Race: Aborigines in Sport*. Kensington: UNSW Press, 1995.

Tatz, Colin. "Race, Politics and Sport." *Sporting Traditions* 1, no. 1 (1984): 2–36.

The University of Sydney in Collaboration with the Koori Centre. "Dr Charles Perkins AO Program: Annual Memorial Oration and Memorial Prize." October 22 2009.

White, L. "Cathy Freeman and Australia's Indigenous Heritage: A New Beginning for an Old Nation at the Sydney 2000 Olympic Games." *International Journal of Heritage Studies* 19, no. 2 (2013): 153–170.

Willacy, Mark. "Senator Herron Repeats Claim of No Stolen Generations. Sydney: ABC." *The World Today*, August 18, 2000.

The Universe is Shaped like a Football: Football and Revolution

Alon K. Raab

Department of Religious Studies, University of California, Davis, USA

Football has had a long and rich history as a liberating force. It has been an important agent of social integration and a major arena in which ethnic and religious identities – local, national and regional – and conceptions and practices of gender and class are played out. It has created a culture where fraternity and cooperation are common and has served as a vehicle for independence and dignity. This essay pays homage to some of the football players, teams, fans, projects and dreams that have been in the front lines of struggles for social justice, community and a better world. It focuses on men and women who have understood the game's connection to larger social and political transformations and, in word and deed, helped further its equalitarian and inclusive nature, thus also helping to transform society.

Introduction

With the final whistle, as Iran ensured its place in the 1998 World Cup, millions streamed into the streets, honking car horns, waving flags and singing. Among the multitude were many women. Barred after the Islamic revolution from stadiums and public life, on this night they removed their veils and celebrated. Some climbed atop cars of the hated morality police, dancing and laughing. Others joined male compatriots hailing the national team's achievement and using the occasion to denounce the regime, shouting 'Death to the Mullahs'.[1]

On December 24, 1914, in the killing fields of Ypres, Belgium, British and German troops decided to lay down their arms. After recovering dozens of bodies and burying them, the troops met in no-man's land. Food and souvenirs were exchanged and they played football. A day later, they were back at slaughtering each other but the memory of the match and its promise remains.[2]

When not scoring fantastic goals, employing the 'Hand of God' or being in drug rehabilitation centres, Diego Maradona, one of the game's greatest players, expressed sympathy for the poor and downtrodden. He admired the Cuban Revolution and opposed most things about America, foremost President George W. Bush. When the Hero of Baghdad arrived in Argentina, Maradona was out in the streets, denouncing the latest US invasion. He also devoted considerable energy to organising a players' union and battling the leaders of FIFA, many of them men with shady pasts and links to military rulers.

In Brazil, until the 1920s, black professional players were a rarity, due to racial prejudice and the football federations' exclusionary policies. Unlike most big clubs, Rio de Janeiro's Vasco da Gama refused to adhere to the racist laws and integrated teams and its coaching staff. In 1924, it was threatened with expulsion by The Sao Paulo league if it did not drop its black, mulatto and poor players. The team refused and gradually other teams joined it, leading to full integration. It took however another decade for the first non-white player, Leônidas da Silva (known as 'The Black Diamond'), to join the national team, and several more years before racist abuse by white players and fans subsided.[3]

Women adapting football as a liberating force, soldiers recognising their brotherhood by playing together, and players and teams in the forefront of battles against war and racism – these are but some of the lives and events exemplifying football's capacity for freedom, joy and social change.

Ancient ball games and their modern variation of football have intersected with important cultural and historical processes such as religion, colonialism, nationalism, women's liberation, urbanism, industrialisation, state building, globalisation and political revolt. Football has been influenced by these developments and has shaped them as well. When writing about football (and especially at its professional level), many authors focus on the negative aspects of the game, including violence, racism, nationalism and commercialisation. Some note how leaders and regimes have cynically used the game to further their aims, and how matches have sometimes been a locale where conflicts were manifested and violence has erupted. Without ignoring these unsavoury connections, it is important however to pay heed to football's long and rich history as a liberating force. Football has been an important agent of social integration and a major arena in which ethnic and religious identities – local, national and regional – and conceptions and practices of gender and class are played out. It has created a culture where fraternity and cooperation are common and has served as a vehicle for independence and dignity. This essay pays homage to some of the football players, teams, fans, projects and dreams that have been in the front lines of struggles for social justice, community and a better world. It focuses on men and women who have understood the game's connection to larger social and political transformations and, in word and deed, helped further its equalitarian and inclusive nature, thus also helping to transform society.

There are many ways to define a 'Revolution'. Seizing political power, often through violent means, is usually invoked, and while these are important, lasting and revolutionary changes appear in many forms. Some revolutions (such as the Russian Revolution) are accompanied by bloodshed, while others (such as 'the Velvet Revolution' that swept Czechoslovakia in 1989) are peaceful. Toppling an oppressive regime is easy to identify but a 'revolution' must also include a radical break with the past and a deep transformation in the order of things. The 1949 Chinese revolution that ushered decades of state communism and the 1979 revolution that transformed Iran into an Islamic republic are two examples. The impact of radical change is often difficult to assess and Chinese leader Zhou Enlai's response when asked what he thought about the impact of the 1789 French Revolution – 'it is too soon to tell' – could apply to other revolutions as well.

Along with earth-shattering political uprisings are the social transformations that are formed of many individual and collective actions and add to the radical break with the past. The changing status and lives of African-Americans and of women worldwide in the latter half of the twentieth century are recent examples. These transformations in politics and culture, social structures and individual and collective consciousness are ongoing and their impact are unfolding and deepening. In this essay, 'Revolution' will be used in its broadest political and cultural sense.

Origins

Organised ball games first emerged in the ancient world in Japan, China, Egypt, Mesopotamia and Meso-America, reserved for priests and the nobility, and were connected to religious celebrations, often simulating the movements of the sun, moon and stars. We have no recorded accounts of attempts to change the rules but perhaps the first football rebel was an Aztec participant in the game of Tchatali who one day decided that the laws proscribing the sacrifice of the defeated left something to be desired and refused to go on. If such a rebel existed, hopefully he was not offered to the gods, a fate much more severe than being sent off the pitch by a referee brandishing a red card.[4]

Gradually, commoners were allowed to participate, a response to their insistence on inclusion and rulers' realisation that they could aid in achieving victory. Later, community-wide games (known as Folk Football) appeared, often lasting for days and involving entire villages. A cross between a bacchanalia and war, they invoked wild emotions and behaviours and the space they provided, free of church or state control, began to worry the rulers. A 1314 decree of Edward the Second warned of

> a great uproar in the city, through certain tumults arising from great footballs in the fields of the public, from which many evils may arise. We command and forbid on behalf of the king, on pain of imprisonment, such game to be used in the city in future.

This action and King Edward III's law requiring able-bodied males to devote their energy to archery were motivated by military considerations. It is clear however that the inability of the authorities to control the crowds and the food riots that occasionally erupted following matches were also a deciding factor.[5]

The modern game that developed in the middle of the nineteenth century was limited at first to the elites, often through laws proscribing participation. Working people quickly adapted the game and insisted on being part of it. Churches and industrialists, recognising football's value in disseminating religious and class ideas and its ability to deflect from possible revolutionary activity, formed teams and sponsored tournaments and leagues. Some radicals found this development worrisome, as expressed by the Spanish anarchist journal La Protesta rallying (in 1917) against the 'pernicious idiotization caused by the constant running after a round object'. The Anarcho-Syndicalist Freie Arbeiter Verein Deutschland (Free Workers' Union of Germany) further exhorted – 'May God punish England! Not for nationalistic reasons, but because the English people invented football'. These revolutionaries deemed the game to be counter-revolutionary, leaving youngsters no time for revolutionary discussion and actions. They noted that to the players and the multitude of enthusiastic spectators all that matters was the fate of their beloved team. The only ones laughing and having a grand time, lamented the revolutionaries, were the capitalists, free to control the stupefied and docile football addicts.

Other activists soon realised that there was no need to leave the game to society's masters and that football is a powerful way to create class solidarity. This recognition gave birth to teams (many still in existence) whose founders were dedicated men of the left. These include Buenos Aires' Argentinos Juniors whose anarchist founders first named it (in 1904) 'Los Mártires de Chicago', in honour of the militants executed for strikes demanding an eight-hour workday. Other teams in the Argentinean capital were Atlético Libertarios Unidos (Libertarians United), El Provenir (The Future) and Chacharita Juniors (named for a neighbourhood) formed on May 1, 1906. Many teams adapted red and black, testimony to their anarchist origins. When local workers were excluded from joining their British employers' team, they formed Independiente, the name and red shirts proclaiming proudly their political ideals. In 1920s Uruguay, the large number of teams with a revolutionary orientation (reflected in names such as Soviet and La Cumuna) led to the formation of the Roja del Deporte (Red Sports Federation) league. Their European leftist brethren formed such teams as Anarch Split, later renamed RNK – an acronym of *Radnički nogometni klub* ('Workers' Football Club') – of Croatia. Formed by radical shipyard workers, during the Spanish Civil War the team organised a contingent of players and fans to join the Republican fighters, and in the Second World War many players and supporters fought the Axis invaders and puppet government. In London, iron workers formed West Ham United and munitions workers Arsenal, teams that are now owned by oligarchs but whose logos, bearing the tools of the trades, still testify to their proletarian origins. In Germany, workers formed in the early twentieth-century sport associations and a league of teams associated with the communist and socialist parties. They stressed sport as the right of all and class solidarity and internationalism as paramount. This rich working-class sporting life ended with the Nazi seizure of power.[6]

Teams

Throughout the game's history, several teams have represented the working class and the poor, and have become symbols of struggles for justice and independence. These include Turkey's Adana Demirspor and Karabuskspor whose players join in May First demonstrations and the Cypriot AC Omonia Nicosia. In the island's politically turbulent 1940s, players of APOEL who refused to align themselves with the right-wing forces founded Omonia and since then its fan base has included many men and women of the left. In the Netherlands, Sparta Rotterdam and Blauw-Wit Amsterdam also represented labourers. Some of the radical top echelon teams are connected with universities. Mexico City's Pumas is the team of The Universidad Nacional Autónoma de México, an institute where many organising campaigns and confrontations with the authorities have taken place; Peru's Club Deportivo Universidad César Vallejo – named for the radical poet jailed for his part in an insurrection, who went to Spain to support the Republic and Chile's Club Universidas de Chile whose supporters opposed the military dictatorship and continue to scorn Colo-Colo – General Pinochet's favourite team.

Under dictatorships, some teams have represented people's longing for freedom, including Spartak Moscow, 'the people's team'. Founded in 1921 and led for seven decades by the four Starostin brothers, star players and managers, it was named for Spartacus. The team's creative style of play and flamboyant leaders conveyed a sense of independence. Victories over teams affiliated with the army and the secret police offered many citizens a measure of satisfaction and revenge. After Spartak beat Dynamo Tblisi in a 1939 cup semi-final, it aroused the ire of the Georgian team's patron, NKVD chief Lavrenty Beria. (He was a passionate football fan and played in his youth, earning a reputation as a dirty player.) 'I knew then we would be going on a long trip', Nikolai Starostin later said. Beria ordered the arrest of the referee and a replay, won again by the Muscovites. To many, humiliating the hated torturer was a victory. Accused at first of conspiring to assassinate Stalin, charges against the Starostins were changed to black-market activity, and each brother was sentenced to 10 years in the Gulag. They survived, however, thanks to their athletic skills. Camp commanders' 'unlimited power over people was nothing compared with the power of football over them', as Nikolai wrote. The brothers were assigned indoor jobs, thus avoiding physical labour in sub-zero temperature and were well fed. In return, they became coaches of the prisoners' soccer teams, each commander eager to have his charges triumph. Outside the camps, fans defiantly continued to support a club so closely aligned with the convicts. Released after Stalin's death they returned to lead the club to further success, with Nikolai coaching and managing the team from 1955 until his 1992 retirement from football at age 90.[7]

Another team that has become a symbol of resistance is Dynamo Kiev. Following the Nazi invasion some players were imprisoned, while others played on FC Start, in a league created by the invaders to demonstrate that life has returned to normal. On August 9, 1942, the Kiev players went up against a Luftwaffe team and were ordered to give the Nazi salute before the game and to lose the match or suffer consequences. They disobeyed these commands, beating the Nazis 5:3 and becoming a symbol of resistance. The players were sent to a concentration camp, where they were tortured and three were executed. The game became known as 'the match of death'.[8]

Some teams and associations have played a vital role in the struggle against colonialism. These include The Indonesian Soccer Association (PSSI) established in 1930 by nationalists promoting independence from Dutch rule. In many lands, including Burma and India, when a local team beat the colonisers it was a cause for celebration. A team representing the Algerian FLN resistance movement included French national team players Rachid Mekhloufi and Mustapha Zitouni (along with six other Algerians playing professionally in France), who chose to forgo the 1958 Mundial and sailed to Tunis to join the government-in-exile and form a team. As a child, Mekhloufi witnessed a massacre by French troops and therefore felt he could never be on the side of the oppressors. 'I was a bit like the spoilt child of football and of Saint-Etienne ... What I got out of that FLN team couldn't have been bought with all the gold in the world'. The team toured countries friendly to the rebels and played before Algerian refugees, offering their countrymen hope.[9]

Sometimes the colonised learned the game from their masters and turned it against them. Unlike in the North African countries under French control where the game was restricted to Europeans, in Egypt the educated elites were allowed to play. Sports were an essential way of introducing western civilisation, and instilling discipline and respect for authority, values useful in ruling the vast empire. After the First World War, football became an area where resistance to British rule was manifested. Starting in 1920, a football team representing Egypt participated in the Olympics, and its performance, particularly in the 1928 games where it reached the semi-finals, was viewed by many Egyptians as proof that they were as good as their rulers, and therefore equality on the pitch ought to be carried into all areas. The urban poor joined clubs and there encountered nationalist and socialist ideas as well as the ideology of the Muslim Brotherhood. Political divisions were expressed most strongly in the struggle, on and off the pitch, between the two main Cairo teams: Al-Ahly and Zamalek. Al-Ahly, whose name translates as 'The National', was formed in 1907 and Zamalek in 1911. In 1940, the latter was named Farouk, after the (puppet) king who supported the team generously, but after the 1952 revolution it was renamed Al Zamalek for its locale. Al Ahly was from its inception supported by the nationalist and liberal elements, with opponents of the British meeting before and after games to exchange ideas and plan actions, and was seen as standing for independence, while Zamalek was supported by royalists and conservative elements, in cahoots with the British. Other teams, such as Port Said's Al-Masry team, also represented political aspirations. Founded a year after the Egyptian Revolution of 1919, the team, unlike other teams of this Suez Canal's city, included only Egyptian players, and was a symbol of national identity and independence.[10]

Some teams that have represented the national aspirations of groups denied political autonomy. In the Iberian Peninsula, FC Barcelona and Athletic Bilbao have long been connected with Catalan and Basque national struggles. During Franco's four decade long rule, Barca's Camp Nou and Bilbao's Estadio San Mamés were among the few public places where opposition to the regime was expressed by displaying the banned national flags and speaking the forbidden languages. This resistance harks back to the 1930s when many players joined the Republican forces. Barcelona's team toured abroad to raise funds and increase support for the cause, while team president, Josep Suñol, leader of the left-wing group Esquerra Republicana and founder of the weekly 'La Rambla' (whose motto was 'sport and citizenship'), was executed by fascist troops. After the war, fascist militiamen bombed the team's headquarters and many players were imprisoned or forced into exile. Shortly after the dictator's death, two Basque players, Jose Iribar of Athlethic Bilbao and Inaxio Kortabarria of Real Sociedad, raised the banned Basque flag during league matches.

In Jordan, the refugee camp team Al Wihdat has long represented the Palestinian community and has created a space for expressing anger at the Hashemite regime's discriminatory polices as well as strengthening a separate identity. (At the same time, the team has also helped in integration into society.) Palestinian leader Yasser Arafat who exclaimed that 'one day when we had no voice, al-Wihdat was our voice' has underlined the importance of the team to Palestinian national life.[11] In the states of Iraq, Syria and Turkey, the pitch has become an important arena where Kurds expressed suppressed nationalistic sentiments with matches sometimes followed by anti-regime riots and calls for political and cultural autonomy. Many of the teams representing nations without states have come together to participate in an alternative tournament, the VIVA World Cup.

In South Africa, football has played an essential political role. During Apartheid, it enjoyed great popularity in the black townships. Many activists, including James Mpanza, a leader of the 1946 Orlando squatters' movement, were involved as players and administrators. At games, political organisers, using portable speakers, made speeches without requesting police permission, disseminated banned information and coordinated political actions, while the banned flags of the African National Congress were held high. Players such as Darius Dhlomo, among the first South Africans to play professionally in Europe, served as role models for youth, as they competed successfully against white players, demonstrating the absurdity of the regime's claims of white superiority. Dhlomo went on to become a teacher and political activist. In 1992, two years before the collapse of the Apartheid system, the four segregated football associations united and formed the integrated South African Football Association with a stated goal of ending segregation.[12]

In 1964, prisoners on Robben Island petitioned their jailors for the right to play football and for three years were denied. They played in their tiny cells with balls made of paper and rags, but once granted permission organised the Makana Football Association and a league of three divisions. The league operated according to FIFA rules, found by chance in a prison library book. During the week, the prisoners were employed in back-breaking labour but on Saturday they were allowed to play for two hours. Even inmates placed in isolation followed the games via clandestine communications. The leagues operated for 25 years, with many of the men who later assumed important roles in the new South Africa, active players.

After liberation, players spoke of the game helping maintain their sanity, sense of dignity and a feeling that they were still part of the 'normal world'. Football fostered political organising skills and camaraderie and united activists from different political factions. South African president Jacob Zuma stated that he and his comrades knew that 'if we can run a league in these extreme conditions, then maybe we can run a country', while Nelson Mandela spoke of how 'the energy, passion, and dedication this game created made us feel alive and triumphant despite the situation we found ourselves in'.[13]

Likewise, political prisoners in other lands experienced purpose and hope by playing or following the game. Among these is Iraqi Emad Nimah. He first saw Tottenham Hotspur FC in 1961 and was entranced. He maintained his love even during 3080 days as a prisoner of war in an Iranian jail. 'My grief was made worse due to total ignorance of how Tottenham were getting on', he later wrote. Owning a radio would result in 60 lashes but after seven years of captivity he bribed a guard to smuggle a tiny radio in a packet of salt.

Listening to the BBC, Nimah heard occasional mention of his beloved team. After returning to Baghdad, he defied the ban on listening to foreign broadcasts (which carried a six-month prison term and a large fine). The American occupation meant being able to watch games via satellite; sometimes the action on the pitch was interrupted by bombings outside his home.[14]

The Tibetan monk Palden Gyatso also found solace in football during his 33 years of imprisonment by the Chinese. In his autobiography *Fire Under the Snow*, he describes a steady diet of Chinese TV as part of the re-education process, including games of the Chinese national team, and the prisoners' joy when the occupiers' team was defeated.[15]

The Arab Spring

One of the most dramatic expressions of football as a force for radical change is taking place across the Arab world. In December 2010, the Middle East erupted, with violence by regimes refusing to relinquish power, resistance by millions of citizens and struggles for political freedom, economic opportunity and gender equality. These developments have also played out in the sporting arenas as fans and athletes were in the forefront of the revolts. Their involvement came as no surprise since for many years the stadium and the mosque were the only public places where political opposition and demands for accountability could be expressed. This was illustrated in 2009 when five Iranian players, in a qualifying match for the Mundial, donned green wristbands in support of the 'Green Revolution' then being brutally suppressed.

The stadium became also the training ground for militant fans to hone their organisational and street battle skills, later used successfully when joining, and often leading, confrontations with the rulers. The ultras first emerged across Egypt in the late 1980s and included Cairo's Ultras Ahlawi (passionate followers of the Ahli Club) and Ultras White Knights (of the Zamalik Club). At first they focused on traditional displays of fandom, but gradually became increasingly politicised, and resembled – in street marches, chants, uniforms and fights with other groups and the police – the militant nationalist youth groups active between the two world wars. Before the 2011 revolt, their ideology was based on antagonism towards the police, media, corporations and the football establishment, represented in extensive literature, art, graffiti and stadium conduct. Though many members were of the anti-authoritarian left, they were disenchanted with the possibilities of political change. The ultras were mostly working-class and lower middle-class youth acutely affected by the economic disaster.

On January 25, 2011, the ultras joined the mass demonstrations and went on to play a critical role in toppling Mubarak. They were especially effective during battles on the Qasr al-Nile bridge that led to the takeover of Tahrir Square by the demonstrators, and 'The Camel Battle', when armed supporters of the regime, riding on camels and horses, attacked the demonstrators. The ultras' long history of street battles and experience working together were well employed as they held off their opponents. Several members were killed and scores injured.

These confrontations and the courage displayed exposed not only the regime's brutality but also its weakness and suggested that victory was attainable. The ultras also played a leading role in neighbourhood watch committees organised to prevent looting and defend the areas, and in setting up and running such necessary services as medical care, food distribution and garbage collection. After Mubarak's fall, ultras have remained a passionate revolutionary force, still committed to the original slogan of the revolution; *'Iish, Huriya, 'Adala 'jtima'iya*, 'Bread, Freedom, and Social Justice'. While maintaining political independence, they have worked with the secularist-socialist coalitions and have protested against the Muslim Brotherhood regime and the Higher Council of the Armed Forces. On February 2, 2012, 74 fans, mostly al-Ahly ultras, were killed during a game in Port Said against the local al-Masri team. Security forces stood by, leading the public to believe that the massacre had been orchestrated by them. Fans have been in the forefront of calls for trials for the culprits as well as for other security personal responsible for killings during the uprising.[16]

Middle Eastern athletes have expressed political sentiments before the revolts but have joined in large numbers since. Among them were Bahraini footballers Aal'a and Mohammed Hubail, and Syrian national team goalkeepers Abdelbaset Sarout and Mosab Balhous. Many of the athletes were arrested and tortured, and some killed.[17]

Players and Coaches

Despite a widespread perception that professional footballers care only about expensive cars and voluptuous models, the number of politically engaged athletes, coaches and administrators is large. Several adhere to nationalistic and xenophobic ideologies, including Italian player and manager Paolo Di Canio who celebrated scoring a goal by raising the Fascist salute and has spoken admiringly of Mussolini, and Lithuania's Algimantes Liubinskas who quit his post as national team coach in order to represent the right-wing *Tvarka ir teisingumas* (Order and Justice) party in Parliament. During the Nazi era, German players, coaches and officials stood by, while their Jewish colleagues were purged from teams and many later murdered.

A roster of those on the left side of the political map could form a team of the highest quality, managed by five exceptional coaches: Cesar Luis Menotti, Joa Sadahnha, Bill Shankly, Brian Claugh and Pia Sundhage.

Menotti led Argentina to the Mundial title in 1978 and on the winner's stand refused to shake the hands of the Generals ruling his country and murdering its citizens. 'We aren't playing for the military generals in the stadium. We are playing for every worker of this country, for every missing person, and for every mother who has lost her child', he explained. Menotti has also spoken of 'right wing football' and 'left wing football' (the first mechanical and dull, the other creative and joyful) and how 'A country has no future without an organized left. Who else would otherwise stand up for a life in dignity and justice, for respect and solidarity with the poor?'

Brazilian leftist coach Joa Sadahnha prepared his nation's team for its resounding 1970 World Cup triumph but shortly before the tournament was sacked by the military rulers and their football federation yes-men due to his criticism of their policies.

Shankly and Claugh were two skilful British players turned successful managers who often supported progressive causes. Shankly, who during his 15 years at Liverpool's helm led the Merseyside team to national and European glory, grew up in a Scottish mining village, an upbringing that influenced his identification as a socialist and lifelong support of workers' rights. 'The socialism I believe in is everyone working for each other, everyone having a share of the rewards. It's the way I see football, the way I see life', he has said. Claugh, who led Nottingham Forest to the pinnacle of European football in the late 1970s, joined striking miners on the picket lines and was active in the Anti-Nazi League. 'For me socialism comes from the heart', Claugh stated. 'I don't see why certain sections of the community should have the franchise on champagne and big houses'.

The four men would be joined by Swedish Pia Sundhage who led the US women's team to two Olympic gold medals and a second place in the World Cup and has long been open about her lesbian identity.

Among politically engaged footballers of earlier eras, Matthias Sindelar stands out. Nicknamed 'The Mozart of Football' and 'papierane', ('the Paper Man') for his virtuosity and ability to float upon the field and evade his pursuers, he starred in the 1930s for FK Austria Vienna (a team with many Jewish players and fans) and for Austria's national team. Sindelar detested the Nazis and opposed the Anschluss. He ignored the new race laws and kept associating with Jewish friends. An 'Alliance Game' between Germany and Austria was arranged in order to symbolise the soon to be united nation and the players were instructed to settle for a draw. In the first half, Sindelar toyed with his opponents but to show that the game was fixed chose to miss in front of the empty net. In the second half, he scored a goal and demonstrated Austrian superiority. Refusing to play in the new united team he retired from football. A Gestapo report described him as a pro-Jewish social democrat, and warned of his hostility towards the Nazis. Shortly afterwards, Sindelar was found dead in his apartment. Few believed the official story of accidental gas poisoning, and his funereal, attended by thousands, served as one of the few acts of resistance by the collaborating Austrian population.[18]

During World War Two, several players were active in the resistance. These included Rino Della Negra, goalkeeper of the Parisian Red Star FC 93 team who participated in dozens of attacks on German soldiers and trains and assassinations of Nazi officers. Della Negra was captured and executed a few weeks before liberation; Two other anti-Nazi footballers, French Etienne Mattler, captain of the French national team, and Norwegian star Asbjørn Halvorsen, were imprisoned and tortured but survived.

Some players choose to build communities across lines of hatred. Bosnian Predrag Pasic played for the unified Yugoslavian team in the 1980s. When the Balkan wars erupted, he chose to remain in Sarajevo. While bombs were raining on his city and leaving it in rubble he operated a multiethnic football school. 'All around the building, people were spreading hatred and firing shells. People were killing each other. But this was a place filled with dreams. The dreams born in the heads of those boys', he later said.

> It was crucial for us that the school had kids from all of Sarajevo's communities, just like before. They played football, wore the same jerseys and were together. Outside, there was hatred between their fathers and between our politicians. But in here, we were all together.

Pasic also spoke of how the children's dreams gave him the power to survive.[19]

During the Fascist era, Mussolini's henchmen controlled Italian football while today oligarchs call the shots but Italy has always produced players who fought the good fight. Paolo Sollier was a factory worker, 1970s footballer and member of the militant group Avanguardia Operaia. Playing for Perugia, a left-leaning town with a rich tradition of anti-fascist resistance, Sollier celebrated goals with the clenched fist symbolising resistance to imperialism and war. Still politically active today, in his autobiography he critiqued the game's commercialism and its function as the opiate of the masses. Another politically minded player is Christiano Lucarelli who rejected a lucrative contact in order to sign with his beloved team of Livorno, a town considered as the birthplace of Italian communism and rich in working-class culture.

As befitting a country where the ideas of Liberté, Egalité, Fraternité were first expressed, France too has produced outstanding footballers with strong political convictions. These include Robert Pires who protested the US invasion of Iraq; Frédéric Kanouté who led a campaign protesting Israeli military attacks on Gaza that killed thousands of civilians, including several football-playing youngsters. Dozens of top players joined him in demanding that UEFA cancel the planned international youth tournament in Israel. Kanouté also established a children's village in Mali; Guadeloupe born French national team defender Lilian Thuram who has been active for many years in immigrant-rights and anti-racism campaigns and supported asylum seekers who barricaded themselves in Paris; Eric Cantona, the mercurial winger whose maternal grandfather was injured fighting Franco's army, attacked banks' greed and role in destroying the economy, and has called for withdrawing all savings from these institutions. 'Football is more than the opium of the people', said Cantona. 'It's about good intentions and noble hearts. When your country is at war, your friends are killing each other and children are given rifles rather than footballs, so what if the whole world admires you! You have to act'. This view led also to producing and narrating the five part series Football Rebels that focused on footballers fighting for justice and freedom.

Across the Pyrenees, players who made their radical beliefs known include Catalonian Presas Oleguer who is a strong supporter of his region's independence as well as that of the Basque nation. 'At its core, football is only a game, but as long as there is oppression it is also a vehicle for people to express dissident opinions, whether we like it or not', Oleguer has stated. A university graduate in Economics, he protested the Iraq war, supported the occupation of abandoned buildings owned by speculators, and was a member of the editorial board of a radical paper. Oleguer wrote, with poet and activist Roc Casagran, a book about Barcelona's 2005 campaign that addressed the corrupting powers of the market and connected Barça's championship to the fight against Franco. A dedicated environmentalist, he rode public transportation to his team's games. An arrest for opposing the removal of squatters and his opposition to heavy sentencing of Basque ETA members has led to accusations by some that he is a supporter of terrorism. Another politically active player in Spain was Sporting Gijon's Javi Poves. Finding the new forms of the professional game too materialistic and that 'football is capitalism, it's death', he retired early from his beloved sport.

In Germany, Volker Ippig, St. Pauli's FC goalie during the 1980s, has combined playing with activism, explaining 'my heart beats left. I cherish social and communal values'. Ippig lived in a squat, joined a work brigade to Nicaragua, and once took a break from the game in order to live and work at a centre for disabled children. His compatriot, player and manager Ewald Lienen, was a vegetarian peace activist, candidate on the Peace List for the European Parliament and a member of the 'Future Council' that advises the Government of North Rhine-Westphalia on sustainable development. Lienen was also one of the organisers of the German players' union. Other politically engaged European players have included Swede Rueben 'the red' Svensson who contributed to communist publications and Swiss star Alain Sutter who before a match against France unfolded a banner to protest French nuclear testing in the Pacific. Sutter was also active against logging in the Amazon forest.

Among politically minded Latin American players are the Brazilians Sócrates, the Chilean Carlos Caszely, and the Argentineans Javier Zanetti and Maradona. In the 1980s, the players of the popular Sao Paolo Corinthians team refused to abide by a requirement to stay in hotels the night before matches. Supported by their coach (and soon management), they formed the 'Corinthians Democracy' movement, demanding at first greater say in managing the club and then the democratisation of Brazilian society, ruled by a military Junta. They participated in demonstrations and displayed the word 'Democracia' on their shirts, earning the authorities' ire and the public's admiration. They were led by players Walter Casagrande and Sócrates Brasileiro Sampaio de Souza Vieira de Oliveira, better known as Sócrates. A creative playmaker who attained a medical degree during his playing days, his childhood heroes were Che Guevara, Fidel Castro and John Lennon.

After retiring from football, and until his death at age 57, Sócrates worked as a physician among the poor and wrote articles about sports and politics.[20]

Chilean Carlos Caszely, born into a family with many members active in leftist politics, was involved with the Players' Union and was a strong supporter of Salvador Allende's government. After the 1973 coup, many of his friends and family members were tortured, including his mother. Caszely continued playing for the national team but expressed his opposition to the military regime, risking his life.[21]

Javier Zanetti, Argentinean international and supporter of the Zapatista movement, convinced his team, Inter Milan, to send money to the rebels after a Mexican military attack on a Chiapas village, and raised funds for medical and sport supplies. In an open letter to the insurgents, Zanetti wrote:

> We believe in a better world, in an unglobalised world, enriched by the cultural differences and customs of all the people. This is why we want to support you in this struggle to maintain your roots and fight for your ideals.

In his autobiography, Zanetti further explained that one must be on the side of 'the losers of the Earth, of the forgotten' and that 'solidarity knows no colour, no religion and no political side'.

Among African players, in addition to the Egyptian and South Africans mentioned above, is Ivorian Didier Drogba, one of the best forwards of his era, who challenged President Gbagbo to end the Civil War and made a passionate plea to the warring sides, helping to bring a peaceful solution.[22]

Several Middle Eastern players have also been at the forefront of struggles for human rights and dignity. Metin Kurt was a Turkish player and coach as well as a trade union activist. When starring for Galatasaray in the 1970s he protested promised bonuses left unpaid, and as a result, along with four teammates, he was dropped from the team. Fans protested and the players were reinstated. Kurt viewed athletes as exploited workers and hence advocated 'democratic struggle'. He was a founding member of the Amateur Athletes' Association and the Revolutionary Sports Workers' Union (Spor-Sen) but the 1980 military coup ended all union activities. In 2011, he ran for Parliament as member of the Turkish Communist Party.[23]

Azeri-Iranian Parviz Ghelichkhani, former captain of the Iranian national team, opposed the Shah's regime and in 1972 was arrested by Savak (the secret police) and held in prison for two months. His opposition caused him to be dropped from the team before the 1978 World Cup. After the Islamic Revolution, he continued supporting leftist causes until, facing arrest, he left the country, and for several decades has served as editor and publisher of a dissident magazine.

Iraq's greatest player and coach Emmanuel Baba Dawud (known as Ammo Baba, Uncle Father) was an Assyrian Christian whose courage extended beyond the pitch. Born in 1934, as a poor child he played with a ball made of fabric and stuffed into a sock. Encouraged by his mother, he soon distinguished himself, eventually becoming captain of the national team. In 1964, he refused to join the Ba'ath party and was stripped of his military rank and forced to leave his Air Force team. After his playing days ended he became a successful coach, leading the national team to three Olympic tournaments. Unlike other sports figures, he openly confronted Uday Hussein, the dictator's son and Iraqi Football Association President, about the mismanagement of sports, lack of resources allocated and the way the matches were fixed to reward Hussein's favourite team. In 1992, at the deciding title game between Baba's Al-Zawraa team and Al-Jawiya, the referee ruled out a legitimate equaliser for Al-

Zawraa. Ammo refused to climb to the podium to receive a medal from Saddam's son. The 50,000 fans cheered, a rare chance to exhibit displeasure with the regime. Hussein retaliated by sending Baba to prison several times and having him tortured. He also forced Baba's family into exile. Upon release, kept out of top level Iraqi football, Ammo established a football academy for poor children. He died in 2009, beloved for his footballing skills and his courage, and was buried in Baghdad's main stadium.[24]

Notable Middle Eastern women football pioneers who persist in their efforts to play and coach, despite religious opposition and legal obstacles, include Egyptian Sahar Al-Hawari[25] and Saudi Reem Abdullah, founder of the Jeddah Kings United Team, Saudi Arabia's first (semi-clandestine) women's team.

In Australia, Aborigine footballers and activists Charles Perkins and John Kundereri Moriarty (born in 1936 and 1938, respectively) blazed a trail. There were Aboriginal footballers in the early twentieth century but after being forced into reservations they were cut off from participation in the professional game. Like many Aborigine youth, Perkins was removed from his home and placed in a school established to eradicate his people's traditions and memory. Perkins studied to be a machinist but his footballing skills led to a successful professional career. In the 1960s, he became an outspoken critic of Australian discrimination and racism, and was among the leaders of many campaigns including the Freedom Ride, which like its American namesake challenged exclusionary practices and raised awareness among all segments of society. Until his death in 2000, he continued with his political work, which included being the first Aborigine to serve as Secretary of the Department of Aboriginal Affairs. In 1960, his comrade Moriarty became the first Aborigine selected to play for the national team but had to get permission from the government to travel outside his reservation. Moriarty too became a leading activist as well as an artist.[26]

Revolutionary Writers and Activists

While many male writers and activists are football enthusiasts, few women have written yearningly about the game. (The female rebels and dreamers of tomorrow will most likely include many who grew up playing and watching football and thus have a strong emotional connection leading to reflection on it.) These writers include the Uruguayan Eduardo Galeano, whose *Soccer in Sun and Shadow* is a poetic homage to the game and its liberatory tradition,[27] fellow-countryman Mario Benedetti and Argentinean Osvaldo Bayer, who (along with Galeano) were forced into exile after the military seized control of their countries and their lives were in danger. Other leftist football lovers included Italian poet and film-maker Pier Paolo Pasolini; French Nobel Prize winner Albert Camus, goalie for his high-school team and for the Racing Universitaire Algerios junior team until TB, forced him to abandon play. His statement 'All that I know most surely about morality and obligations I owe to football' testified to a deeply felt connection; Turkish poet and communist activist Nazim Hikmet, during his long imprisonment, wrote lovingly of childhood games of football; Palestinian national poet Mahmud Darwish, who in the summer of 1982, in the besieged city of Beirut, as bombs fell, wrote in his journal about the Mundial; and Bob Marley, whose music celebrated spiritual and political revolution, had a life-long passion for the game.

Not all radical thinkers embraced football. Antonio Gramsci and George Orwell, astute critics of the many ways mass and totalitarian regimes control life, wrote dismissively of it, not understanding its magic and revolutionary promise. In his *Prison Notebooks*,

Gramsci noted that 'football is a model of individualistic society', while Orwell, commenting on the violent games between Dynamo Moscow and British teams (held in 1946, shortly after the wartime allies became enemies) concluded that while sport is not one of the main causes of international rivalry it is nevertheless 'an unfailing cause of ill-will'. Orwell ignored the fact that the majority of games, by amateurs and professionals, are played in a spirit of camaraderie and fun.[28]

Leftist political leaders display a range of interest in the teeming masses' favourite sport. The voluminous writings of Karl Marx and Friedrich Engels contain no mention of football, while Lenin, a passionate cyclist, cared little for organised sports, surprising in light of his love of organisation. Decades after his death, the Bolshevik leader was resurrected as footballer *Lenin of the Rovers*. This BBC comedy centred on Ricky Lenin, captain of the communist football team Felchester Rovers. Other characters included the defender Terry Trotsky who fortunately for him did not have to encounter a player named Joe Stalin. Employing quotes and events from Vladimir Illich's life, the show satirised the growing commercialism of the game as well as imperial wars.

Several contemporary revolutionaries are lovers of the game. These include Kurdish Abdullah Ocalan, Mexican Subcomandante Marcos, Bolivians Evo Morales and Felipe Quispe Huanca, and Italian Antonio Negri. Ocalan, serving a life sentence in a Turkish prison, has spoken of his support for the national team of the country he battled for decades; Marcos, a former philosophy professor radicalised by the 1968 massacre of Mexican students, wrote from his home in the forests of Chiapas to Inter Milan's president to suggest a game between the wealthy Italian team and the Zapatistas. He proposed that the rebels wear a chameleon-like outfit to confuse their skilful rivals, and that banners supporting political prisoners Mumia Abu-Jamal and Leonard Peltier and struggles for national liberation adorn the field. Marcos emphasised that the game must be like a carnival, 'to reclaim the game from business into the realm of joy and feelings'.[29] Bolivian president Evo Morales, member of the Aymara indigenous people, is a committed socialist and a capable midfielder. His compatriot Huanca is a former guerrilla leader and union activist who has been instrumental in establishing the Pachakuti Club whose goals include strengthening the indigenous population's sense of pride and solidarity. Negri, a staunch internationalist who spent four years in jail for his membership in groups engaged in the armed struggle against the Italian state and corporations and is the author of such works as *On Empire*, is also a passionate supporter of the Italian national team. He has addressed this paradox and that of being a fan of A.C. Milan, a team owned by Silvio Berlescuni, a love inherited from his father.[30] (The author of this essay has always rooted for teams representing workers and minorities but his loyalty is to Maccabi Tel Aviv, one of Israel's wealthiest teams whose political base is the liberal centre. The reason for this unending devotion is simple – his father, Israel Tzvi Z'L, was a Maccabi player in his youth.)

The Bolivian Marxist Tupac Amoru Revolutionary Movement and The Situationist international (SI) are two revolutionary groups connected to the game. Accounts of Latin American revolutionaries often contain descriptions of guerrillas enjoying football in their jungle hideouts and sometimes playing matches with friendly villagers. The love of the game has been however to the detriment of the 14 Tupac Amaru who in December 1996 seized the Japanese embassy in Lima. Their demands to free political prisoners and end neoliberal economic policies were ignored and government forces stormed the building, taking advantage of the daily football game that the guerrillas were engaged in. All the rebels and one hostage died, with three of the Tupac Amaru captured and immediately executed.

Active in the 1960s and 1970s, The SI critiqued professional sports as yet another manifestation of 'the spectacle' but some of its members were enthusiastic fans. During the May 1968 French uprising, they supported the Footballers' Action Committee whose members occupied the French football association offices and rallied against the growing exploitation of the game by the moneyed classes. The committee demanded the retaking of the game from the clutches of the bureaucrats 'who have their egotistical interests as sport profiteers' and demanded their resignations. Under the slogan 'Football for the footballers!' they called for government subsidies and supported students and workers striking across the land. 'United we will make football once again what it ought never to have ceased to be- the sport of joy, the sport of the world of tomorrow which all the workers have started building'.[31] These demands were ignored but footballers in other lands have also gone on strike demanding better pay and conditions, with a recent action taking place in Columbia in 2005.

Fans

From the game's earliest days, fans have played an important role in establishing their beloved teams' identity and in battling to maintain historical links with past traditions. In the last three decades, groups of politically conscious fans have emerged. These groups, including the Polish Never Again Organisation, the Basque Herri Norte Taldea and the Chilean Los de Abajo ('The Ones from Below'), are united in their opposition to the growing commercialisation of the game and to war, racism and sexism. Members view themselves as an integral part of the club rather than mere consumers, with activities in the arena of football but part of their engagement in the world, as they desire to remake not only sport but also society. Fans of FC St. Pauli, a team based in a Hamburg district that is home to dock workers, sex workers and squatters, have been especially active and have prevailed upon their team to remove sexist ads and cancel the naming of the stadium after a former team president who was a Nazi. In Italy, Perugia, Genoa and Modena have active leftist fan groups. Members of Brigate Autonome Livornessi 99 of Livorno sing before each match 'Bandiera Rossa', the hymn of the anti-fascist resistance during the war. Hundreds of these fans have also attacked the offices of the local Alleanza Nazionale fascist party, setting the place on fire and celebrating.[32] In Israel, Ha'poel Tel Aviv's Ultras Ha'poel have been vocal in their opposition to anti-Arab expressions rampant in Israeli stadiums and life and have supported their team's sponsorship of Jewish-Arab youth academies and games. Hapoel ('The Worker') is the association historically aligned with the labour unions and though wealthy individuals currently own many of its teams, the original logo of a player formed out of a hammer and sickle still adorns the players' shirts.

In the early 1990s, groups such as Reds Against the Nazis (comprised of Manchester United fans) fought National Front supporters. Most members were working-class youth and part of the anti-fascist movement. FARE (Football Against Racism in Europe) and the organisation Women in Football were all-European networks that increased visibility and allowed for greater coordination of actions. Many of these fans joined the Kick It Out and Show Racism the Red Card campaigns which employed creative protests, education and legal challenges. Gradually, the football establishment adapted some of their anti-racist programmes.

Some fans, alienated by their local teams and national federations becoming the playthings of wealthy individuals with no love of the game or concern for football traditions (exemplified in changing historical stadiums' names to those of multinationals with shady business practices), have fought back. During the 2008 UEFA Euro tournament, members of the Swiss Brot und Aktion (Bread and Action) group occupied

Zurich's Hardturm stadium and held a sport festival 'without sponsors or security forces'. Some fans, wishing to create a new model of play – one based on solidarity, equality and camaraderie – organised their own teams. Adapting consensus decision-making, they emphasise community connections and involvement, mutual aid and the creation of an alternative culture. FC United of Manchester, Autônomos FC of Sao Paulo and Córdoba's Atletico y Deportivo Ernesto 'Che' Guevara are among these teams. In 1992, anarchists and punks in Bristol formed the Bristol Easton Cowboys/Cowgirls, whose members work with local groups on immigrants' rights, anti-gentrification and in defence of open spaces. The team has travelled to Chiapas and to Palestine, playing local teams and joining in building projects.[33]

Some groups such as the Anarchist Soccer Club of Montreal, reacting to the competitive model eliminated score keeping, field boundaries and team captains, emphasising enjoyment rather than results. They also include players of many ages and skill levels and change team compositions during the game. Similar teams include FK Utopia of Denmark, FC VOVA of Vilnius, Lunatics FC of Antwerp, the San Francisco Bay area's Kronstadt FC (named for the short-lived 1921 Russian commune established by soldiers and sailors rebelling against Bolshevik repression), FC Bakunin of Zurich (established in 1970 and named for the Russian anarchist), the Emma Goldman Anarchist Feminist Club and Republica Internationale FC of Leeds. Players discuss such issues as how to respond to aggression by other teams, in a way that is effective and that reflects the commitment to a peaceful world. Many of these teams come together in events such as the 2010 Poor People's World Cup held in Cape Town, organised by activists upset over the eviction of thousands of poor people whose homes stood in the way of new Mundial stadiums. In Japan, activists held tournaments protesting the meeting of G8 leaders, and a plan by the Nike Corporation to turn a public park into a private space. Other events aimed at creating a 'social forum for sport' include The Alternative World Cup, a week-long celebration of football, music and networking. Other tournaments that encourage individual and societal change include the Homeless World Cup and the Amputee World Cup, which offer their participants a sense of accomplishment, pride and belief in change.[34]

Fans have also played an important role in making their teams more aware of the ecological destruction caused by modern sport practices. Some teams have responded by taking important steps towards ecological sustainability. These include the eco-friendly Forest Green Rovers of Nailsworth, Gloucestershire, England, who use solar panels on the stadium roof, collect rainwater for future use, aim to increase biodiversity around the grounds by building nest boxes and planting wildflowers, and offer vegetarian food for purchase. Fans and athletes have also campaigned against child labour employed in the manufacturing of balls, kits and equipment. There have been some gains and a growing public awareness but the practice still continues

The Revolutionary Potential of Women's Football

Football has played and continues to play an emancipatory role in the lives of girls and women, fostering personal autonomy and changing societal perceptions. Everywhere, women's participation in the game has served as a measure of their status in society and the strides they have made.

This participation is long-standing. Women played a form of the game in the Japanese royal court, as indicated by Lady Murakami's twelfth century *The Tale of Genji*, and participated in English Folk Football. When in the middle of the nineteenth century the game became codified, women were excluded as their participation was deemed unfeminine and damaging reproductive organs. Gradually, the modern game was introduced into elite women's schools and soon women from other sectors and classes adapted football. Nevertheless, male opposition continued and resulted in Dutch and German bans. During the First World War, when long-held opposition to women's equality declined, spurred by economic necessity, a space was created for women's football. Women filled factory jobs left by men and factory owners established teams. Most famous of these was Dick, Kerr Ladies FC, created at a Preston munitions plant. The men's team played poorly and women mocking them were challenged to a game. They went on to play other women's teams but also competed successfully against men. The team drew large crowds, including 53,000 fans that watched, in 1920, a game in Liverpool against St. Helens Ladies.[35] The men running the English Football Association decided however that the game was unsuitable for females and banned women's football from all their facilities. The ban was abolished only in 1970 with the emergence of the feminist movement.[36]

In the last four decades, the game has enjoyed growing popularity reflecting the gains made by women in all areas of private and public life. In the USA, Title IX, mandating equal funding for females and males in educational programmes including sport, has had a significant impact. Worldwide, 25 million females participate, a small number compared with the 240 million males participating, but growing. While football is widely played in lands where women's status is relatively high (Germany, Scandinavia, France, Canada and the USA), women are claiming their right to play in many lands.[37]

Most dramatic has been the long and arduous struggle of Middle Eastern girls and women to fully participate in sport despite familial and religious prohibitions. Their efforts have been receiving increased public and scholarly attention since they intersect with societal attitudes to sports and to the body, notions of modesty and honour, and ideas about women's place. Regional women participated in sporting events in the ancient world and through the centuries, and emerging national movements heralded sports as uniting people, strengthening the body and the spirit and preparing for confrontations with the foreign conquerors. The clubs and groups (such as the Egyptian Civil Committee for Physical Education and the Palestinian (Christian) Orthodox Club of Jaffa) that they spawned included both men and women, who also engaged in educational and political organising. With independence, Syria, Iraq and Egypt, following the Soviet model of sport for the masses, established sport centres and encouraged both genders' participation.

It is important to note that levels and forms of participation vary from country to country and are in flux. In 1930s Iran, the Women's Awakening movement was instrumental in getting the wearing of the veil banned. For over four decades, the participation of women, wearing western athletic outfits, in local and international sporting events was regarded as a sign of their political progress. Shortly after the 1979 revolution, new laws were enacted. These prohibited females over the age of nine from participating in gymnastic events and all international competitions (except shooting), banned them from stadiums men attended, required the wearing of long coats and head scarves and eliminated sport facilities in schools. Women have resisted these restrictions by exercising at home or in public parks before dawn, attempting to enter stadiums, publishing manifestos calling for equal participation in sports and society, and organising. As of 2013, Iranian women are allowed to participate in sports, with football and basketball popular, but must wear the hijab and are still barred from mixed sport facilities. In Saudi Arabia, millions of girls and women are still prohibited from practicing sports, even in schools. A small but increasing number of women have participated in sports clandestinely, including football.[38]

Women's worldwide participation in sports, as players, fans, writers and administrators, is bound to grow in number and result in greater general public acceptance. While fundamentalist religious response is expected, the courage and dedication that women have shown, in the sport arena and in society at large, will prevail.

The Future

Radicals often critique the modern game of football for being a spectacle that exhibits the worst aspects of class society and diverts the attention of the masses from revolutionary action. Football indeed reflects prevailing power relations and a society's consumerism, nationalism and violence. However, to ignore the game's rich tradition of solidarity and resistance is to omit football's profound impact.

The game's individual and communal benefits are many. In a world where community life and traditions are under attack, teams offer a connection to a specific place and to local history. Football imparts important lessons about individual contribution to the common good, cooperation, overcoming obstacles and hope. In a world where selfish behaviour is often held as the norm, football demonstrates that history is created by all, and while individuals excel, in order to succeed, collective action is necessary.

In summer 2013, as Brazil hosted the Confederation Cup, millions took to the streets to protest corruption in the organising of the games and next year's Mundial, the eviction of thousands to build stadiums and neoliberal policies that have increased inequality. Players voiced support for the protesters and their demands including Neymar who stated that 'I'll get on the pitch inspired by this mobilization'. Former national team star Romário, a member of the National Congress representing Brazil's Socialist Party, lambasted the way the games embody his country's many ills. Throughout the history of football, many such aware and caring players have emerged, players who have chosen not to forget their often humble origins, and have stood for their beliefs. It is a history abundant with friendships across lines, including between Jewish and Palestinian players that during the British Mandate competed peacefully and sometimes were part of 'mixed' teams, notably of refinery workers and citrus fruit packers. And it is a heritage where bringing warring people together, as in Sierra Leone after the Civil War, via 'Football diplomacy' between the two rival Yemen in the 1980's and between Turkey and Armenia in 2009, and through programmes such as Search for Common Ground that operate in areas of ethnic conflict, has long been present. A powerful example of this solidarity emerged in July 2007 when the Iraqi national team won the Asian Cup. Sunnis, Shiites, Christians, Kurds and members of other ethnic and religious groups were elated. Surviving decades of Saddam Hussein's dictatorship, a bloody war with Iran, an American invasion and occupation, destruction, poverty and continual sectarian bloodshed, the spirited never-say-die attitude of the united national football team offered a measure of hope for cooperation and unity.[39]

What will the game be like in a world of justice and equality? The many games played daily by amateurs will continue. The professional game, increasingly controlled by a few wealthy individuals and teams, might be disbanded or greatly modified. Perhaps, new forms of the game will take root, such as Three Sided Football. Created in the 1960s by Danish artist and SI member Asgner Jorn, it is played on a hexagonal field, as three teams and three goals create changing alliances and tactics. Jorn aimed to 'deconstruct the mythic bipolar structure of conventional football' and instead of having a supposedly neutral referee (the state) arbitrating between two opposing forces (Labour and Capital) and a winner-take-all result, wished to reflect society's complexity and the possibility of shifting alliances and cooperation.[40]

'First of all, our young men must be strong. Religion will come afterwards. Be strong, my young friends; that is my advice to you. You will be nearer to Heaven through football than through study of Gita' taught, over 100 years ago, Hindu monk Swami Vivekananda, one of the first to introduce Vedanta and Yoga to the west. Vivekananda was talking about spiritual benefits (applicable to men and women of all ages), but perhaps the heavenly connection is based also on the idea, suggested by NASA space probes, that the universe is shaped like a football.[41] Reaching heaven through football is a lofty goal. What is clear, however, is that as long as it is played and loved, football will continue to be an important force for personal and societal transformation.

Notes

1. Shahidian, *Women in Iran*, 222–4.
2. Foreman, *War Game*, 1–68.
3. Bellos, *Futebol*, 30–6.
4. Whittington, *The Sport of Life and Death*, 22–37.
5. Goldblatt, *The Ball is Round*, 16–18.
6. Kuhn, *Soccer vs. the State*, 18–21, 142–4.
7. Edelman, *Spartak Moscow*, 114–63.
8. Riordan, "The Match of Death."
9. Nait-Challal, *Les dribbleurs de l'indépendance*, 95–9.
10. El-Sayed, "Ruled by the Game," 681; Lopez, "Football as National Allegory."
11. Tuastad, "Al-Wihdat."
12. Alegi, *Laduma!*, 32–7, 186–92.
13. Korr, *More than Just a Game*, x–xii
14. Nimah, *Tottenham 'Til I Die'*, 77–97.
15. Gyatso, *Fire Under the Snow*, 222.
16. Dorsey, The Turbulent World of Middle East Soccer; El-Zatmah, "From Terso into Ultras"; and Tuastad, "From Football Riot to Revolution."
17. Free Syrian Translators , "Revolution Icon."
18. Bosi, "Matthias Sindelar."
19. Perez and Rof, "Football Rebels: Predrag Pasic."
20. Perez and Rof, "Football Rebels: Sócrates."
21. Elsey, *Citizens and Sportsmen*, 207–42; Perez and Gilles, "Football Rebels."
22. Perez and Rof, "Football Rebels: Didier Drogba."
23. "Kurt, Turkish Football's 'Left Winger', dead at 64," *Hürriyet Daily News*, August 25, 2012, 362. http://www.hurriyetdailynews.com/kurt-turkish-footballs-left-winger-dead-at-64.aspx?pageID=238&nID=28559&NewsCatID=362
24. Mubarak, "The Amazing Story of Iraq's Football Legend."
25. Mueller-Kroll, "Soccer Pioneer."
26. Maynard, *The Aboriginal Soccer Tribe*, 62–84.
27. Galeano, *Soccer in Sun and Shadow*.
28. Orwell, "the Sporting Spirit," 110–5.
29. Marcos, "Let the Games Begin," 159–65.
30. Negri, "On Futbol and Class Struggle."

31. Vienet, *Enrages and Situationists*, 113–4.
32. Kennedy and Kennedy, "Fan Culture in European Football," 167–82, 246–61.
33. Easton Cowboys & Cowgirls. http://eastoncowboys.org.uk/
34. Homeless World Cup. http://www.homelessworldcup.org/; World Amputee Football. http://www.worldamputeefootball.com/
35. Jacobs, *The Dick, Kerr's Ladies*, 98–102.
36. Williams, *A History of Women's Football*, 55–9.
37. Grainey, *Beyond Bend it Like Beckham*, 260–79.
38. Benn, Jawad and Pfister, *Muslim Women and Sport.* 1–35.
39. Turnbull, "Pride of Lions."
40. InEnArt, "Three Sided Football."
41. Whitehouse, "Cosmos is 'Shaped like a Football'."

References

Alegi, Peter. *Laduma!: Soccer, Politics and Society in South Africa, from its Origins to 2010*. Scottsville: University of KwaZulu-Natal Press, 2010.

Bellos, Alex. *Futebol: The Brazilian Way of Life*. New York: Bloomsbury, 2002.

Benn, Tansin, Haifaa Jawad, and Gertrud Pfister, eds. *Muslim Women and Sport*. London: Routledge, 2010.

Bosi, Emiliano. "Matthias Sindelar: More than a Footballer." http://thepositive.com/matthias-sindelar-more-than-a-footballer/

Dorsey, James. "The Turbulent World of Middle East Soccer." www.http://mideastsoccer.blogspot.com

Edelman, Robert. *Spartak Moscow: A History of the People's Team in the Workers' State*. Ithaca, NY: Cornell University Press, 2012.

El-Sayed, Muhammad. "Ruled by the Game." *Al-Ahram Weekly* March 11–17, 2004. http://weekly.ahram.org.eg/2004/681/op61.htm

Elsey, Brenda. *Citizens and Sportsmen: Fútbol and Politics in Twentieth-Century Chile*. Austin: University of Texas Press, 2011.

El-Zatmah, Shawki. "From Terso into Ultras: The 2011 Egyptian Revolution and the Radicalization of Soccer's Ultra-Fans." *Soccer and Society* 13, no. 5–6 (September–November 2012): 801–813.

Foreman, Michael. *War Game*. London: Pavillion Books, 1993.

Free Syrian Translators. "Revolution Icon, Activist Abdelbaset Sarout." http://freesyriantranslators.net/2012/03/12/syrian-revolution-icon-activist-abdelbaset-sarout-documentary/

Galeano, Eduardo. *Soccer in Sun and Shadow*. London: Verso, 1998.

Goldblatt, David. *The Ball is Round: A Global History of Football*. London: Viking, 2006.

Grainey, Timothy F. *Beyond Bend it like Beckham: The Global Phenomenon of Women's Soccer*. Lincoln: University of Nebraska Press, 2012.

Gyatso, Palden. *Fire Under the Snow*. New York: Grove Press, 1997.

InEnArt. "Three Sided Football." http://www.inenart.eu/?p=8605

Jacobs, Barbara. *The Dick, Kerr's Ladies*. London: Robinson, 2004.

Kennedy, David, and Peter Kennedy. "Fan Culture in European Football and the Influence of Left Wing & Progressive Ideology." *Soccer and Society* (Special Issue) 14, no. 2 (2013): 117–290.

Korr, Chuck. *More than Just a Game: Soccer vs. Apartheid*. New York: Thomas Dunne Books, 2010.

Kuhn, Gabriel. *Soccer vs. the State: Tackling Football and Radical Politics*. Oakland: PM Press, 2011.

Lopez, Shaun. "Football as National Allegory: Al-Ahram and the Olympics in 1920's Egypt." *History Compass* 7, no. 1 (January 2009): 282–305.

Marcos, Subcomandante. "Let the Games Begin." In *The Global Game: Writers on Soccer*, edited by Alon Raab, John Turnbull, and Thom Satterle, 159–165. Lincoln: University of Nebraska press, 2008.

Maynard, John. *The Aboriginal Soccer Tribe: A History of Aboriginal Involvement with the World Game*. Broome: Magabala Books, 2011.

Mubarak, Hassanin. "The Amazing Story of Iraq's Football Legend." http://www.goal.com/en/news/1775/asian-editorials/2009/05/29/1292246/ammo-baba-the-amazing-story-of-iraqs-football-legend

Mueller-Kroll, Monika. "Soccer Pioneer Builds Her Own Revolution in Egypt." 2012 NPR, May 24. http://www.npr.org/2012/05/23/153512361/soccer-pioneer-builds-her-own-revolution-in-egypt

Nait-Challal, Michel. *Les dribbleurs de l'indépendance*. Paris: Prolongations, 2008.

Negri, Antonio. "On Futbol and Class Struggle, Interview with Liberation, 2006." http://antonionegriinenglish.wordpress.com/2010/07/30/futbolclassstruggle/

Nimah, Emad. *Tottenham 'Til I Die'*. Middlesex: Legends Publishing, 2008.

Orwell, George. "The Sporting Spirit." In *Shooting an Elephant, and Other Essays*, 168–175. New York: Harcourt, Brace, 1950.

Perez, Gilles, and Rof Gilles. "Football Rebels: Caszely and the Demise of Allende." Aljazeera TV 2013.

Perez, Gilles, and Gilles Rof. "Football Rebels: Didier Drogba and the Ivorian Civil War." Aljazeera TV 2013.

Perez, Gilles, and Gilles Rof. "Football Rebels: Predrag Pasic and the Siege of Sarajevo." Aljazeera TV 2013.

Perez, Gilles, and Gilles Rof. "Football Rebels: Sócrates and the Corinthians' Democracy." Aljazeera TV 2013.

Riordan, James. "The Match of Death: Kiev, 9 August 1942." *Soccer and Society* 4, no. 1 (2003): 87–93.

Shahidian, Hammed. *Women in Iran: Emerging Voices in the Women's Movement*. Westport, CT: Greenwood Press, 2002.

Tuastad, Dag. "From Football Riot to Revolution. The Political Role of Football in the Arab World." *Soccer and Society* 14, no. 2 (February 2013): 1–13.

Tuastad, Dag. "Al-Wihdat: The Pride of Palestinians in Jordan." In *Sports and the Middle East* (Special issue of MEI Viewpoints), edited by John Calabrese, 24–27. Washington, DC: The Middle East Institute, May 2010.

Turnbull, John. "Pride of Lions: Iraqi Asian Cup Victory Reminds a Civilization What 'Normal' Feels like." *The Global Game*, August 9, 2007. http://www.theglobalgame.com/blog/2007/08/pride-of-lions-iraqi-asian-cup-victory-reminds-a-civilization-what-normal-feels-like/

Vienet, Rene. *Enrages and Situationists in the Occupation Movement: France, May 1968*. New York: Automedia, 1992.

Whitehouse, David. "Cosmos is 'Shaped like a Football'". BBC, October 8, 2003.

Whittington, Michael E. *The Sport of Life and Death: The Mesoamerican Ballgame*. New York: Thames & Hudson, 2001.

Williams, Jean. *A History of Women's Football: Gender, Power and the Rise of a Global Game*. London: Routledge, 2002.

Noteworthy Websites

Soccer Politics The Politics of Football. http://sites.duke.edu/wcwp/

http://fromaleftwing.blogspot.com

http://muslimwomeninsports.blogspot.co.il/

http://insunandshadow.com

Index

Aboriginal peoples: Aborigines Advancement League (AAL) 90; activism at the Brisbane Commonwealth Games, 1982 94–5; activism over land rights 95; experiences, 1960s 90; Federal Council for the Advancement of Aborigines (FCAA) 90; formal process of reconciliation 96; Foundation for Aboriginal Affairs 93; policy of forced separation (lost generation) 86–7, 96–7; Student Action for Aborigines (SAFA) 92–3; *see also* Perkins, Kwementyaye (Charles)

Alcindor, Lew 71

Algeria 107

Amla, Hashim 9

Arab Spring 43, 109–10

Argentina: Cesar Luis Menotti 110; Diego Maradona 103; football and political activism (Javier Zanetti) 113; football clubs in 59, 63; influence of British cultural ideals 62–3; influx of Spanish refugees 60

Arlott, John 6–7

Australia: Brendan Nash 9; Brisbane Commonwealth Games, 1982 94–5; formal process of reconciliation 96; policy of forced separation (lost generation) 86–7, 96–7, 114; radicalism, cricket 5–6; Royal Park Reds Cricket Club 6; Sydney Olympic Games, 2000 95–6; *see also* Aboriginal peoples

Austria 111

Baird, Bruce 96

baseball: consultancy roles, Harry Edwards 77–8; in Cuba 47–8, 50; exhibition baseball games, Cuba 48; Negro League (USA) 79

Bolivia 115

Bolshevism: knowledge of the people 32–3; role of physical health 33–4; *see also* Soviet Union (USSR)

Booth, Douglas 1

Boston, Ralph 70

Bowker, Albert 75

Brazil: fan activism, World Cup 119; football and political activism (Sócrates) 112–13; Joa

Sadahnha 110; racial prejudice against black players 103–4

Caldwell, Malcom 6

Cantona, Eric 112

Carlos, John 71, 79

Carte, Rebecca 56

Cartwright, Tom 6

Castro, Fidel 47, 48–9

Castro, Raúl 50

Caszely, Carlos 113

Chavez, Hugo 48

Chernyshevsky, Nikolai (*What is to Be Done?*) 33

Chile 113

Chinese Revolution 44, 45, 104

Collins, Michael 18, 19, 23, 26

Constantine, Learie 8, 9

Craig, James 14

cricket: and apartheid 6–7, 9–10; Basil D'Oliveira 9; black players in 7–9; Brendan Nash 9; C.A. Ollivierre 7–8; C.B. Llewellyn 8; C.L.R. James 8–9; Frank Hyett 5–6; George Francis 8; George Headley 8; H.M. Hyndman 5, 6; John Arlott 6–7; Learie Constantine 8, 9; Malcom Caldwell 6; and race barriers 9–10; as social/politically conservative 4; Tom Cartwright 6; in Zimbabwe 10

Cuban Revolution: concept of the 'New Man' 49–51; exhibition games (baseball) 48; as a process 46–7; sport and Cuban identity 47, 51–2; sport and guerrillas 47–8; sport as a constitutional right 49

Dawud, Emmanuel Baba (Ammo Baba) 113–14

Della Negra, Rino 111

Demetr, G.S 34, 35

Dobbyn, Séamus 21, 23

D'Oliveira, Basil 9

Downtown Abbey 6

Drogba, Didier 113

Edwards, Harry: academic writings about 79–80; academic writings by 72; activism and sporting boycotts 70–2; college demonstrations, San Jose State 69; criticism of Jesse Owens 70–1; denial of tenure at Berkeley, University of California 74–5; early career 68–9; on education of black athletes 75–6; influences of Paul Robeson and Louis Lomax 73; later career 78; legacy of 78–9; memoir, *The Struggle That Must Be* 72–3; and the Olympic Project of Human Rights (OPHR) 69–72; as a revolutionary 80; on role/meaning sport for African Americans 76–7; on sociology of sport 73; sporting consultation roles 77; surveillance by the FBI 71, 73

Egypt: history of football in 107; the ultras (football fans) and the Arab Spring 109–10; women's football 118

Elwood, Carter 32, 33

Engels, Friedrich 34–5, 39

England: black cricket players in 7–9; export of cultural ideals to Argentina 62–3; John Arlott 6–7; socialist football coaches 110; Tom Cartwright 6

football (soccer): as counter-revolutionary 105; and creation of class solidarity 105–6; fans and the Arab Spring 109–10; leftist fan groups, 116–17; leftist political support for 115; as liberating force 103–4; origins of 104–5; and pan-national solidarity 119; and resistance, WWII 111; revolutionary writers and activists 114–15; sense of community and 119; socialist players and coaches 110–11; as solace for imprisoned political activists 108–9; teams and colonialism 107; teams as expressions of nationalism 107–8; teams as symbols of resistance 106–7; women's involvement in 103, 110, 114, 117–19

Foreman, George 71

France 111–12

Francis, George 8

Freeman, Cathy 97

Gaelic Athletic Association (GAA): arrest of Monaghan players 24–5; drilling and marching with *camán* 18; Gaelic games and the Garda 26; growing sedetionary membership 16; growth in nationalist feelings within 18; growth of, 1910s 13; impact of the Tan War 21; increasing politicization of 18–21; infrastructural weakness 13–14; links with Irish Volunteers 14; members in British forces, WWI 15–16, 18; members in the IRA 22; members' involvement in the Easter Rising 16–17; monitoring by the security forces 25–6; and oath of allegiance, civil servants 20; response to entertainment tax 17; Sunday matches,

resistance to 13–14; suspension of matches, WWI 15; *see also* O'Duffy, Owen

Galeano, Eduardo 114

Germany: football and political activism 112; football as counter-revolutionary 105; football as working-class sport 106; leftist fan groups 116

Ghelichkhani, Parviz 113

Gramsci, Antonio 114–15

Granado, Alberto 56, 57, 58, 59, 60, 61, 63–4

Gregory, Dick 70

Guevara, Ernesto 'Che': analysis of early life 56; as asthmatic 57; care for leprosy sufferers 57, 59, 64; as chess player 60; cultural ideals and sport 62–3; exhibition baseball games, Cuba 48; as football player 58–9; on the formation of the socialist body 50; as a golfer 58; love of literature 61; love of sport 49; medical training 61; motorcycle journey 56, 57, 58, 59, 60, 63–4; as popular icon 55–6; as rugby player 49, 60–2; sport as early socialising activity 57, 58, 59, 63–4; swimming 57

Guevara Lynch, Ernesto 58, 60, 61, 63–4

Hartmann, Douglas 79

Hawkins, Billy 80

Headley, George 8

Hogan, Dan 19–20, 22, 23, 24, 25

Holsinger, Alfred 7

Hyett, Frank 5–6

Hyndman, H.M. 5, 6

Indigenous peoples, Australia *see* Aboriginal peoples

Ippig, Voker 112

Iran: football and political activism 109, 113; Parviz Ghelichkhani 113; women's involvement in football 103, 118

Iraq: Emad Nimah 108–9; football and political activism 113–14; football as unifying force 119; protests against Iraq War 111, 112; women's football 118

Ireland: Anglo-Irish treaty, 1921 23; Irish Civil War 26; partition of 17, 21–2; police permits for sports events 17, 19; War of Independence 20–1; *see also* Gaelic Athletic Association (GAA); O'Duffy, Owen

Irish Republican Army (IRA) 20–5

Irish Volunteers 14, 15

Israel: leftist fan groups, football (Ha'poel) 116; protests against, football players 111

Italy: anti-fascist activism, football 111; leftist fan groups, football 115, 116

Ivory Coast 113

James, C.L.R. 8–9

Johnson, Jay 79

Johnson, Rafer 69–70
Jordan 108
Jorn, Asgner 119–20

Kanouté, Frédéric 111–12
Kiaer, Christina 38
King, C. Richard 79
Kurt, Metin 113

leftist critiques 1
Lenin, Vladimir, I.: interest in physical activity 32, 33–4; Marxist-Leninist concept of 'New Man' 33; myth of 33–4, 35, 36; *see also* Soviet Union (USSR)
Lenin of the Rovers (TV show) 115
Leonard, David J. 79
Lienen, Ewald 112
Llewellyn, C.B. 8
Lomax, Louis 70, 73

Maradona, Diego 103
Marquesee, Mike 10
Marx, Karl 34, 39
Masucci, Matthew A. 79
Menotti, Cesar Luis 110
Mexico: proposed boycott of 1968 Olympic Games 69–70, 71; socialist football teams 106; Subcomandante Marcos 115
Morales, Evo 115
Moriarty, John 89, 114, 90

NAACP (National Association for the Advancement of Coloured People) 74
Nash, Brendan 9
National Collegiate Athletic Association (NCAA) 75–6, 78
National Socialist Party (UK) 5
National Volunteers 15
Negri, Antonio 115
NEOsport 45
'New Man,' concept of the: in Cuba 49–51; in the Soviet Union 33, 37, 39
Nimah, Emad 108–9
Noffs, Rvd Ted 92, 93

O'Duffy, Owen: affiliations with Sinn Féin 20; defiance of police permit regulations 19–20; detention in Belfast Gaol 19–20, 21; IRA/ GAA roles combined 24; joined the Irish Volunteers 18; resistance to entertainment tax 17; role in the GAA, post-revolutionary decade 26–7; role in the IRA and republican movement 22–4; support for Anglo-Irish treaty, 1921 23–4; work as GAA secretary 13, 14–15; *see also* Gaelic Athletic Association (GAA)
Oleguer, Presas 112
Ollivierre, C.A. 7–8

Olympic movement: black power salutes, Mexico 1968 71; boycotts by black athletes 69–72, 79; neoliberalism and 45; Sydney Olympic Games, 2000 95–6
Olympic Project for Human Rights (OPHR) 69–72
Orwell, George 114–15
Owens, Jesse 70–1

Palestine 114
Pasic, Predrag 111
Perkins, Kwementyaye (Charles): Black Protest Committee (Brisbane Commonwealth Games, 1982) 94–5; career in Aboriginal Affairs 93–4; career overview 114; death of 97–8; education 87, 89, 91; football career 88–9, 91–2; ill health of 91, 93–4; increasing political activism of 89–90, 93; influence of Rvd Ted Noffs 92, 93; involvement in school sports 87–8; marriage 90–1; move to Adelaide (forced separation) 86–7; move to Sydney 91; on the Olympic bid team (Sydney 2000) 95–6; presidency, Student Action for Aborigines (SAFA) 92–3
physical culture (Soviet): creation of the 'New Man' 33, 37, 39; and growth of the individual 35, 37, 45; health of the revolutionary 34–5; involvement of young people 36–8; society-wide participation in 38
Polite, Fritz G. 80

race: anti-racist programmes, football 116; black cricket players 7–9; exclusionary policies, Brazilian football 103–4; race, sport and American Culture 69–72, 79; race relations board, UK 9; racial prejudice against black players, cricket 9–10; sport and race relations, USA 69–72
revolution, defined 44, 104
revolutionary, term 4–5
Riordan, James 34, 35, 45
Robeson, Paul 73
Royal Park Reds Cricket Club 6
Royal Ulster Constabulary (RUC) 25–6
Russia: Dynamo Kiev 106; Spartak Moscow 106; *see also* Soviet Union (USSR)

Sadahnha, Joa 110
San Francisco 49ers 77
Semashko, Nikolai 36
Shankly, Bill 110
Sindelar, Matthias 111
Situationist International (SI) 115–16, 119
Smith, Tommie 71, 79
Sócrates (Sócrates Brasileiro Sampaio de Souza Vieira de Oliveira) 112–13
South Africa: Basil D'Oliveira 9; black cricket players in 8; boycotts (cricket) 6–7, 9–10;

fan activism, World Cup 117; football, political role of 108; Hashim Amla 9; rugby tour, New Zealand 94

Soviet Union (USSR): communist *vospitanie* 35; military training of young people (*Vsevobuch*) 35–7; role of sport 44; worker's sports clubs 36; *see also* physical culture (Soviet)

Spain: FC Barcelona 107–8; football and nationalism 107–8, 112

sport: as conservative social institution 4, 43, 44–5; cultural context and 44–5; as developing good character 62–3; for the formation of the social person 35–9, 45–6, 49–50; health of leaders and health of the state 48–9

Sri Lanka: Alfred Holsinger 7; cricket and ethnic barriers 10

Subcomandante Marcos 115

Swami Vivekananda 120

Switzerland 116–17

Trotsky, Leon 37–8

Tupac Amoru Revolutionary Movement 115

Turkey 113, 114

Ulster Special Constabulary 22–3

Ulster Volunteer Force (UVF) 14

United States of America (USA): global promotion of neoliberalism 45; race, sport and American Culture 69–72, 79; role in Cuban politics 46–7; *see also* Edwards, Harry

Uruguay 114

Venezuela 48

West Indies: black cricket players in 7–9; C.A. Ollivierre 7–8; Learie Constantine 8, 9

Whelan, Patrick 14, 16, 18, 19, 20

Whitfield, Mal 70

Williams, Raymond 1

women: involvement in football, Iran 103, 118; Middle Eastern players/coaches 114, 118–19; Pia Sundhage (football coach) 110; women's football 117–19

Yugoslavia 111

Zanetti, Javier 113

Zimbabwe 10